DATE DUE

The Image of the Popular Front

The Image of the Popular Front

The Masses and the Media in Interwar France

Simon Dell

palgrave
macmillan

First published in 2007 by
PALGRAVE MACMILLAN
Houndmills, Basingstoke, Hampshire RG21 6XS and
175 Fifth Avenue, New York, N.Y. 10010
Companies and representatives throughout the world.

PALGRAVE MACMILLAN is the global academic imprint of the Palgrave Macmillan division of St. Martin's Press, LLC and of Palgrave Macmillan Ltd. Macmillan® is a registered trademark in the United States, United Kingdom and other countries. Palgrave is a registered trademark in the European Union and other countries.

ISBN-13: 978–0–230–00328–6 hardback
ISBN-10: 0–230–00328–1 hardback

This book is printed on paper suitable for recycling and made from fully managed and sustained forest sources.

A catalogue record for this book is available from the British Library.

Library of Congress Cataloging-in-Publication Data
Dell, Simon, 1969–
The image of the Popular Front : the masses and the media in interwar France / Simon Dell.
p. cm.
Includes bibliographical references and index.
ISBN 0–230–00328–1 (cloth)
1. France – Politics and government – 1914–1940. 2. Front populaire. 3. Socialism – France – History – 20th century. 4. Press and politics – France – History – 20th century I. Title.

DC396.D34 2007
944.081′5—dc22 2006044835

10 9 8 7 6 5 4 3 2 1
16 15 14 13 12 11 10 09 08 07

Printed and bound in Great Britain by
Antony Rowe Ltd, Chippenham and Eastbourne

The working men have no country.
Karl Marx and Friedrich Engels, *The Communist Manifesto*, 1848

The communists ... love their country.
Maurice Thorez, speech in the Chamber of Deputies, 1934

... factory workers are somehow rootless, exiled within the borders of their own country.
Simone Weil, *Experience of Factory Life*, 1941–1942

Contents

List of Illustrations

Acknowledgements

This book would not have been completed without the support of a number of individuals and institutions.

I am grateful to the Leverhulme Trust for the award of a fellowship which permitted both research in Paris and a crucial period of study leave. I am also grateful to the following for permission to reproduce photographs: the Bibliothèque nationale de France; Magnum Photos; the New York Times and the Victoria and Albert Museum. For help with gathering illustrations, and for the permission to reproduce them, I am particularly indebted to staff at the Bibliothèque Marxiste de Paris, the Bibliothèque de l'Office Universitaire de Recherche Socialiste and the Musée Social. The illustrations were skilfully prepared for publication by Max Adcock.

Many people have helped me during work on this book and I would like to thank Paul Arblaster, Karen Bowen, David Hopkins, Dirk Imhof, Ludmilla Jordanova, Penny Rook, Karen Rosenberg and Hugo and Ane Thøfner. I am particularly grateful to Christopher Green and Graham Smith for their academic support. Colleagues in the School of World Art Studies and Museology at the University of East Anglia have offered many forms of encouragement; I am indebted to Joanne Clarke, Clare Haynes, Sandy Heslop, David Hulks, Ferdinand de Jong, John Mitchell, Stefan Muthesius and John Onians. I am also indebted to Neil Cox and Duncan Forbes for careful readings of the manuscript. Chas Savin and Ruth Wood have shown me more kindness than I deserve and I am very happy to be able to record my gratitude to them. Yet my greatest thanks go to Margit Thøfner. This book is dedicated to her with love.

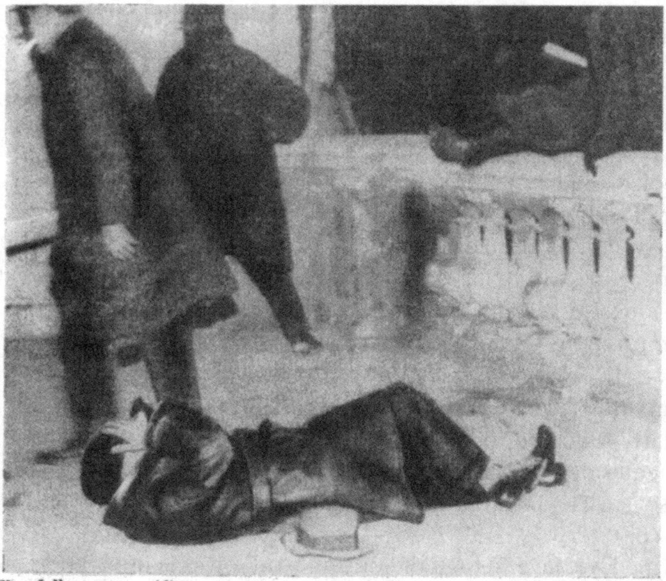

Il a fallu un magnifique sang-froid au photographe qui, balayé lui-même par la charge, a pu prendre un cliché de ce manifestant... fraîchement matraqué.
Photo N. Y. T.

Fig. 1 Anon. (Credited: New York Times/Wide World), 'The photographer needed a cool head to be bowled over in the charge and still be able to take a photo of this demonstrator ... just knocked down', *Marianne*, No. 70, 21 February 1934, p. 8. Photograph: Max Adcock. Copyright: New York Times. Private Collection.

Introduction: 6 February 1934

Coincidence is one of the materials of modern journalism. It has a number of different forms, which may be exploited to different ends. For example, the coincidence on the page of different narratives may be used to figure a cultural trend by making it specific, punctual. Consider in this light the following scene, from an article written sometime in the middle of February 1934; the author is Carlo Rim, a journalist, caricaturist and sometime scriptwriter, thus amongst other things a professional of coincidence.

> The other Tuesday, at the Place de la Concorde, a dark crowd advanced with menacing steps towards another more disciplined group ... The black wave of demonstrators broke with a roar against the firm line of the police. Then the first shots were fired. 'They're using blanks!' shouted an old soldier – who hadn't been hit. But at the same moment a boy a bit like Gavroche, who was holding a large box up to his pale face, cried out: 'S***! My hat!' The first bullet had gone through the felt to finish up heaven knows where. This 20-year-old kid, a joker, skinny and a bit scruffy, was just doing his job, the job of the photographer.[1]

The coincidence here is of an event and a practice: the event is a riot, that of 6 February 1934, and the practice is that which will eventually be defined as photojournalism. The riot scene works, in fact, as the pivot of Rim's article. The ruining of a perfectly good hat is the incident which attracts the author's attention to the young photographer and this serves to shift a general discussion of photography into an account of the new relations between photography and the press. The sartorial misfortune distracts Rim from the riot and from the unfolding crisis which will later find its place in the mythology of the Popular Front. And in permitting himself this distraction, Rim transgresses the principles of political journalism. By the time his article was published on 21 February, the events of the 6th had assumed great significance due to the subsequent fall of the government; yet Rim is studiedly unconcerned with this narrative. For his article was destined for the centre pages of a weekly, not the front page of a daily; events elsewhere linked to political machinations and the effects of the Depression are here simply a means of locating a practice, providing a snapshot of the photographer at work. Thus the reader's attention is here directed towards aspects of the riot deemed irrelevant and suppressed in other accounts. Accordingly, in both Rim's text and its accompanying illustration, the actions of the rioters compete with the presence of a discarded hat (Fig. 1).

Now I am certainly not the first to begin a history of the Popular Front with a discussion of the evening of 6 February 1934, and indeed the riot features in all accounts of the Popular Front. Yet these later historical accounts most frequently rehearse events from the perspective of privileged figures, privileged not least in the ability to direct their own histories through the medium of autobiography. Take for example the memoirs of André Delmas, the general secretary of the national union of schoolteachers. Delmas relates that he was having dinner near the Gare de l'Est when he was interrupted by news of the shootings. The owner of the restaurant bursts in on Delmas and his friends and announces: 'It seems the police have fired on the crowd at Concorde. People have been killed.'[2] Delmas, however, feels he knows better than to let such a story take away his appetite. He was from Montauban and regarded Parisians as too easily excited. Even the fact that his bus cannot take the normal route home does not trouble him too much. This incredulity and this physical distance from the Place de la Concorde are perhaps best understood as signs of a certain respectability. As an activist Delmas might take part in demonstrations, but on his wing of the labour movement one was not supposed to be found within earshot of gunfire. Others, such as Daniel Guérin for example, took pride in the violent aspects of their militancy, and in their presence at the Place de la Concorde; Delmas is measuring a distance from this attitude.[3] To note this is not to denigrate the account Delmas provides, nor yet to suggest an invidious comparison with Rim's article. However, a brief consideration of the differences between these narratives may serve to introduce the materials and problems this book addresses.

Delmas is not privileged simply because he may finish his dinner in an unhurried fashion whilst the young photographer, as Rim notes with avuncular concern, has to carry a half-eaten sandwich in his pocket. Delmas is also favoured because his directive role in the union affords him a perspective on the causes and consequences of the riot. And in due course he will convey his opinions to the reader. A reported conversation between Rim and the photographer makes it clear that the latter does not have time for such reflections. One might conclude from this that the young photographer is of little value to the historian but I think this would be too hasty. For such a judgement rests on a narrow conception of the historian's materials, as if one's attention were more properly directed to the front page of the newspaper than to page eight. It is this conception which makes affairs of state the province of the political historian and consigns seemingly more trivial matters to the social historian. Yet political transformations cannot be understood simply as affairs of state and they cannot be grasped simply by reading the front pages. The riot of 6 February 1934 produced a whole series of political transformations but these events involved a number of protagonists not normally featured on the front page. As much may be clarified if I return once more to the matter of hats.

Published just alongside Rim's article on the young photographer was a piece by Marcel Aymé which addressed the consequences of the riot. This article also featured a discussion of headgear. This, of course, is just another coincidence of journalism, but once again it has its own significance. Aymé's concern is with the distinction between bowler hats and caps, and their respective roles as markers of identity. The date is now 9 February and the Communists have organised a demonstration to protest against the events of the 6th. In the hours before this demonstration the Parisian police frisk suspects on the boulevards. Yet Aymé notes that the searches were not conducted at random. 'The well-dressed were not subjected to examination, and the bowler hat, even when worn at a rakish angle, was the most effective passport.'[4] The article, then, is about the everyday injuries of class but the very fact that Aymé reports the attitudes of the police suggests that their established prejudices cannot be indulged quite as freely as had previously been the case. And if for the police the cap is supposed to be the sign of the working-class demonstrator, then what of the discarded trilby in the photograph accompanying Rim's article? What does this indicate of the class composition of the riot? These questions at least suggest something of the complexity of this moment. They suggest something of the difficulty of defining the mass movement which emerged from the events of February 1934.

This returns me to my first coincidence. For in choosing to describe the photographer at the riot, Rim is gesturing towards a shift in practice;

the riot of the 6th becomes his means of demonstrating how 'photography has become anonymous – and has come down onto the street'.[5] Of course the first anonymous photograph does not date from 1934, any more than the first political demonstration does. Yet Rim's coincidence of event and practice is one aspect of the relationship this book explores. This relationship, stated in the simplest possible terms, is that between the Popular Front as a mass movement and the press as a mass medium.

The simplicity of this last statement immediately prompts qualification, however, precisely because the significance of the Popular Front lies in its complexity, and the complexity of its failures. The Popular Front was a left-wing coalition formed to combat fascism in France; it had a popular base and a parliamentary presence. In the Chamber of Deputies the Front was represented by the Socialists, the Communists and the Republicans of the centre-left, the Radicals. This coalition succeeded in forming a government in 1936 and this government committed itself both to maintaining the bourgeois state and to recasting the relations between capitalist production and the state. That there was a potential conflict between these commitments should be clear enough. And that this conflict might threaten the unity of the coalition should also be evident. The task of the Popular Front thus became that of maintaining its commitments whilst also preserving a relationship between its base and its parliamentary presence. To this end the Front sought both to reform and exploit the channels of mediation offered by the press. Yet ultimately, the Popular Front failed to transform the relations between capital and the state. It did not presage a revolution. Nevertheless, I believe the failure of the Front remains important. For the failure of its negotiations and compromises is more revealing of the relationship between state, capital and public sphere than the extremity of the revolutionary situation.

* * *

Exploring the relationship between mass movement and mass media is a means of exploring the central contradiction of the bourgeois constitutional state. Marx describes this contradiction as that between political power and social slavery: it is the contradiction between the equality of universal suffrage and the inequality of capitalist and wage-labourer.[6] My contention is that the Popular Front is best understood as an attempt to recast this contradiction. This recasting was to be a renewal of what was threatened by the night of rioting, a renewal of nothing less than the Republican ideal of government by and for the people. This ideal – as the locution 'by and for' reveals – involved a specific relationship between the mass of the electorate and their representatives. One could term this a relationship of exchange, a relationship in which government was not reified as the task and privilege of a political caste but was instead an open process. A figure for this relationship would be the Communist Alfred Costes. Fredo, as he was known, had been a metalworker at the Renault factory at Boulogne-Billancourt, yet was elected to the Chamber in 1936. Costes is perhaps best described as the figure for a possibility; the French Republican ideal did not demand that all Deputies emerged from behind factory gates (any more than the American variant requires all Presidents to step forth from log cabins). Yet the possibility of a metalworker entering the Chamber went to the heart of the contradiction between political power and social slavery. Whilst Marx had traced the emergence of this contradiction in France to the revolutions of 1848, it certainly endured in the Third Republic. And in another form it endures as I type these words onto the screen. Its analysis therefore remains pressing.

My further contention is that the prison notebooks of Antonio Gramsci provide the most appropriate framework for analysing the contradiction within the Republic. Gramsci was arrested in 1926 as part of the Fascist repression of the Partito Comunista d'Italia; when he was granted permission to write in his cell in February 1929, the former general secretary of the party planned a campaign of research centred on nineteenth-century Italy. Yet his wider aim was to account for the failure in Italy of both democracy and the socialist revolution and for Gramsci the fragmentation of the Italian state was thrown into relief by the success of the French Third Republic. At numerous points in the prison notebooks Gramsci seeks to clarify Italian failures, and especially those of the Action Party during the Risorgimento, by drawing comparisons with developments in France. Thus Gramsci arrived at a new and more penetrating analysis of the republican institutions which, 80 years earlier, Marx had felt able to dismiss.

Gramsci's analysis turned on the development and transformation of Lenin's concept of hegemony. Gramsci understood hegemony as more than the simple assertion of the interests of a dominant class and argued that a hegemonic class is one which moves beyond the confines of the economic group to embrace the interests of subordinate groups.[7] It was this understanding which led Gramsci to a reassessment of the Third Republic. He explored how the bourgeoisie came to exercise hegemony within the Republic, yet he also addressed the status of intellectuals as the organisers of hegemony and the status of the press as a key element of this organisation. Thus the notebooks offer abundant proof that Gramsci read the centre pages as well as the front page, proof that he was concerned not only with the official accounts presented by parliamentary reporting, but also with some of the things which distracted Carlo Rim.

I return then, once more, to Rim's coincidence. If the contradiction within the bourgeois state is a matter of general interest, its analysis in the context of the Popular Front is of a specific historical interest because of its relationship with the print media. As I shall show, in the period following the First World War capital came to exert a new measure of control over the French press. This new control was to transform relations between the press and the political parties. And second, it was to shift the balance between the daily and the weekly press, which in turn was to result in the consolidation of photojournalism. Thus the organisers of the Popular Front were presented with both new constraints and new possibilities. And so the experiment of the Popular Front marked a particular moment in the transformation of the public sphere; it marked a particular stage in that transformation whereby the critical functions of the mass media were superseded by economic imperatives.[8] This is the wider significance of Rim's coincidence.

The importance of the Popular Front, then, lies both in its attempt to restore a form of Republican government and in the means it exploited to that end. My argument will be that this Republican government required a relationship between leaders and led which confirmed popular sovereignty and that, in turn, it was this relationship which defined an image of the Popular Front. This is to say that the image of the Popular Front was a site of exchange between viewers and viewed, between leaders and led. The Front of course had its iconography, its gestures and symbols, but its image was not reducible to these elements. Instead I shall argue that the image of the Popular Front was the site at which the iconography was recognised and affirmed. It was this recognition and this affirmation which secured the Popular Front.

The opening chapter of this book surveys the materials used to construct the image of the Popular Front and reviews the agents marshalled for that task. In this chapter, Gramsci's account of hegemony is used to analyse the contradiction within the Republic and to assess the means by which a French Republican ideology was produced and then reproduced to negotiate the contradiction.

The second chapter traces the creation of the image of the Popular Front following 14 July 1935. On that day, Socialists, Communists and Radicals demonstrated together for the first time to commemorate the storming of the Bastille; this commemoration of the people's intervention in the Revolution was a means of declaring a new popular resolve. On 14 July, demonstrators swore an oath to defend the Republic against fascism and thereby renewed a link between the working classes and French nationalism. The celebrations of the 14th were commemorated in a widely circulated brochure, an analysis of which concludes the chapter. I shall argue that this brochure – designed by the Radical politician Robert Lange with the assistance of the photographer Marc Réal – finally established the image of the Popular Front for it succeeded in defining the Front as both a popular and a national movement.

The third chapter traces the fate of this national–popular conjunction. In 1935, the conjunction was oppositional; it was defined against the threat of fascism and also against the policies of the presiding government. This conjunction was a crucial factor in the election campaign of 1936. In the second round of voting in these elections the Popular Front parties emerged with a clear victory and Léon Blum, the leader of the Socialist party, announced that he would form a government to 'occupy' power. Yet such an occupation was a refusal of hopes of revolutionary transformation and Blum was greeted with a wave of strikes which reasserted the Front as a movement of popular militancy. The press coverage of the strikes provided the Popular Front with a new mythology and a new imagery, yet it also revealed the tensions which were emerging between the cabinet and the electorate. The coverage thus threatened the image of the Front as a site of exchange.

In the final chapter, I explore how the tensions within the Popular Front were transformed into an open conflict following the outbreak of the Spanish Civil War. If the image of the Front was predicated on the oath of July 1935, in which the people of France swore to remain united to fight fascism, then the outbreak of the civil war in July 1936 immediately gave the fight against fascism a new urgency. Yet although Blum initially wished to support the elected government of Spain – another Popular Front government – he was forced to adopt a policy of non-intervention. Whilst the press photographs of the Spanish Republican militia presented an image of the people taking up arms to defend democracy, such an image of the Popular Front could no longer be sustained in France because Blum's government refused to act.

The epilogue addresses the effacing of the memory of the Popular Front by considering the image of the general strike of 1938. If the Front's mythic origin is most often located in the aftermath of 6 February 1934, its demise is most frequently located in the failed strike of 30 November 1938. This event was the last attempt to revive the popular militancy of the preceding years. Yet whilst the strike marked the end of the Popular Front as a mass movement, the manner in which it was reported also confirmed the centrality of the mass media.

* * *

The main chapters of this book thus explore three images of the Popular Front, as presented at three distinct moments. In a sense these images can only be the equivalent of snapshots, given that historians – like viewfinders – tend to exclude more than they embrace. Yet the three successive moments to be examined are selected not by arbitrary divisions of date but by tracing the creation of an image and then the contests which transformed it. My concern, then, is less with individual photographs than with photographic series. This is not just because the image of the Popular Front could not be defined by a single photograph. The Front was not simply a figurehead such as Léon Blum or even a crowd at the Place de la Bastille. And so the image of the Front could not just be that of a leader or a group. Instead, the image of the Front was defined by the exchanges between crowds and figureheads, between leaders and led. Each of the three main chapters addresses a transformation of these relations and a transformation of the photographic series. (As will become clear, I shall also have cause to address other series and other media, including film and the novel; the principal investigation, however, is of the photograph.) Yet viewing the image of the Popular Front as a site of exchange has a number of methodological consequences, consequences perhaps best explored through a brief historiographical review.

It is now widely accepted that the development of a critical history of photography has been hampered by the problematic unity of 'photography'. The earliest histories invented a technical unity and recounted a sequence of innovations in the manufacture of lenses, papers, shutters and so forth.[9] This model produced and has continued to produce resistance. Yet the technical history has at least the virtue of coherence. This is not the case for the more recent histories which have simultaneously marginalised the technical and maintained a technical definition of their field of enquiry. Such histories multiply accounts of the divergent uses to which photographs are put whilst marshalling these accounts by reference to the technical, that is, by appealing to a body of images defined by their production through the chemical action of light on a sensitised surface.[10] Yet this attention to the divergent uses of photography has made the conventional history of photography increasingly problematic. It does not seem a coincidence that the materials for a critical history have emerged not from the history of photography itself but from sociology and art criticism. These alternative approaches have taken the use of the photograph as their point of departure – the use of the photograph in domestic and social rituals and the use of the photograph in art practice.[11] In turn, these investigations have contributed to a more complex understanding of the operation of photography.[12] These critical works provide a foundation for this book. Yet they cannot provide the point of departure. For my enquiry is not limited to photographic materials and thus is neither a history of photography nor a history written via the photographic image.[13] I have to adopt a wider remit; for considering the photograph as a site of exchange entails an investigation of how photographs are used to maintain (or destroy) social formations.[14] Thus my point of departure has to be not a body of images or an archive but a set of developing social relations. Here two sets of historiographical problems converge.

Writing in 1988, Julian Jackson noted that French accounts of the Popular Front could be divided into three historiographical traditions and that these traditions could be identified with different fractions of the left wing. Broadly speaking, the traditions could be described as Trotskyist, Socialist and Communist.[15] However, the most important recent work on the Popular Front has moved beyond the confines of these traditions to explore the complexities of the interaction between the popular base and the parliamentary parties.[16] Such work is a step towards a subaltern history, and it provides another important part of the foundation for this book. Whilst I cannot pretend that what follows is a subaltern history, I do believe that tracing an image of the Popular Front as a site of exchange will allow one a clearer view of the interactions defining the Front. And this should provide one means of escaping from affairs of state, a means of escaping from the history defined by policy and policymakers. If this is generally desirable it is perhaps particularly appropriate in the case of the Popular Front, for the Front was precisely an attempt to renew a political process which had decayed in the charge of a caste.

Finally, if the image of the Popular Front is understood as a site of exchange, it has to be acknowledged that the terms of the exchange were not stable, and were, on the contrary, subject to constant revision. The very possibility of a fruitful exchange between viewers and viewed, between leaders and led, is a possibility founded on contingency, and it is important to acknowledge this. Analyses of imagery, and in particular analyses of imagery designated 'political', have tended to treat the arbitrary nature of the sign as a condition to be defeated in the interests of coercive communication or propaganda. This type of account posits a centre of power which seeks to legitimate itself before a relatively passive audience. Yet if images are considered not as coercive but as sites of exchange then viewers are properly endowed with agency. And the successful image is not one that simply legitimates but rather one that is recognised as legitimate by its viewers. This recognition is elective, it cannot be compelled. Such recognition is founded on the possibility of divergent interpretations; it is founded on the contingency of the image.

One could imagine an art history which took the investigation of this contingency as its central task. And in such an art history the development of press photography would have a special place. For contingency was not just the condition for the reception of press photographs; it was also a condition for their production. As I shall show in the first chapter, press photography as it developed in interwar France was largely the province of press agencies and the aim of these agencies was to maximise the profit to be extracted from a negative by maximising its circulation. The photographs which circulated most freely were those which were most easily appropriated, those with the weakest coding. These photographs were of course made specifically for reproduction and their meanings were to be secured in the context of that reproduction. In this sense press photographs were radically contingent and were exploited as such to create the image of the Popular Front. Analysing the image of the Front may thus reveal some of the methods and materials for an art history of contingency. I hope this will be understood as a contribution to a Gramscian art history.

1
The Republican Imaginary: Hegemony and its Reproduction

The photograph in *Marianne* first appeared in *Paris-Soir* on the evening of 7 February 1934 (Fig. 1). It was perhaps there that Rim first encountered it and it is quite possible that his narrative was constructed around the suggestive detail of the discarded hat. Yet this detail probably remained submerged for most viewers. The photograph was first reproduced with ten others on the back page of *Paris-Soir*. Here the caption identified the scene as taking place close to the Hôtel de Ville, whilst other captions indicated the Boulevard de Sébastopol and the Avenue des Champs-Elysées; the suite of images served to show the extent of the rioting in central Paris. On 7 February, then, it was the extremity of the violence that was the salient fact. This was not because street violence was exceptional at this moment. There had been a good deal of unrest in the previous weeks, prompted by the political corruption revealed during the investigation of the financial dealings of one Alexandre Stavisky. Violence was exceptional on 7 February because of its consequences. The front page of *Paris-Soir* carried news of the riot and also announced that Edouard Daladier had resigned as president of cabinet. The violence had brought down the government.

On 7 February, then, the photographs of the rioting were representations of a particular threat, a threat to the Third Republic. It was not simply that a set of institutions were threatened, what was also endangered was the political process, the manner in which debates were conducted, the means by which dissent was voiced. Thus the riots threatened what I shall term the Republican imaginary. They threatened a particular relationship between Republican ideology and its subjects. How this relationship was constructed and how it was reproduced are the matters to be explored in this chapter.

My account of the image of the Popular Front has to begin here because it is my contention that the principal task of the Popular Front was to secure the threatened relationship between Republican ideology and its subjects. This involved not only the parliamentary arena but also the popular arena of the streets. The fundamental issue is that of the interaction between these arenas. My argument shall be that an image of the Popular Front was constructed to permit this interaction and that this, in turn, secured the relationship between subjects and ideology constituting the Republican imaginary. Yet before proceeding further I should offer a definition of this imaginary.

To say that the Republic was the governmental system of France between September 1870 and July 1940 does not allow one to proceed very far. However, to say that the Republic was the attempt to realise the Revolutionary ideals of *liberté, egalité, fraternité* is to say everything and nothing. Everything, because the three terms offer a complete programme; and nothing, because, as I shall show, the terms remained largely without content. Nevertheless, *liberté, egalité, fraternité* were central to the Third Republic. This Republic, like any other, may be defined most simply (and therefore most evasively) as a state in which power rests with the people. Yet what is entailed in this sovereignty of the popular will? Again, to say that the popular will is made manifest in universal suffrage does not mark a rapid progress in understanding. An alternative is to consider universal suffrage as a specific instance of the relationship between subject and ideology described by Louis Althusser.

Using concepts (and locutions) derived from Lacan, Althusser argues that ideology interpellates 'individuals into subjects'.[1] He develops this point with reference to the relationship between the individual Christian and the Godhead, respectively designated 'the subject' and 'the Subject'. Here ideology '*subjects* the subjects to the Subject, while giving them in the Subject in which each subject can contemplate its own image (present and future) the *guarantee* that this really concerns them and Him'.[2] Thus for Althusser the relationship of subject and Subject is one of apparent reciprocity. This last point is crucial. Althusser is not concerned simply with describing patterns of oppression or manipulation, instead he is attempting to account for how consciousness inspires subjects to act. For Althusser, the actions of subjects are governed by rituals and these rituals ensure 'the mutual recognition of subjects and Subject, the subjects' recognition of each other, and finally the subject's recognition of himself'.[3]

Such acts of recognition characterise universal suffrage. The casting of the vote may be understood as a ritual of subjection, for this ritual is a recognition of and acquiescence before the state. Yet it should also be acknowledged that the apparent autonomy of the voter permits the act of voting to appear as an expression of will, as something which 'really concerns' the voter. Thus, in the case of the Third Republic, the voting individual constitutes himself as a citizen and places himself amongst peers as a member of a polity. (The gendered status of these voters is a matter to which I shall return.) In the mutual recognition of subjects and Subject, the power of the electorate is conferred by the state, whilst the voters, in voting, confer power on their representatives, giving them the mandate to govern. The ritual of the ballot box is, then, one of apparent reciprocity. And in this reciprocity, the sovereignty of the popular will is ensured.

Yet it must be emphasised at once that the ritual of the ballot box is distinct from those earlier ceremonies in which the people acclaimed the sovereign. In such rituals the people would witness the sovereign taking an oath to respect the rights and privileges of the territory and, in turn, the people would offer allegiance to the sovereign. However, under universal suffrage, sovereignty is vested in the people; here, then, the people can only acclaim the people. I define the set of rituals confirming the sovereignty of the people as the Republican imaginary.[4]

In a postscript to his own definition of ideology, Althusser concedes that his account is schematic and abstract. He suggests that this abstraction will be overcome when ideologies are understood in relation to the social division and organisation of labour.[5] Thus I cannot content myself with a description of rituals. I have to offer an account of how these rituals emerged and of the ends they served within the Third Republic. In short, I have to offer an account of the exercise of the hegemony. Such an account has to address not only the ways in which capital reorganised class relations in the nineteenth century but also the ways in which it reorganised the functions of the public sphere. These are matters which cannot be treated in isolation from each other and accordingly this chapter has to embrace issues as diverse as the legislation on rights of association and the contracts given to agency photographers. However, the exercise of hegemony in the Third Republic was above all a means of containing the contradiction within the Republic, the contradiction between political power and social slavery. This contradiction is my point of departure. In what follows I do not wish to offer a history of nineteenth-century France and much less do I wish to present a *bildungsroman* in which, after many travails and some picturesque diversions, a lost inheritance is restored to the people with the foundation of the Third Republic. Instead, I will present the emergence of the contradiction and the attempts to negotiate it.

The contradiction of the people

For many, the Popular Front was baptised on 14 July 1935. The storming of the Bastille was commemorated by rallies and demonstrations held across France, events organised by the Comité national du rassemblement du 14 juillet 1935. At a huge Parisian rally the chair of the Comité, Victor Basch, declared: 'As on 14 July 1790, when it was not only the People of Paris but all of France who swore loyalty to the Revolution, so on 14 July 1935 it is the entire country which pledges allegiance to democratic liberties, to their consolidation and extension and to the safeguarding of peace.'[6] Basch was confident that the celebration of 1935 could be taken as a new *fête des Fédérations*. He believed in a kinship between the people of 1790 and the people of 1935. Yet such a kinship must be questioned and the vicissitudes of universal suffrage in France would offer sufficient reason to do so. However, Basch, like many others in 1935, wished to see 14 July as the final entrance of the people onto the political stage. He hoped the Popular Front would be the final act of that drama attended by Napoleon, the drama which began when Figaro appeared and brought with him the Revolution. My first task, then, is to sketch out what followed Figaro's entrance.

The Emperor was still only an artillery officer when the people stepped onto the political stage for the first time, in June 1789. This was the occasion when the Third Estate, recalled to Versailles by Louis XVI, declared itself the National Assembly. The principle of the nation as the source of sovereignty was entrenched by the declarations of rights drafted by the Marquis de Lafayette and then by Thomas Paine. Yet the liberal bourgeoisie of 1789 were perhaps less democrats than constitutionalists, at least judging by the property-franchise incorporated in the Constitution of 1791. However, following the creation of the Republic in 1792, the promulgated Jacobin Constitution did offer universal suffrage and thus the means of realising the sovereign will of the people. Of course, the Jacobin Republic was short-lived and the language of *liberté, egalité, fraternité* was only given a new urgency with the proclamation of the Second Republic in February 1848.

The effects of this proclamation are analysed by Marx in *The Class Struggles in France*. Here he observes that at this moment, 'not just a few fractions of the bourgeoisie but all classes of French society were suddenly propelled into the arena of political power; they were forced to quit the boxes, the pit, the gallery and to act for themselves on the revolutionary stage!'[7] And with the entrance of these classes, the emancipation of the proletariat was declared. 'The phrase which corresponded to this imaginary abolition of class relations was *fraternité*, universal fraternization and brotherhood. This pleasant abstraction from class antagonisms, this sentimental reconciliation of contradictory class interests, this fantastic transcendence of class struggle, this *fraternité*, was the actual slogan of the February Revolution.'[8] Thus, at the very moment when all classes were propelled onto the stage, a division emerged between a political language and a set of unequal social relations. A vocabulary was emptied of content; emancipation was declared in February 1848 as Louis Philippe fled to England but unequal social relations were preserved. In June of the same year the Parisian proletariat was defeated on the orders of the Constituent Assembly.

For Marx, the Republic proclaimed in February was in fact a consolidation of the financial bourgeoisie.[9] A dictatorship of bourgeois republicans followed the defeat of June. Thus many of the actors on the crowded stage were compelled to take minor supporting roles and others were forced off altogether. The consequences of this were evident in the constitution drafted between 4 September and 23 October 1848. Both the transcendence of class struggle and the struggle itself had left their marks on this document, but the constitution did, at least, preserve universal suffrage for men. Yet, as Marx was at pains to emphasise, the division between the political and social was now codified. For the constitution gave 'political power to the classes whose social slavery it is intended to perpetuate: proletariat, peasants and petty bourgeoisie'.[10] This Marx described as 'the most comprehensive contradiction' in the constitution.[11]

In many respects the contradiction within the constitution is of greater significance than those thrown up by the Revolution. Cries of *liberté* were certainly heard in 1789 as the Bastille was stormed and proposals for universal suffrage were made in 1792. Yet these slogans and programmes did not confront a ruling bloc dominated by the bourgeoisie as they were to do in 1848. Of course, capitalism was not fully developed in France at this date and the dominant fraction of the ruling bloc was the 'financial aristocracy' rather than the industrial bourgeoisie.[12] Nevertheless, in October 1848 the contradiction of the bourgeois constitutional state was revealed, just as in February the nature of revolution in the nineteenth century had been revealed with the 'emancipation' of the proletariat.

Yet if *fraternité* represents the 'fantastic transcendence of class struggle' its significance may only be grasped by analysing the conditions of that struggle, the conditions of labour. For Marx these conditions assumed their own 'fantastic form' in societies 'based on commodity production'.[13] The analysis of this fantastic form is the point of departure of the first volume of *Capital*. Here Marx returns to the contradiction between political freedom and social slavery in analysing the contradiction between the juridical freedom exercised by the enfranchised worker and the freedom to exploit exercised by the capitalist. These matters thus require a brief review.

The capitalist epoch arises only with the appearance of wage-labour, with the appearance of workers able to alienate their own labour-power. It 'arises only when the owner of the means of production and subsistence finds the free worker available, on the market'.[14] Yet what is the freedom of the free worker? Marx addresses this in his analysis of the sale and purchase of labour-power. In his discussion of these transactions, he returns to the root of the contradiction of 1848. He revisits the language of rights, the language which developed in France into the trinity of *liberté, egalité, fraternité*. Yet for Marx the political language of freedom is not a universal language but the product of a specific social formation. Marx's presentation takes the form of a parody of a fundamental text of the French Revolution: Paine's *Declaration of the Rights of Man and of Citizens*. With reference to the second article of Paine's declaration, Marx notes:

> The sphere of circulation or commodity exchange, within whose boundaries the sale and purchase of labour-power goes on, is in fact a very Eden of the innate rights of man. It is the exclusive realm of Freedom, Equality, Property and Bentham. Freedom, because both buyer and seller of a commodity, let us say of labour-power, are determined only by their free will ... Equality, because each enters into relation with the other, as with a simple owner of commodities, and they exchange equivalent for equivalent. Property, because each disposes only of what is his own. And Bentham, because each looks only to his own advantage.[15]

In this account the juridical relation of the contract governs the interaction of those exchanging commodities in the marketplace. This is the relation on which political economy is based and it is this which Marx subjects to a critique. To do so Marx has to leave the marketplace. For outside the sphere of simple circulation or the exchange of commodities

> which provides the 'free-trader *vulgaris*' with his views, his concepts and the standard by which he judges the society of capital and wage-labour, a certain change takes place, or so it appears, in the physiognomy of our *dramatis personae*. He who was previously the money-owner now strides out in front as a capitalist; the possessor of labour-power follows as his worker. The one smirks self-importantly and is intent on business; the other is timid and holds back, like someone who has brought his own hide to market and now has nothing else to expect but – a tanning.[16]

The transaction in the marketplace may be fair and equal, but the money-owner and the possessor of labour-power do not meet as two equals in some imagined state of nature, as if Robinson Crusoe were confronting his double. In the transition from the market to the hidden abode of production, innate rights cease to apply. It becomes clear that the two entering into relations meet as capitalist and worker, that is, as exploiter and exploited.

In the marketplace the capitalist purchases not only labour-power but also the means of production; in the hidden abode of production the one commodity is set to consume the other. This labour process is initiated by the capitalist and the result, the product, belongs to the capitalist. Yet in initiating this process the capitalist does not seek only to produce commodities but to produce surplus-value. This is possible because of the specific property which labour-power possesses, the property 'of being a source not only of value, but of more value than it has itself'.[17] All the capitalist has to do is to ensure that the value which the worker produces is of a greater magnitude than the value of labour-power the capitalist has purchased.[18] 'If the process is not carried beyond the point where the value paid by the capitalist for the labour-power is replaced by an exact equivalent, it is simply a process of creating value; but if it is continued beyond that point, it becomes a process of valorization.'[19] Whatever language is used in the marketplace, the abode of production, as the site for the process of valorisation, is not a realm of freedom or equality, but the site for the exploitation of the purchased labour-power.[20]

The conditions of exploitation imposed by wage-labour therefore stand in contradiction to the political power conferred by the constitution of 1848. Thus there are two contradictory roles for 'the people'. *Le peuple* defined as *les hommes français* are free to exercise their will as political subjects. But *le peuple* defined as *le populaire* remain an exploited class despite this freedom. French men under universal suffrage act as the sovereign will of the nation but this role is quite distinct from that occupied by the social class possessing nothing but its own labour-power.[21]

However the tension between these roles was not immediately worked out. The contradiction of the constitution of 1848 did not emerge in a developed political form as the Republic of 1848 was itself short-lived. Marx argued that the bourgeoisie recoiled from its own class rule; its public interests were abandoned for private business, and whilst clamouring for order it acquiesced in the coup d'état of 2 December 1851.[22] The bourgeoisie would not regard the state as a favourable terrain until the débâcle of the Franco-Prussian War. The contradiction of 1848 had to await the capitulation of Napoleon III at Sedan on 2 September 1870 and the subsequent proclamation of the Third Republic.

The programme of the Republic was already known. Its most celebrated formulation was that adopted by Léon Gambetta for his election campaign of 1869. In the name of universal suffrage, Gambetta appealed once more for the realisation of the great formula of *liberté, egalité, fraternité*.[23] In essence this programme was a repetition of that proposed in 1849 by the Montagne, the party of the republican petty bourgeoisie. Marx's judgement of the earlier programme holds as an assessment of the later one: 'democratic republican institutions are demanded as a means of softening the antagonism between the two extremes of capital and wage-labour and transforming it into harmony'.[24] He continues in a caustic but measured vein:

> However varied the measures proposed for achieving this goal, however much it may be edged with more or less revolutionary conceptions, its content remains the same. This content is the reformation of society by democratic means, but a reformation within the boundaries set by the petty bourgeoisie. Only one must not take the narrow view that the petty bourgeoisie explicitly sets out to assert its egotistic class interests. It rather believes that the *particular* conditions of its liberation are the only *general* conditions within which modern society can be saved and the class struggle avoided.[25]

Yet whatever the beliefs, the class struggle was not to be avoided. In 1871 the Paris Commune was created and destroyed. With the Commune the contradiction between 'the people' as a sovereign will and 'the people' as a class was transformed into a bloody conflict. This may be taken to demonstrate the bankruptcy of the Montagne's programme, whether in the form of 1849, 1869 or 1870. And yet the Third Republic endured. Could its programme be described as truly bankrupt if it survived not only the Commune but also the First World War? Marx, of course, was not compelled to answer such a question. But Gramsci was. At the moment in 1929 when he was granted permission to record his own thoughts the resilience of the Third Republic could not be in doubt. And so Gramsci was led to reconsider the Republican programme. He was led to review the relationship between the particular conditions of a class and the general conditions of a society.

The Jacobin Republic

Gramsci's account of the Third Republic is one aspect of his analysis of nineteenth-century Italian history. But this is not to say that for Gramsci the Republic is only of secondary interest. The success of the Republic, its relative longevity and relative stability, affords Gramsci, *contra* the Italian case, his clearest example of the operation of hegemony. He proposes that this hegemony is a complex legacy of the Revolution.[26]

Gramsci argues that 'the internal contradictions in the French social structure that took shape after 1789 were resolved, relatively speaking, only with the Third Republic'.[27] With the Republic the new class of the bourgeoisie 'demonstrated its vitality in contrast to both the old and the very new'.[28] 'In fact, it was only in 1870–71, with the attempt of the Commune, that all the seeds that sprouted in 1789 were historically exhausted'.[29] That is, it was at this point that the French bourgeoisie finally defeated not only the representatives of the *ancien régime* but also the revolutionary fraction of the working class, the Communards. As a result, 'France now has sixty years of stable political life after eighty years of progressively longer waves of upheaval: 1789–94, 1794–1815, 1815–30, 1830–48, 1848–70'.[30] This stable political life was the great achievement of the Third Republic. Gramsci describes it as the 'formal perfection' of Jacobinism.[31]

For Gramsci, the new Jacobinism of the Third Republic is actually a perverse development of Revolutionary Jacobinism. He argues that the success of the first Jacobins lay in their willingness to impose themselves on the French bourgeoisie and to discover the interests that this class shared with the other strata of the third estate. And conversely, Gramsci argues that the failure of the Jacobins lay in their repression of the urban workers; here the decisive act was the passing of the Chapelier law which meant the suppression of the workers' right of coalition. This 'broke up the Parisian urban bloc' by asserting the rights of the bourgeoisie over those of the workers.[32] Yet if the Jacobins failed in 1794, 'Napoleon was their continuator and today they are the French radical socialists'.[33] However, whilst the Revolutionary Jacobins were the leaders of a revolutionary class (or, more precisely, the drivers of the most politically advanced segment of the third estate), the new Jacobins were not. This, for Gramsci, is their perversity. For the new Jacobins the task was not to lead a revolution but rather to overcome one.

The new Jacobins had to overcome 'the attempt of the Commune'. Thus what had led to the failure of the first Jacobins, the repression of the workers, was the initial condition for the success of their latter-day counterparts. In a note on the history of French suffrage, Gramsci observes that in 1871 the Parisian working class 'takes a great step forward because it rebels against the National Assembly created by universal suffrage'.[34] The attempt of the Commune was to cut through the contradiction between political power and social slavery by rejecting the compromised and tainted freedom of universal suffrage. Yet the attempt failed and the 'invaluable historical experience is immediately wasted because its bearers are physically suppressed: there is, therefore, no normal development'.[35] As a consequence of the suppression of the Commune, 'Paris loses its revolutionary unity and its [revolutionary] "democracy" breaks down into classes'.[36] Thus with the suppression of the Commune the Parisian people can no longer be the bearers of the Jacobin tradition; '1871 destroyed the umbilical cord between the new people and the tradition of 1793'.[37]

Yet the cutting of this umbilical cord also delivered the Third Republic. Breaking the unity of Paris and suppressing the revolutionary fractions of the working class were the acts which secured the foundations of the Republic. Democratic republican institutions could now proceed more easily with the task of softening the antagonism between the two extremes of capital and wage-labour. Thus Gramsci observes that universal suffrage and 'democracy go increasingly hand in hand with the ascendancy of the French Radical Party and anti-clerical struggle'.[38] This ascendancy marked the formal perfection of Jacobinism.[39]

The exercise of hegemony

In Gramsci's account of the Third Republic 'the people' as defined by universal suffrage triumphs over 'the people' as defined by class relations. Yet the Jacobin ascendancy was checked following the First World War and would be thrown into crisis by the events of February 1934. At this point there was (almost) a reversal of the earlier triumph, for 'the people' defined as the working class was now called to the rescue of the Republic and its institutions. But this very transformation prompts the question: what was the nature of the Republic that it might command such loyalty? What did it mean to exercise hegemony within the Republic? Whilst these questions were posed with a particular urgency by the crisis of 1934, they had already compelled Gramsci's attention.

Gramsci's account of the success of the Third Republic was, implicitly, a reassessment of Marx's account of the republican programme of the Second Empire. Marx had recognised that the programme of the Montagne should not be interpreted narrowly, for the petty bourgeoisie at least 'believes that the *particular* conditions of its liberation are the only *general* conditions within which modern society can be saved'.[40] Yet for Marx, such a belief amounted to little more than Alphonse de Lamartine's perception of class conflict as a 'terrible misunderstanding' which the mere proclamation of the Republic would remove.[41] Writing almost 80 years after Marx, Gramsci saw that the relation of particular and general conditions had to be recast. The success of the Third Republic could not be attributed simply to one class's misrecognition of its particular case as the general case. Rather, Gramsci argued that the Republic was successful to the extent that a class was able to present its own interests as universal interests. For Gramsci, the leading class had not simply to be conscious of its own interests but also conscious of the interests of others.

Gramsci's account of this type of consciousness has as a point of departure Marx's assertion 'that humans become conscious of their tasks on the ideological terrain of the superstructures'.[42] Given this, Gramsci asserts, *contra* Benedetto Croce, that ideologies 'are anything but appearances and illusions: they are an objective and operative reality'.[43] And for Gramsci this is a crucial point. He argues that Marx's own theory is a superstructure, with, precisely, the aim of making 'a specific social group "become conscious" of its own tasks'.[44] The terrain of the superstructures is thus defined as a terrain of ideological struggles with its own concrete value. And as this terrain ceases to be a realm of illusions and sophistries, the question of the nature of the relations between structure and superstructures arises with a new urgency. To this end Gramsci introduces the concept of the 'historical bloc'; this bloc is constituted by a 'necessary and vital connection between structure and superstructures'.[45] The successful formation of an historical bloc is exemplified for Gramsci by the transition from the Second Empire to the Third Republic, the transition from the ersatz legitimacy of Napoleon III to the 'formal perfection' of Jacobinism. This historical bloc is secured through the exercise of hegemony.[46]

For a class to exercise hegemony it has to attain what Gramsci terms a level of 'political' consciousness. In fact, in his account of hegemony Gramsci distinguishes three levels of political consciousness, each defined by its relation with the economic sphere. The first level is the most rudimentary. Gramsci describes it as 'the primitive economic moment' in which there is only an awareness of the professional group.[47] At a second level, during a 'politico-economic' phase, there develops an awareness of a solidarity amongst all members of a social group.[48] However, the third level marks the transition to hegemonic relations with a new degree of self-consciousness. At this level,

> one becomes conscious of the fact that one's own 'corporate' interests, in their present and future development, go beyond the 'corporate' confines – that is they go beyond the confines of the economic

> group – and that they can and must become the interests of other subordinate groups. This is the most patently 'political' phase, which marks the clear-cut transition from the structure to complex superstructures; it is the phase in which previously germinated ideologies come into contact and confrontation with one another, until only one of them – or, at least, a single combination of them – tends to prevail, to dominate, to spread across the entire field, bringing about, in addition to economic and political unity, intellectual and moral unity, not on a corporate but on a universal level: the hegemony of a fundamental social group over the subordinate groups.[49]

It is this unity which was attained by the Jacobins of the Third Republic. Their Revolutionary precursors had perceived that the language of *liberté, egalité, fraternité* addressed not only their interests, but also those of the other social strata of the third estate, nevertheless the interests of the first Jacobins had come into conflict with those of the Parisian workers. Thus the Revolutionary Jacobins 'always remained grounded in class', that is, they ultimately remained within corporate confines.[50] Hence their failure. By contrast, the distinctive feature of the bourgeois class of the Third Republic was its ability to move beyond corporate confines and to make 'sacrifices of an economic-corporate kind' to exercise hegemony.[51] If the Revolutionary Jacobins had foundered on the Chapelier law and the suppression of the workers' right of coalition, the exemplary 'sacrifice' of the new Jacobins would be the Waldeck–Rousseau law of 1884, the law which legalised trade unions.

Such sacrifices secured the historical bloc of the Third Republic, for these sacrifices demonstrated the 'political' consciousness of the bourgeoisie in a twofold sense. Not only did they demonstrate that the class had moved beyond the narrow pursuit of its own interests but also that it had recognised that 'the state-government' was 'the group's own organism for creating the favourable terrain for the maximum expansion of the group itself'.[52] If under the Second Empire the bourgeoisie had recoiled from class rule, under the Republic it was prepared to act within the state. However, Gramsci emphasises that this transition was not simply for the expansion of the group; the interests pursued were tied to those of subordinate groups and were 'viewed concretely as universal'.[53] Certainly, the trinity of *liberté, egalité, fraternité* could not simply be summoned, however much Lamartine might have wished this to be the case. Yet, under the Third Republic, the bourgeoisie came to recognise, with Gambetta, that this trinity constituted a programme to be realised. This recognition had specific consequences for the protagonists of the Republican hegemony.

The actors on the stage

That Marx had a fondness for metaphors drawn from the theatre is well known. The comment Marx attributed to Hegel on the playing out of history first as tragedy and then as farce is perhaps the most famous example of this predilection. And I have already had cause to cite a further example, of February 1848 as the moment when all the classes of French society were propelled on to the revolutionary stage. In a note on Marx and Machiavelli, Gramsci observes that a study of the connections between the two theoreticians might lead to a book 'that is, in a certain sense, "dramatic," an unfolding historical drama in which political maxims are presented as a specific necessity and not as scientific principles'.[54] For Marx, the protagonists in such a historical drama would necessarily be the classes; for Gramsci, this was not quite the case. The development of the concept of hegemony entailed a reassessment of the tasks a class might undertake, and a rewriting of the script. This was also a reassessment of the concept of class, part of Gramsci's revision of the 'official' Marxist tradition.[55]

Gramsci's account of hegemony is an account of the process whereby one group comes to exercise leadership over others. It is not, therefore, an account of simple dominance but rather of the connections between groups. In the case of the Third Republic, the exercise of hegemony involved two quite distinct protagonists, neither of whom automatically spoke the lines of a given class: these protagonists were 'the intellectuals' and 'the people', and the relationship between them was that between leaders and led. It is this relationship between protagonists which was to become central to the drama of the Republic, but each protagonist first requires a separate introduction.

In considering the transition from the Second Empire to the Third Republic as the securing of a hegemony, Gramsci had implicitly reassessed the scope of the Montagne's programme. This, in turn, entailed another revision: of Marx's account of 'the cult of the people'.[56] Marx saw that the universal suffrage of 1848 ultimately served to break the mythic unity of 'the people' and to reveal antagonisms between classes. And he recognised that under the Second Empire universal suffrage was the tool of Napoleon III. However, Gramsci saw that under the Third Republic the situation was transformed. Under the Republic, the parliamentary regime provided the appropriate institutions for universal suffrage, the institutions so obviously lacking under the Empire. Although universal suffrage remained an instrument of class rule, the character of this rule had changed. Now it appeared in a properly 'universal' guise. So if the hegemony of the Republic was secured by the bourgeoisie, this hegemony was not to be exercised in the name of that class, but in the name of 'the people'.

The Third Republic did not fully resolve the contradiction Marx had noted in the constitution of 1848; the bloody suppression of the Commune can in no way be described as a resolution. However, during the Third Republic the terms of the contradiction were recast. Above, I described the Republic as the triumph of 'the people' defined by universal suffrage over 'the people' defined by class relations. This description may now be refined: the revolutionary fraction of the working class had been defeated, but the Republic held out the promise that 'the people' as an oppressed class were to be liberated by 'the people' as the sovereign will of the nation. The freedom of the latter, ensured by the institutions of the Republic, would lead to the freedom of the former. Just as the sovereign had been acclaimed for promising to protect the rights and privileges of the territory, so 'the people' would protect *liberté, egalité, fraternité*. It was this imaginary which provided the guarantee that 'the people' acted in its own interest, the guarantee that its actions really concerned itself. Thus within the Republican imaginary 'the people' became both agent and acted upon; in Althusser's terms both subject and object.

Yet if 'the people' became the central protagonist in the Republican imaginary, the actual exercise of the Republican hegemony entailed a particular relationship between this protagonist and 'the intellectuals'. For Gramsci, this latter group has the function of educating and leading. Therefore, to complete his analysis of hegemony, Gramsci provides an analysis of the status of the intellectual.[57] Extending the account of hegemony to embrace its agents is not simply a means of shifting from bloodless abstraction to the physically embodied, a means of transforming a dry text into a lively performance. Nor is the extended account simply a means of identifying the agents of hegemony. This identification is important, but the question of who occupies the leading role is preliminary. It leads to a larger question: how was the leading role acquired?

Gramsci sketches a first answer to this question by considering the nature of the relationship between 'the people' and 'the intellectuals'. This he describes in terms of the transition

> from *knowing* to *understanding* to *feeling* and vice versa from feeling to understanding to knowing. The popular element 'feels' but does not understand or know; the intellectual element 'knows' but does

not understand and, above all, does not feel ... The error of the intellectual consists in believing that one can *know* without understanding and, above all, without feeling or being impassioned: in other words, that the intellectual can be an intellectual if he is distinct and detached from the people. One cannot make history-politics without passion, that is, without being emotionally tied to the people, without feeling the rudimentary passions of the people, understanding them and hence explaining [and justifying] them in the specific historical situation and linking them dialectically to the laws of history, that is, to a scientifically elaborated superior conception of the world: namely, 'knowledge' ... Only if the relationship between intellectuals and people-masses, between the leaders and the led, between rulers and ruled is based on an organic attachment in which impassioned sentiment becomes understanding and hence knowledge (not mechanically but in a living manner), only then is the relationship one of representation, and only then does one get an exchange of individual elements between the rulers and the ruled, the leaders and the led; in other words, only then does a life of connectedness, which alone is a social force, become a reality, and the 'historical bloc' come into being.[58]

This is at once a description of the interaction between leaders and led and a description of the interaction between levels of consciousness. As such it foreshadows Gramsci's account of the hegemony of a fundamental group as brought about when the group becomes conscious that its interests can and must meet with those of other, subordinate groups. This coming to consciousness is central to Gramsci's account of the intellectuals.

Gramsci develops his discussion by distinguishing between two categories of intellectuals: the organic and the traditional. For Gramsci, the distinction between the former and the latter corresponds in part to the distinction between the 'politico-economic phase' and the 'patently "political" phase', a distinction between a consciousness of an internal, group solidarity and a consciousness which extends beyond corporate interests. In the note on the operation of hegemony, this distinction is drawn through the contrast between two different relationships with the state. In the politico-economic phase 'the question of the state is posed, but only in terms of rudimentary political equality', that is, at a corporate level, whereas in the patently political phase the state is finally seen as a 'favorable terrain' for an expansion which may be viewed as universal.[59]

The full significance of this distinction is revealed when Gramsci turns to consider the tasks intellectuals undertake in civil society and in relation to the state. According to Gramsci, 'intellectuals have a function in the "hegemony" that is exercised throughout society by the dominant group, and in the "domination" over society that is embodied by the state, and this function is precisely "organizational" or connective'.[60] So, following Gramsci's examples, organic intellectuals in the cities, such as engineers, serve to establish the relations between entrepreneurs and masses and their peers in the country, such as notaries, serve to establish relations between the local administration and the peasantry. Yet above the connective tasks performed within civil society are those performed within the state by traditional intellectuals in, for example, those legal and educational tasks now controlled by the state but previously monopolised by the clergy and the *noblesse de robe*.

Gramsci acknowledges that the task of 'organizing social hegemony and state domination has various levels and among these levels some are purely manual and instrumental'.[61] However, Gramsci also argues that from an intrinsic point of view, 'intellectual activity can be differentiated by levels that in moments of extreme opposition become a genuine difference in quality'.[62] Thus on the 'highest rung' of the ladder there are the 'creators' whilst on the lowest there are the humble 'administrators and disseminators' of intellectual wealth.[63] Yet despite this differentiation there is 'a sense of solidarity' between creators and disseminators.[64] They may stand on different rungs but these various figures all belong on the same ladder. And such a metaphor is not simply a means of restating the distinction between the categories of 'traditional' and 'organic'. This much is made clear when Gramsci turns to that specific level of intellectual activity which is political leadership.

I have argued that the hegemony of the Third Republic was secured by a twofold consciousness on the part of the bourgeoisie, demonstrated not only by the ability to move beyond the pursuit of its own interests, but also by the ability to recognise the state as the terrain for expansion. For Gramsci this twofold consciousness is that of the individuals prepared to take up political leadership. And this leadership is characterised by a shift of terrain. Rather than standing on one's rung, dutifully performing one's tasks, one may step off onto 'the mechanism' that is the political party.[65] This mechanism serves 'to lift the "economic" members of a social group to the level of "political intellectuals," that is organizers of all the functions intrinsic to the organic development of an integral civil and political society'.[66] Here the transition to hegemonic relations is embodied in an intellectual development. Producing this development, lifting its members to a new level, is a function which belongs to the party proper and not to professional organisations such as the unions. The unions exist to serve an 'economic-corporate function' and thus only pose the question of the state at a rudimentary level.[67] By contrast, in the political party 'the elements of an economic social group go beyond this moment of their historical development and become agents of general activities that are national and international in character'.[68] Those who attain this consciousness through the political party become capable of exercising hegemony; it is precisely these actors who are able to perform on the national stage.

The material organisation of hegemony

On 14 July 1935, a national stage was set up at the Buffalo Stadium. On this day Victor Basch gave a speech which he considered as the culmination of nearly four decades of campaigning. Entering political life in 1897, when he became engaged with the Dreyfus Affair, Basch was a central figure in the Ligue des droits de l'homme, and was president of that organisation when it played a key role in the formation of the Popular Front. More closely than any other figure, Basch tied the struggles of the Popular Front to the struggles of the Dreyfusards. At the Parisian rally of 1935, it was Basch who called for silence in memory of Captain Dreyfus, whose funeral was by chance to take place the same day. And in his speech, Basch declared that the Popular Front was to mark the true conclusion of the Dreyfusard campaign. With this declaration, Basch acknowledged that the Popular Front belonged to a particular moment in the development of the Republic. If the Republic is to be seen as the final victory of the bourgeoisie over the representatives of the older classes, then this victory was sealed not with the reforms of 1875 nor with the ministries of Jules Ferry, but with the Affair. Indeed, for Gramsci, the exoneration of Dreyfus marked the moment at which 'the clergy and military caste' were 'subordinated to secular politics'.[69] With this subordination of the vestiges of the older order, the 'political intellectuals' of the Republic had secured their hegemony. Basch was one of those involved in this process and he certainly saw the significance of the moment. In recalling the Affair at the inauguration of the Popular Front, Basch self-consciously embodied a connection between the Dreyfusards and the antifascists. He made himself an exemplary figure.[70]

Basch was, then, a traditional intellectual; a professor of philosophy at the Sorbonne, a committee chair, an author and public speaker; he was also engaged in no less an undertaking than the protection of the Rights of Man. And if that task was not identified directly with the state, it nevertheless claimed a universality. Basch stood on one of the highest rungs of the ladder. Yet Carlo Rim's young photographer would have stood on the same ladder. He certainly would have occupied a lower rung. Rim does not present him as having either the time or the temperament for introspection. The differences between such a photographer and such a philosopher would be great enough to suggest, in Gramsci's terms, 'a genuine difference of quality'. Basch should be described as a 'creator', whilst Rim's photographer would be much closer to being a humble 'disseminator'. Nevertheless, the interaction between such figures was central to the hegemony of the Republic.

But under what conditions could such an interaction take place? For Gramsci, the question of 'how the ideological structure of a ruling class is actually organized' was a pressing one.[71] Answering this question requires a careful study of 'the material organization meant to preserve, defend, and develop the theoretical or ideological "front" '.[72] The second part of this chapter is dedicated to such a study and specifically to the study of 'the most notable' and 'most dynamic part of the ideological structure', namely the press.[73]

Certainly the press of the Third Republic required creators and disseminators; it solicited contributions from figures such as Victor Basch and Léon Blum but also from Carlo Rim and from nameless photographers. Yet to recognise that different ranks of intellectual occupy different levels within the press is simply to recognise that it is both structure and superstructure. For Gramsci the press, as part of the printing industry, is 'an object of property and hence of class division and struggle'; yet 'it is also an inseparable element of an ideological activity'.[74] So any adequate history of the press has to trace both those demands imposed by capital and those demands imposed by the defence of the ideological front. During the Third Republic, the interaction of these demands redefined the material organisation of hegemony.

Gramsci's prison notebooks offer two points of departure for an account of this material organisation. First, and most obviously, the notebooks provide a conceptual framework. Second, the very concerns which the notebooks address have their own historical status. In identifying the activity of party intellectuals with the organisation of hegemony, and in identifying the press as the most dynamic part of the material organisation of hegemony, Gramsci's notebooks are a response to a particular series of developments. Of course, the intellectuals, parties and the press were hardly recent inventions at the date of Gramsci's imprisonment. Yet at that date, relations between these protagonists were being redefined by processes of centralisation which were transforming the public sphere. In what follows I shall sketch the shape of this transformation in France after the First World War. During this period a new relationship developed between the daily and the weekly press which affected both the composition of the dailies and their forms of reporting. These changes were preconditions for introducing new techniques to the press, new techniques of communication and above all new forms of photographic coverage. So, if the first part of this chapter has sketched the nature of the hegemony secured under the Third Republic, the second part may be considered an inventory of the materials which were to be exploited by the Popular Front in the reconstruction of that hegemony.

Information, opinion and entertainment

During the interwar period in France the dominant form of both economic and ideological development was that of concentration. And in both respects this form entailed a shift of emphasis from the regional to the national. The economic concentration involved the rise of the large circulation press at the expense of smaller, local papers, an internal development conditioned, however, by the relationship between the press and newer media. The ideological concentration involved the growth of the political party at the expense of more informal groupings of independent politicians. Here it should be remembered that the parties comprising the Popular Front were quite youthful. The Radical party was formed in 1901 and the Socialist party, the Section française de l'internationale ouvrière (SFIO), in 1905. The Parti communiste français (PCF) was formed in 1920 after the majority of the SFIO decided to adhere to the Third International. Precisely as these parties assumed national and international tasks, so the relationship between politician and local electorate was weakened.[75]

The electoral reforms of 1919 introduced a form of proportional representation which placed an emphasis on the parties at the expense of individual candidates. As a result, the small newspapers which served the interests of particular Deputies quickly declined in number. And as this section of the press shrank, the large circulation dailies expanded their market share.[76] These papers attempted to dominate the market by further increasing circulation. Thus they diversified their coverage to appeal to a broader readership. The consequence was that political reporting occupied a smaller proportion of these papers than had previously been the case and a larger proportion was now given over to features, to fashion and to sport. The exemplary development of the 1920s was the introduction of various dedicated pages catering to these interests.[77] In this transformation, the dailies were guided by the model of the weeklies, the latter being perhaps the most dynamic sector of the press during the interwar period.[78] The impact of this model was clearest in the case of the evening press; the two largest circulation papers, *Paris-Soir* and *L'Intransigeant*, led the way in translating the practices of the weekly magazines into new contexts.

Thus the continued rise of the political party served to undermine the prewar organisation of the political press and to facilitate a shift of emphasis whereby the demands of the market exerted a new degree of control over the French press. The consequences may be illustrated by a review of the failure and the success of the Popular Front in this field: the failure to reform the organisation of the press and the success in adapting to the new diversification.

During the Third Republic the press was divided into two types of publication, the *presse d'information* and the *presse politique*. Here a distinction was drawn between what could be termed independent publications and those which served political groups. During the Popular Front the largest circulation dailies in the former category were *Paris-Soir* and *Le Petit Parisien*, and in the latter category the Communist *L'Humanité* and the Socialist *Le Populaire*.[79] The circulation figures of the different publications in these categories might offer one means of assessing the forces contesting the ideological front. Yet the distinction between the neutral communication of facts and forms of political commentary is a spurious one. It is the clearest indication of the relative strength of the forces; the right-wing publications claimed to be trading with the pure coin of information whilst the left wing was assigned the debased currency of political reporting.

It is hardly a new insight that the distinction between fact and commentary is spurious. In the interwar period a number of commentators, largely on the left wing, observed that the independent press was controlled either directly or indirectly by capitalist interests and merely claimed an impartiality whilst pursuing right-wing editorial policies.[80] The venality of the press was a central concern of the supporters of the Popular Front. If the Popular Front was committed to fight against the new Bastilles held by capital, then a decisive struggle would be that to liberate the press from the clutches of the newspaper trusts.[81] This was a preoccupation of the bulletin of the Comité de vigilance des intellectuels antifascistes from its first publication in April 1934. And the reform of the press was accordingly made a feature of the Popular Front programme published in January 1936. A project for reform was submitted to the government by Lucien Vogel after the election victory in May.[82] Whilst this particular project came to nothing, the campaign for reform was further intensified after the outbreak of the Spanish Civil War when the wilful manipulation of reports became increasingly obvious.[83] Yet the decisive event was the suicide of Roger Salengro, a Socialist cabinet minister who had been hounded by the right-wing *L'Action Française* and *Gringoire* over his war record. Salengro's suicide, in November 1936, was swiftly followed by legislation for press reform. However, whilst the law passed through the Chamber of Deputies it was delayed in the Senate. When a neutered version of the project was finally returned to the Chamber it was buried by the fall of Blum's government.[84]

The failure of the campaigns for reform was the failure to deal effectively with the increased control which capital exercised over the press. Yet, by the same token, other Popular Front policies met with success when the effects of this control were acknowledged and accommodated. This much is clear from the publishing practices of the PCF.

The PCF was the most recently founded party in the parliamentary coalition of the Popular Front, and as a consequence responded most effectively to the transformation of the French press.[85] Beyond *L'Humanité*, the party also supported the photojournal *Regards* from 1932 and the evening paper *Ce Soir* from 1937.[86] Such a portfolio corresponds closely with the dominant trends of the period, especially the ascendancy of the weekly press and the evening paper. Yet that the PCF would sponsor first a photojournal and then an evening paper also indicates a shift in its attitude towards its potential readership, which was no longer to be defined by reference to militancy.[87] It is not a coincidence that *Regards* was launched in the period during which the PCF rejected the policy of fighting 'class against class'. The party now opened its press to a range of everyday issues.[88] In the following years, the embrace of republican traditions led the party towards new audiences and this success in turn prompted the launch of *Ce Soir*. This evening paper was to be a rival to *Paris-Soir* and imitated its rival in the adoption of the practices of the weeklies. This, in turn, was a consequence of the market position of the evening papers; Jean-Richard Bloch, an editor of *Ce Soir*, noted that the evening papers had an additional cause for innovation in their need to distinguish their coverage from that of the morning editions.[89] For Bloch the evening paper had to offer a summary of the day's events but had also to provide a guide to the potential entertainments of the evening and, moreover, its feature articles were to be numbered amongst such distractions. The considerable coverage of leisure interests in *Ce Soir* was thus in accord with the established editorial policies of the other evening papers. Yet the coverage was also a response to the leisure policies of the Popular Front. Perhaps the clearest example of this was the attention paid to aspects of tourism, which responded to the introduction of paid holidays and the projects subsequently pioneered by Leo Lagrange at a newly created ministry for sport and leisure.[90]

Just as the morning papers had followed the pattern set by the evening press and progressively adopted the practices of the weeklies, so the editorial policies of *Regards* and *Ce Soir* came to condition those of *L'Humanité*. There is no irony to be found in the ability of Communist journalists to track the conditions imposed by capital on their work. For these journalists were in the service of a populist party. Yet for precisely this reason the development of the Communist press remains one of the clearest indices of the transformation of the press in the interwar period. As the political coverage of the party organ was increasingly supplemented by fashion pages, film reviews and enhanced sports coverage, so the operation of the market became increasingly clear.

Techniques of communication

The diversification of coverage was not only a matter of introducing new rubrics. It was also a question of new techniques and here the evening papers were again important mediators. From its relaunch, the front and back pages of *Paris-Soir* were largely dedicated to photography.[91] This emphasis on the image seems to have been a key factor in the jump in the paper's circulation, which almost doubled between October 1931 and March 1932.[92] The decision of the PCF to launch the photojournal *Regards* should in part be seen as a response to this success, as should the extensive space dedicated to photographic coverage in *Ce Soir*. Yet just as the expansion of rubrics in the evening papers was a translation of the editorial policy of the weeklies, so the expansion of photographic coverage followed a similar precedent. Here the principal model was *Vu*, the first French photojournal, launched in 1928 by Vogel.

Now, the narratives of the development of photojournalism are frequently couched in terms of technical obstacles overcome. In the case of *Vu*, publication was doubtless facilitated by technical improvements in the later 1920s, improvements in the rotary printing press and the photomechanical process of heliogravure.[93] Yet the increased speed of a printing cylinder would not constitute a sufficient cause for the transformation of photojournalism any more than the introduction of the

Leica would. An account of this transformation needs to address the shifting demands of the market and not simply the means by which these demands were met. Thus, in trying to complete the account, various commentators have invoked the impact of other technologies, those of radio and film. It would certainly seem that the introduction of regular news programmes to radio in 1923 and the development of cinema, and especially the development of synchronised recorded sound in 1929, had an impact on the existing news media, however delayed.[94] In 1937 Paul Vaillant-Couturier felt able to explain aspects of his own editorial policy for *L'Humanité* by generalising about an armchair public, a public with ready access to all manner of information thanks to the radio.[95] That radio bulletins fulfilled some of the most basic and immediate functions of the newspaper seems clear enough. However, it is extremely difficult to trace and measure the impact of one medium on another. Indeed, rather than concentrate on the competition between technologies it may be more productive to consider innovations in patterns of consumption. Here it is important to register that radio broadcasts and cinema screenings were forms of entertainment before they were means of communicating news.

Just as the technology of film involved a synthesis of existing means, so the earliest film programmes combined existing genres of domestic, urban and landscape photography. Moreover these films were screened within the context of pleasure and distraction, presented as they were at fairgrounds and café-concerts. The first programme presented by the Lumière brothers in 1895 did contain one film of a contemporary event which could be described as 'news', if one considers newsworthy the arrival of members of a photographic congress at Lyon.[96] However as the industry developed over the next decade fiction film came to prominence. Not the least of the reasons for this was that, given the complexities of location filming, simple studio fictions were cheaper to produce than film of current affairs.[97] The earliest cinema established a pattern that endured, in which the newsreel was perhaps one reel amongst five in a weekly release. And the coverage on this weekly reel was less that of the front page of a daily than that presented by another form of weekly, the illustrated magazine. Here *L'Illustration* probably offered the most important model.[98]

Whilst the radio offered a different form of temporality, like the cinema its programming was dominated by forms of entertainment. The first regular radio broadcasts, commencing on 6 November 1922, were of concerts.[99] The first regular news broadcasts followed almost a year later, beginning on 26 October 1923.[100] This first news programme,

Journal sans fil, was put out at 5.00 p.m., thus positioning itself in relation to the evening papers. Of course by 1934 a Parisian wishing to find out about the events of 6 February would have had a range of options. Radio-Paris, Tour Eiffel, Paris-P.T.T. and Poste Parisien all had daily news programmes and these ranged from short bulletins and press reviews to analyses of the debates in the Chamber.[101]

Both radio and cinema offered new platforms for journalism, then, yet neither supplanted the newspaper. However, both the newer media did succeed in placing journalism within a new hierarchy, in which consuming information was subordinate to other pleasures. Not, of course, that consuming information should be considered as an entirely sober activity. Proust has the narrator of a short story reflect on 'that abominable and voluptuous act called *reading the paper*', in which

> all the misfortunes and cataclysms suffered by the universe in the last twenty-four hours – battles which have cost the lives of 50,000 men, crimes, strikes, bankruptcies, fires, poisonings, suicides, the cruel emotions of politicians and actors – are transmuted, for our own amusement, into a matutinal accompaniment, at once exciting and invigorating, for a cup of coffee.[102]

Such transmutations are not uncommon in Proust's narratives; they are signs of a certain disposition. Whilst I would not suggest that the daily press sought to cater directly to this disposition, there was nevertheless in the postwar period a reordering of the morning paper in which various amusements were given a freer rein. If radio and cinema presented competition for the daily press, and thereby encouraged its diversification, then it is important to recognise this diversification as a reordering of pleasure and information. Such a reordering is after all to be found in the shifts in readership of the interwar period, in the rise of the weekly press and the relative decline of the daily paper. The expansion of rubrics and the introduction of new levels of photographic coverage were not ends in themselves or simple responses to developing technologies, but means of addressing a developing readership with developing forms of attention. These forms of attention are perhaps most clearly revealed by comparing the different genres of text employed in the press.

The most basic genre is that of the communiqué, an official statement issued by a body, say the PCF, or a representative, say Basch as the president of the Ligue des droits de l'homme. The communiqué is presented as a statement of fact; it most commonly opens with location in time ('yesterday, at 6.00 pm'), and space ('in the Parisian region'), and then proceeds to a narration of a sequence of events ('the decision to strike …'), presented in chronological order. In this presentation, events are primarily physical; the communiqué is the genre of the positivist. And it goes without saying that the positivist writes in the third person.

At the opposite end of the scale is the report which exploits the resources available to the first-person narrator; Rim's account of the young photographer is one example of this type of report. This genre, which might be referred to as the genre of the eye witness, is a careful expansion of the communiqué. The eye-witness report preserves the location in time and space ('the other Tuesday, at the Place de la Concorde'), but does so to locate the individual witness. This witness expands the range of the communiqué in offering subjective impressions, and using adjectives quite freely (demonstrators may form a 'black wave'). But to preserve the integrity of the report the author may use only certain forms of description and speculation. For example Rim may see the photographer as a reincarnation of Gavroche, the street urchin of *Les Misérables*, but he may not enter the mind of this figure. In the eye-witness report interiority is to be externalised in dialogue.

The communiqué and the eye-witness report were distinct genres of journalism, yet, depending on the situation, aspects of these genres could be combined in different measure. In the period immediately after the First World War a key determinant was the type of publication in which an article appeared. For several years after 1918 newspapers tended to rely on variants of the communiqué. This was because the price of paper limited dailies to four pages and accordingly limited the length of articles and their discursiveness. However, as such effects of the war receded, so did the reliance on the communiqué.[103] Precisely as the daily press diversified and increasingly adopted the practices of the weeklies, so it exploited an increasing number of genres. The neutral account of the communiqué was supplemented by the descriptive range, telling detail and reported conversation offered in the eye-witness account. Thus the austere language of positivism was supplemented by the range of pleasures afforded by the techniques of the realist novel. These techniques would be less those of Victor Hugo than of Georges Simenon. Individual articles did not of course seek the range of *Les Misérables*, yet they would track across the ground familiar to Inspector Maigret. And whilst Simenon's prose is hardly florid, the detective novel certainly commands the forms of description and dialogue exploited in the eye-witness report. The frequent serialisation of Simenon's work would only have served to underline the connection. (For example, the issue of *Marianne* containing Rim's article on photographers also featured an installment of Simenon's *Le Locataire*.) Newspapers provided new literary forms, as Walter Benjamin observed.[104] Thus the reordering of information and pleasure addressed and transformed the way newspapers were read. For whilst the communiqué effaced itself, attempting transparency, and positing a relatively passive consumer of information, the eye-witness report exploited a range of techniques and addressed a more complex subjectivity, one prepared to exercise the range of skills proper to the reading of fiction.[105]

In a market responding to the arrival of new media, the press increasingly sought to address this latter readership and to this end editors increasingly sought the assistance of photographers. In the presentation of an event such as the riot of 6 February 1934, an eye-witness report like Rim's could draw attention to incidents, such as the loss of a photographer's hat, which would not feature in a communiqué. And in turn, the description of such incidents could encourage an examination of photographs in which details such as discarded hats become salient (Fig. 1). Yet of course not all photographs would reward such attention in equal measure. Less than revealing were the studio portraits of public figures, usually by Henri Manuel, which frequently accompanied newspaper articles. Thus in the postwar period the practice of press photography was transformed. This was precisely to provide an imagery which could appeal to skills analogous to those of the reader of fiction and which could sustain similar forms of attention. A key agent of this transformation was a new professional figure, the reporter-photographer.[106] Tracing the emergence of this figure, the final task of this chapter, is a means of tracing the emergence of a new practice of press photography.

The press photograph and the reporter-photographer

When Rim sought to define the activity of the reporter-photographer, his first recourse was to a contrast with the practice of a Man Ray or a Kertész, that is, a contrast with the practice which made of photography an art. The photography Rim describes is not the work of a famous individual, it is 'anonymous'. It does not belong in the studio, it has 'come down onto the street'.[107] These are familiar oppositions and familiar locutions, suited to the centre pages of the weekly. The descent to the street is as commonplace as the evocation of Gavroche for the description of those found there. Perhaps the most one can say is that the banality of these terms is appropriate to the anonymity discussed. The terms, then, by themselves, are insufficient to frame an analysis of press photography. However, the anonymity Rim describes may be given its own specificity when one observes that the photograph accompanying his article is credited not to an individual, or even to a publication, but to a photographic agency.

These agencies created a form of anonymity which, paradoxically, became the defining feature of French press photography in the interwar period. The anonymity of the agency photograph was twofold. Not only was the image made for reproduction, the site of reproduction was not specified in advance. For the agencies worked without specific commissions. Their images, then, are not just anchorless but to a certain extent rudderless. Yet for precisely these reasons such images could be more readily circulated. It was this new facility of circulation which was fundamental to the interwar period; it created new conditions for the reception of photography, yet it also created new conflicts.[108]

This new form of circulation was a response to the postwar transformation of the press but it was a response shaped at once by the demands of the press and the existing organisation of photography. Measured in terms of titles launched, the French press of the interwar years had its decisive period of expansion between early 1928 and early 1934.[109] This period, with a hiatus between mid-1930 and late 1931 due to the delayed effects of the Wall Street Crash, also saw the decisive expansion of the market for press photography. These parallel phases of growth are nicely marked by the development of journals dedicated to the photographic image: *Vu* first appeared in March 1928, *Regards* first appeared as a monthly in January 1932 and as a weekly in January 1934.[110]

Nearly a decade after *Vu* was founded its artistic director Alexandre Libermann estimated the volume of images circulating with a simple calculation. In 1937 Libermann saw the representatives of between eight and ten agencies every day, each bringing a selection of perhaps 40 photographs, so he saw 320 photographs a day, 2,240 a week, 8,960 a month and roughly 120,000 a year.[111] The situation Libermann describes was the consequence of a specific form of growth. He was not describing a simple increase in commissioned work nor the growth of work produced by staff photographers employed by particular publications. Such work existed of course, but Libermann was emphasising a separate development, the growth of the photographic agency. It was this which gradually transformed the structures of mediation preserved from the prewar period.

In the years before 1914 the French market for press photography was comparatively small. The development of the half-tone process did create new possibilities for editors, but these were not grasped with any alacrity in France. The first half-tone image to appear in a daily newspaper was published in the *New York Daily Graphic* in 1880 but such an image did not appear in France until *Le Matin* adopted the technique in 1902.[112] Yet even after this innovation the market remained weak as only' *Excelsior* developed an editorial policy designed to exploit the photograph.[113] This weakness had two effects, each with its own impact on the postwar period. The first effect concerns the status of photographers. Most newspapers avoided expensive contracts with staff photographers and sought images from freelancers and photographic agencies. The second consequence concerns these agencies, which in the absence of both significant demand and significant competition were not compelled to adjust their existing practices. The agencies founded at the turn of the century were combinations of studio and archive; a studio such as that of Henri Manuel generated negatives in the process of fulfilling commissions and created a second source of income by making this archive available to interested parties. So the practice of the agency was principally geared to a nineteenth-century mode of production organised around the studio.[114] Thus the earliest agencies remained suppliers of *reportages photographiques*, that is, they remained simply suppliers of illustrations.[115] It was only in the postwar period that these agencies were overtaken by newer organisations supplying *actualités*, photographs of current affairs.

The growth of new photographic agencies after 1918 may be traced through the relevant trade directories. For its first year of publication, 1922, the *Photo Annuaire* lists three agencies.[116] By 1928, the first year of the decisive expansion of the press, the list is divided between Paris and the provinces, with 17 entries in the former section and 7 in the latter.[117] Yet perhaps the clearest sign of the emergence of the new photographic agency is the appearance of a rubric for such organisations in the trade directory dedicated to the press. This rubric first appears in the *Annuaire de la Presse* for 1929, with a list containing 18 entries.[118] It is not surprising that the rubric should appear at this date, and nor is it surprising that it should be located in the section dedicated to 'Agences d'Informations et principales correspondances de Presse'. However the emergence of the photographic agency in the sphere of the press agency signals at once a break from and a continuity with the prewar period.

The emergence of the new photographic practice marked the final decline of the studio-based agencies. This much is signalled in the listings of the general trade directory, the *Annuaire de Commerce Didot-Bottin*. Here the number of agencies listed as supplying *reportages photographiques* grows steadily through the 1920s with a marked increase during the period of press expansion. Yet the *Didot-Bottin*, as a general directory, permits comparison between sectors of an industry as it cross-lists entries. This cross-listing shows that, at the beginning of the 1920s, supplying *reportages* was one of a number of activities for an agency. However, by the later 1930s many agencies had refined this activity into a specialism and were only rarely cross-listed as providing studio work.[119] Yet, by definition, the emergence of the new agencies also demonstrated that a significant number of reporter-photographers remained independent of specific publications and this was in continuity with the prewar period.

However, the image presented by the directories is incomplete. Such directories might be considered as communiqués issued on behalf of capital. They have their own locations of time and space, their own methods of sequencing, and their own studied neutrality, all designed to facilitate the exchange of goods and services. The directories are guides to spheres of circulation and offer much less on the complexities and inequalities of production. This is clearest, of course, in the general directory. Indeed it is clear in the very organisation of the *Didot-Bottin*, which uses the classification system that Frédéric Le Play had developed for the universal exhibition of 1867. As several commentators have observed, photography is resistant to such systems for a number of reasons: because it is a hybrid of the chemical and optical, because it has a wide variety of potential uses and because it might conjure different forms of labour.[120] As a result the listings for photography are distributed across a number of Le Play's classes. There is a basic listing for 'Photographes' under 'Instruments et procédés généraux' but also, for example, a listing for 'Photographie (éditeurs de)' under 'Librairie-Imprimerie'. However, the new agencies specialising in press photography created a new problem. In the *Annuaire de la Presse* these agencies are listed with other correspondents, but the listing in the *Didot-Bottin* for 'Correspondance et agences de presse' under 'Librairie-Imprimerie' refers one back to 'Reportage photographique', a sublisting under 'Photographes'. The nineteenth-century categories could not easily accommodate the development of the agency for the hybrid press photograph. These agencies were organised along lines distinct from the conventional studios but were nevertheless classified as such.

Yet rather than operating with fixed categories, the photographic agencies served to facilitate unfixing. The agencies existed to circulate images; that is, they were a form of mediation designed to maximise the occasions on which a photograph might be reproduced, to increase the number of possible exchanges. Such mediation operated most effectively by unfixing signs, and multiplying the categories in which an image might function. Consider for example the distinction between *reportages photographiques* and *actualités*. This distinction fulfilled a task and registered an orientation but the distinction was not absolute. Photographs could be shuttled between the categories. Events which met the editorial criteria for inclusion on the front page could unfold so as to return an image to a status it had lost. The death of a politician might restore an archived studio portrait to the category of *actualités*, if only for a day. Conversely, the signs which anchored an image with a date could soon become unrecognisable, freeing the image to serve other audiences and functions more effectively. So the instability of signs could serve the different demands of the market well enough and there were few photographers who would resist attempts to extract value from an old negative. Thus none of the parties involved would have wished the distinction between *reportages photographiques* and *actualités* to be fixed.

With this unfixing of the photograph in the marketplace, images were defined by their context to a new degree. Walter Benjamin registers as much when he notes that, with illustrated magazines, captions become obligatory.[121] This was the consequence of making anonymous photographs for reproduction. Benjamin describes this in terms of the driving back of cult value by exhibition value. It may also be described, in a different register, as the redefinition of photography in terms of the circulation of imagery.

The taxonomic problems of the *Didot-Bottin* are indications of the ways in which press photography broke free of earlier definitions of photographic practice. The waning of the studio-based practice involved a division of the production process and increased specialisation. For what is press photography but a specialisation in the production of one form of commodity? Yet, once separated from the ensemble of practices defining photography, is the reporter-photographer simply a supplier of commodities? What would be the consequences of such a designation? Here, once again, there was a conflict between the sphere of circulation and that of production. This was a conflict between the site of commodity exchange as 'the exclusive realm of Freedom' and the site for the exploitation of purchased labour-power. Consider the interests involved in the publication of the photograph of the riot in *Marianne*. The credit for this image reads 'Photo N.Y.T.', indicating that it was taken by a photographer working for the New York Times agency Wide World Photos. The photograph was, therefore, precisely a commodity: an object produced not as an end in itself but to be exchanged. As such it was a stake in a struggle between the photographer and the agency. The site for this struggle was the agency office on the Rue Réaumur, and here the struggle was potentially not only over the price for the negative but also over rights for initial and subsequent reproduction.[122] Such a struggle was conditioned by the status of agency photographers and the nature of their contracts, and at the date when the riot photograph was taken these contracts were at the centre of a complex series of negotiations conducted by a special section of the Syndicat national des journalistes.[123] For if the photographers were placed at a distance from the studio, then the value of their skills would have to be asserted in relation to another profession.

One effect of the growing concentration of the press in the postwar period had been the recognition of a new level of *esprit de corps* amongst journalists. As a result of this the Syndicat national des journalistes was founded in 1920. Now the various smaller syndicats were united to protect the interests of the whole sector, including, eventually, the reporter-photographers. For as the market for press photographs grew in the years after 1918 a new hierarchy developed between reporter-photographers and their employers. Accordingly steps were taken by photographers to protect their interests and in 1924 Maurice Boiry attempted to group those collaborating with the press into an association. The group ultimately formed was a *syndicat*, but as the membership was too small for the foundation of a *syndicat indépendant*, the group went through a series of different affiliations. In a further rehearsal of the classifications of press photography the *syndicat* was linked successively with the Syndicats de la chimie and then the Syndicats du livre before finding a home with the Syndicat national des journalistes in 1931.[124]

Henceforth the press photographers had a means of defending their status as *journalistes de l'objectif* as opposed to mere *opérateurs*.[125] To this end on 14 October 1933 the photographers formed their section within the Syndicat national. The negotiations of this section were in turn part of a wider struggle, pursued in the Chamber of Deputies through Henri Guernut's project for a law establishing the professional status of journalists.[126] Even though the passing of the Guernut law in March 1935 confirmed reporter-photographers as journalists, the status of agency photographers remained problematic. This was because to benefit from the protection of the new law photographers needed to be regular collaborators with specific publications and this was not necessarily the case for agency workers.[127] And these photographers remained a significant proportion of those active in this sector of the industry. Boiry calculated that in 1936 there were 55 photographers working for 15 papers and 35 working for 15 agencies.[128] The struggle of this group of photographers was to identify their skills with those of the journalist. Therefore the contract proposed by the reporter-photographers followed the Guernut law in insisting that the photographer was not a mere technician. Rather than simply following a set of instructions, the photographer had to be able to work independently and be able to provide a commentary on any suite of images produced.[129] That is to say that the captions which Benjamin noted had become crucial for the interpretation of the photograph in print were, ideally, to be drafted by the photographers. The anchorless photograph was to be secured. And what was lost in one dimension of the photographers' practice was to be restored in another, when they acted in their capacity as reporters.

Whilst the proprietors of the press formed one front of resistance to these negotiations, the proprietors of the photographic agencies organised another, constituting themselves as the Syndicat de la presse d'information photographique on 12 November 1934.[130] The conception of photography entertained by these proprietors was quite distinct from that of the reporter-photographers. For the proprietors, the role of the photographers was to supply a demand not simply for images but for images with a currency which matched the text they were to accompany. If this required a rapid turnaround on the part of photographers working for the weekly press the speed of response obviously had to increase as photographers came to provide more and more material for the daily press. This situation was simply a local variant of the drive to extract surplus-value through increasing the productivity of labour. This was to be achieved by the intensification of labour and also by the introduction of more efficient instruments. Here the interests of the agencies and the press were expressed in the technology they exploited; the tension between these interests and those of the photographers is evident in the significant disparity between the technical developments of the period and the instruments used by photographers. Throughout the interwar period, photographers used large format 9 × 12 cameras with 12 plates, most usually in the 1930s Klapps produced by Gaumont.[131] These cameras were heavier and certainly less convenient to use than the newer small format models, nevertheless they continued in service because prints could be made directly from their plates, dispensing with the need to use an enlarger. Thus the advantage of the older camera was that its prints could be produced more quickly, and if there were disadvantages in the weight of the instrument this was a burden borne, literally, by the photographer. This concern with speed is made clearer still in the considerable investment which went into refining the technique for transmitting photographs by telegraphic means. Experiments with this technique were first undertaken by Arthur Korn in 1902 and were continued by Edouard Belin, who first demonstrated the *bélinographe* in 1908. By 1933 refinements had produced a suitcase-sized transmitter.[132] With the *bélinographe* the photographic image was separated from its material support and transmission replaced transportation. This was done in the service of the press, and the *bélinographe* belongs properly in a history of the press rather than a history of photography. In a market in which the value of an image stood in direct relation to the speed at which it was communicated, the *bélinographe* was the purest expression of the desire to extract surplus-value.

The *bélinographe* separated the photograph from the photographer, the commodity from its producer. It was the technical expression of a wish that Belin also expressed in 1936 as president of the Chambre syndical française de la photographie et de ses applications. Belin proposed that the Chambre syndicale be affiliated to the Confédération générale du patronat française; that is, he proposed that proprietors of photographic enterprises identify themselves with other proprietors rather than with other photographers. And Belin made this proposal despite the fact that a Confédération nationale des syndicats de photographes had been founded in 1934 to represent photography as a unified practice.[133] Belin's proposal was one further attempt to reclassify and redefine photography; here the practice was to become simply a source of commodities.

So if the transformation of the press in the interwar period was characterised by the new preponderance of the demands of capital, this found its own expression in the organisation of photography. Yet whilst the new demands of capital meant that the ideological operation of the press was reconfigured, this operation was certainly not suspended. That the photograph in *Marianne* was a commodity conditioned but did not destroy its significance. Once an agreement on pricing was reached and the photograph was published, it entered into a further set of struggles, over the meaning of 6 February 1934.

That a meaning for 6 February had not been immediately secured was a sign of the weakness of the Republican imaginary. However, on 14 July 1935 the events of the 6th were given a place and a meaning. This marked the decisive moment in the creation of the image of the Popular Front.

2
'People of France': The Image Created

> We take the oath to remain united to defend democracy, to disarm and dissolve the factious leagues and to place our liberties beyond the attack of fascism. On this day which revives the first victory of the Republic, we swear to defend the democratic Liberties won by the People of France, to give bread to the Workers, work to the Young, and Peace for humanity to the World.[1]

This is the text of an oath sworn on 14 July 1935. On the anniversary of the storming of the Bastille, 'the people' pledged to conquer new citadels and to secure the victory of the Popular Front. Such is the founding myth of the Front. According to the myth, as it was rehearsed in various speeches on 14 July 1935, 'the people' of France had passed through a trial but had been delivered. The events of 6 February 1934 had shown that France was divided, and that a struggle must commence to unite the country. How the battle was fought was a tale that varied with the teller, but most versions included the following sequence of events.

On 6 February 1934 various groups, including the Camelots du roi and the Ligue des Croix-de-Feu, demonstrated against the new government of Edouard Daladier. The night, of course, ended in riots, and the following day Daladier resigned. The PCF then mounted a counter-demonstration on 9 February. Then the Confédération générale du travail (CGT) called a general strike for 12 February. The SFIO decided to hold demonstrations on this same day. The PCF then took the same decision. These two parties had previously been opposed but on the 12th their supporters converged at the Place de la Nation. This moment of unity led to a rapprochement between the sections of the left wing and a pact between the two parties was signed on 27 July. On 9 October

1934 the general secretary of the PCF, Maurice Thorez, called for the pact to be widened to include the middle classes in a 'Popular Front'. This front was finally cemented in 1935 when the Republican party of the centre-left, the Radical party, agreed to participate in a series of 14 July celebrations.

These events are the subject of this chapter. Yet there is no smooth arc from the unity of 12 February to the unity of 14 July. The story I have just retold was an attempt to describe this arc but this involved a number of elisions. For example, the Communists stumble on their heroic march when their participation in the riots of the 6th is included in the narrative. Moreover, 12 February and 14 July represent quite distinct moments. Whilst the rallies of February were ultimately protests, those of 14 July were explicit demonstrations of support for the Republic.[2] Between these events lay a complex series of negotiations and tergiversations in which a number of different groups attempted to respond to the popular demonstrations and to redefine them for their own ends. The 14 July celebrations were the result. However, these celebrations should not be seen merely as the formal collaboration of the parliamentary parties, for they marked the reconstruction of a hegemony. Yet what enabled the reconstruction? What exactly had been destroyed?

The crisis of Jacobinism

The Radical Republic was brought to an end on 7 February 1934. When Daladier resigned on the morning of that day his government became the first since 1870 to be brought down by violence. Yet ultimately this was not a complete collapse of the democratic process. The actual night of violence did not destroy the government; instead, it was brought down by the resignation of Daladier. His resignation was a consequence of his isolation, in turn the result of the decision of the Radicals to satisfy the demands of the right-wing demonstrators. The crisis was of the 7th, not the 6th and it was the crisis of the Radical party, the party which identified itself with the defence of the Republic.[3] Until 7 February the Radical party had been able to present itself as the incarnation of the perfected Jacobinism of the Third Republic. However the abdication of responsibility on the 7th destroyed this legitimacy.[4] The latter-day Jacobins of the Radical party had abandoned the role established by their Revolutionary precursors; they were now reluctant to lead. So the crisis of the 7th was a crisis of the historical bloc of the Third Republic to the extent that it threatened the 'exchange of individual elements between the rulers and the ruled, the leaders and the led'.[5]

Neither the Socialists nor the Communists were able to assume the mantle of Jacobinism in February 1934. The protest demonstration of 9 February organised by the PCF ended in further violence. Yet on the same day the organ of the CGT, *Le Peuple,* carried the announcement of a general strike for 12 February; this strike was to demonstrate popular support for the Republic.[6] Whilst the demonstrations of the 12th were to become central to the myth of the Popular Front, the initial coverage of these events reveals the distance between the participating factions and the absence of the conditions needed for a reconstruction of hegemony.

Both the SFIO and the PCF represented the 12th as a day of united action, however, their conditions for this unity were mutually exclusive. The Communist account in *L'Humanité* presented the demonstrations of the 12th as a realisation of the strategy of the 'united front', which entailed appeals to Socialist workers whilst refusing any cooperation with the actual Socialist party. The PCF had pursued this strategy of unity at the base as one aspect of their policy of fighting 'class against class'. This was a policy formalised in July 1928 by the announcement of the 'Third Period' tactics. Thus in *L'Humanité* the Communist Deputy André Marty argued that while 'the Socialist party has kept in the background in these difficult days, constantly overwhelmed by the militants at its base, the workers have declared that our Communist party was everywhere on guard, and in the thick of the battle'.[7] For Marty, the success of 12 February was simply a vindication of the established policy of the party. 'Yesterday was the triumph of the unity of action of the Parisian proletariat, rising not to defend the bourgeois Republic ... but to prepare the overthrow of the rotten democracy by the true Republic of working people and peasants, the Republic of the Soviets of France.'[8] Such an account was a product of the Bolshevisation of the Communist parties, in which the revolution was envisioned as a united proletarian response to crisis.

The account in the Socialist organ *Le Populaire* presented the unity of the workers in a quite different guise. Whilst *L'Humanité* merely acknowledged the presence of the Socialists in the demonstration, *Le Populaire* emphasised that the 12th marked a moment of reconciliation between the parties.

> 12 February will be a date fixed forever in the history of the French proletariat. For the first time in years, the two rival factions of the working class have abandoned their fratricidal struggles ... How many were there? At least 150,000 workers of the hand and mind.

> They had responded to the call of the Socialist party and that of the Communist party, which had given the order to its supporters to join with ours.[9]

In *Le Populaire* the reconciliation is almost inevitable, cemented by force of circumstance:

> The crowd grows minute by minute. It is now so dense and so compact that ... it is impossible for militants to rejoin their respective organisations. The Communists join with us. Further back, near the Porte de Vincennes, a great number of our friends in the SFIO mix with the Communist marchers. In a moment, all will march shoulder to shoulder, with one spirit and one heart, carried by the same wave of generous indignation, by the same invincible faith in the strength and the sovereignty of the proletariat united before a common enemy.[10]

Here it is the very streets of Paris which force the factions together. The response to the threat becomes one in which the demonstrators are physically united. And in turn this unity is presented as a defence of the Republic; in a speech delivered at the Place de la Nation Léon Blum declared, 'we are all united in order to defend the Republic because we know that only the Republic can enable our forward march'.[11] This is only a partial defence, of course, but it is nevertheless clearly at odds with the declarations of the PCF. Whilst the Communist account emphasised the united front 'from below' which would ultimately overthrow a corrupt, capitalist regime, the Socialist account emphasised a unity of workers, coordinated by the political parties and dedicated to saving 'the Republic of the workers'.[12]

If *Le Populaire* emphasised a spontaneous unity which *L'Humanité* did not, the two newspapers nevertheless had a common approach to the coverage of 12 February; both party organs viewed the events from within the framework of existing policies. Thus the events of the 6th had not yet assumed their full significance. The extent of the Radical crisis was not yet recognised; as a consequence neither the Socialists nor the Communists were able to develop a coherent means of responding to it, let alone profiting from it. So the task of protecting the parliamentary terrain of Jacobinism was not yet to be assumed by the parliamentary parties. In the first instance this task was undertaken by a new formation, the Comité de vigilance des intellectuels antifascistes (CVIA).

The rearticulation of hegemony

The CVIA was the first antifascist organisation to be founded after the events of February 1934. The early vitality of the committee was due to its date of birth, for as a new organisation it was not weakened by the ideological sclerosis which still constrained much of the left in France. The CVIA was therefore able to respond to the conditions which obtained after the 6th. Thus it was able to provide the terms for the reconstruction of the hegemony of the Third Republic.

The manifesto of the CVIA, *Aux Travailleurs*, was drafted by Pierre Gérôme and André Delmas, the latter now being fully persuaded of the danger he had refused to digest with his dinner on the evening of the 6th. Gérôme and Delmas persuaded Paul Rivet, Paul Langevin and Alain to be signatories to the manifesto. These figures represented a spectrum of the left; Rivet was a member of the SFIO, Langevin was known to be sympathetic to the Communists and Alain to the Radicals. At a symbolic level, the manifesto performed the task of uniting the left in the aftermath of 6 February and as such it came to be presented by the CVIA as the first realisation of the Popular Front.[13]

The manifesto was a declaration of support offered to the workers by intellectuals; it was an explicit attempt to initiate exchanges between 'the leaders and the led'. It begins:

> United before the spectacle of the fascist riots in Paris and the popular resistance which was the single response offered to them, we set aside our differences and declare to all workers, our comrades, our resolution to struggle with them in order to save from fascist dictatorship all the rights and public liberties which the people has conquered.[14]

In this formulation of events, the liberties previously won by 'the people' are protected by the most dynamic class, that of the workers. The intellectuals now recognise and support this action. This formulation differs in important respects from those offered by the party organs. Whereas the PCF called for a Republic of the Soviets and the SFIO a Republic of the workers, the manifesto of the CVIA refused to maintain a privileged link between the Republic and a class. The manifesto addresses a broader audience. 'We shall not let virtue be invoked by the corrupt and corrupting. We shall not let the anger provoked by financial scandals be turned against the Republic by the banks, trusts and arms dealers – against the true Republic of the people working, suffering, thinking and striving for emancipation.'[15] Here the Republic is identified with those who are active in its cause, the true Republic belongs to those who struggle for liberty. Thus the manifesto moved beyond the positions previously adopted on the left. It was implicitly a rejection of the united front from below and a rejection of the sectarian positions adopted by the PCF and the SFIO. Yet it was also a rejection of the collapsed position of the Radicals, for it did not mark a retreat to the status quo and a facile identification between the Republic and the sovereign will of 'the people'. 'We do not have to preserve the world as it is, we have to transform it, to deliver the state from the tutelage of capital – whilst maintaining the closest links with the workers.'[16] Thus the three signatories of the manifesto should not be seen as representatives of the three parties active in promoting an alliance. Instead they are figures close to the parties who share a recognition of these parties' failures. The symbolic force of the party allegiances of the signatories derives from this.

Aux Travailleurs was the first effective antifascist statement in France because it was the first to acknowledge that the older responses to fascism were individually inadequate, whether they derived from class solidarity or the reflexes of republican defence. In the manifesto of the CVIA these older responses are offered in a new combination. Fascism is identified with oppression and the Republic with liberty; the agents of fascism are a financial oligarchy and the defenders of the Republic are all those who struggle for liberty. In the antifascist struggle, the workers were to become the guardians of 'the people', the guardians of the sovereign will of the nation.[17]

The working class is thus called back onto the political stage. This class was now to return in a specific role, that which Gramsci described as belonging to the protagonist of French history. In a note on French and Italian culture, Gramsci had argued that the

> very complexity and diversity of French political history during the last 150 years has enabled the historical culture and the general culture of France to develop and become 'popular-national' ... A unilinear national 'hagiography' is impossible, and any effort to produce one appears immediately sectarian, contrived, utopian, and antinational because it has to erase [or to undervalue] indelible pages of the nation's history ... For this reason, the permanent element of these political variations, the people-nation, has become the protagonist of French history: hence a type of political and cultural nationalism that breaks through the limits of the strictly nationalistic parties and impregnates the whole culture[.][18]

Antifascism revived this nationalism and 'the people-nation' moved upstage. This was the consequence of joining the struggle against capital with the defence of the Republic.

The conjoining of these struggles may be described as an 'articulation', a term proposed by Ernesto Laclau and Chantal Mouffe in their revision of Gramsci's theories. This revision is crucial to an understanding of the operation of 'the ideological front' and therefore it is crucial to an understanding of the image of the Popular Front. Laclau and Mouffe use the term articulation in its etymological sense, to designate a joint; articulation is 'a *political construction* from dissimilar elements'.[19] This emphasis on the articulation of the dissimilar is fundamental to their revision of both hegemony and universality. Whilst Gramsci had described hegemony as the process in which a combination of ideologies brings about economic and political unity on a universal level, Laclau and Mouffe emphasise that the universal level is not unified but unstable, precisely because hegemony is a construction of dissimilar elements.

Laclau and Mouffe argue that hegemony is only secured by articulation, by the forging of links between different social groups. If this is done then distinct and dissimilar groups may nevertheless act in concert, and struggle together. The forging of such links requires the participating groups to establish 'relations of equivalence between themselves'.[20] Yet this does not mean that different groups simply identify with one another; relations of equivalence are not to be confused with relations of identity. Acting in concert does not entail the merging of groups. Rather, it entails a group redefining its own sphere of interests. Gramsci had argued that hegemony was secured when a class was able to present its own interests as universal interests. For Laclau and Mouffe this is what is achieved by establishing relations of equivalence. They argue that equivalence is represented by 'one particularity whose body is split, for without ceasing to be its own particularity, it transforms its body in the representation of a universality transcending it'.[21] Thus one group may transform its interests, transcending sectarian concerns and thereby embracing the interests of other groups. It is this transformation which secures hegemony. Yet Laclau and Mouffe take care to emphasise that the transformation remains incomplete; the body does not cease to be its own particularity and thus the universality remains unstable. The universality of hegemony 'is a *contaminated* universality'.[22] And because it is contaminated, the universality cannot be secured absolutely. It is contingent. Thus the practice of articulation 'consists in the construction of nodal points' which may serve to join separate struggles but may only 'partially fix' their meaning.[23]

This account offers, I think, the best means of grasping the complex operations foreshadowed in *Aux Travailleurs*. The new bloc sketched by the manifesto was to be formed by the working class assuming a set of tasks broader than those defined by merely sectarian programmes. As has been seen, such a movement beyond the corporate characterises the political moment of hegemony. This was to be achieved by the articulation of two struggles, that of the workers and that of those defending the Republic. By such means relations of equivalence were to be established between 'the people' as a class and 'the people of France'.

Gramsci had argued that the suppression of the Commune had destroyed the umbilical cord between the 'new people' and the tradition of 1793 because this marked the point at which democracy broke down into classes. However, the publication of *Aux Travailleurs* could be said to mark the point at which the working class was restored to the role of bearer of the Jacobin tradition. The protagonist of French history now spoke with a new accent. Or rather the protagonist spoke with an accent which had not been heard clearly since the very first years of the Third Republic. Yet ultimately this accent could not alter the role that the protagonist was to play.

Relations of equivalence

The Mollard sisters lived together. The eldest, Catherine, had been married but her husband had left her for another woman. Now she acted as mother to Madeleine and Dédé. Catherine had started work at 13; she was the only female glassblower in her factory. The two younger sisters also worked. Despite this, the three together barely earned enough to survive. Unfortunately, in the spring of 1935, there was nothing remarkable in any of this. What was remarkable was that the story of the Mollard sisters was told. The sisters were interviewed by Etienne Constant for *Les Femmes dans l'Action Mondiale*, the journal of the Comité mondial des femmes contre la guerre et le fascisme. Constant was interested in the sisters precisely because their impoverishment seemed unremarkable. The purpose of the interview was to transform privation from a condition into an experience, to make the statistical punctual, and even painful. Constant wanted to represent the sisters at once as individuals and as types: 'there are so many Mollard sisters in this world'.[24] Thus for Constant the Mollard sisters are particularities whose bodies are split; they are themselves but also representations transcending themselves. The sisters are, then, figures of a struggle for hegemony, figures of the antifascist struggle.

The Comité mondiale des femmes contre la guerre et le fascisme was intended to coordinate struggle on the feminist front. As Gabrielle Duchêne explained in the first issue of *Les Femmes dans l'Action Mondiale*, the committee was a 'mobilisation of all feminine forces ... brought about to combat war, to combat fascism and, in general, to resist all attacks on the material and moral condition of women'.[25] Like the CVIA, the Comité mondiale des femmes was formed in the wake of the events of February 1934, and like the CVIA, the committee sought to articulate the struggle against fascism with other struggles against oppression. Each committee carried the struggle against fascism to a different constituency. Each thus required its own form of address, its own appeal to the universal, its own relations of equivalence. Establishing these relations was the precondition for the creation of the Popular Front.

The CVIA addressed Gramsci's caste of traditional intellectuals, the group predisposed to undertake tasks viewed as universal, the group whose members tend to 'think they are themselves the state'.[26] Accordingly, the appeal of the CVIA was made with reference to the state, and couched in terms of the defence of Republican liberties. Here the workers' direct resistance on 12 February was articulated with the intellectuals' principled resistance. Basch, of course, signed the manifesto, as did over 1,200 others, ranging from scientists to sinologists, from grammarians to geologists.

The Comité mondiale des femmes addressed a gender and its appeal could hardly be to a state which stubbornly perpetuated the disenfranchisement of women. Instead, the exploitation of women was related to the exploitation of purchased labour-power. Thus, in the first issue of the committee's journal, Bernadette Cattanéo asked directly: 'Is not the female worker the most exploited under all the regimes where capital is in control?'[27] The oppression of a class compounded the oppression of a sex; it is this that the Mollard sisters were to represent. The feminist struggle was thus articulated with that of antifascism. This articulation also met with success; in 1936 the committee estimated its membership to be 600,000, three times that of the SFIO.[28]

The Comité de vigilance and the Comité mondiale followed the same strategy through different campaigns; the two successes were one. In each case, relations of equivalence were established between particularities, between Victor Basch and André Delmas, between Gabrielle Duchêne and Dédé Mollard, and between Delmas and Duchêne, because the principal organisers of the feminist committee were traditional intellectuals. They too were members of the CVIA, exercising vigilance in specific capacities. These relations of equivalence served, then, to articulate struggles and to form the foundations of the Popular Front. But they also produced contradictions within the Front. Relations of equivalence are not relations of identity, and Paul Rivet recognised this when he assessed the progress of the CVIA on its first anniversary.

In an article in the committee's bulletin, *Vigilance*, Rivet notes that after 6 February 1934 those with 'little interest in public affairs suddenly came to feel a close solidarity uniting intellectuals and workers, despite their different situations'.[29] The events of the 12th made the intellectuals 'understand how their love of independence corresponded to the great desire for liberty felt by the popular masses'; and so the '"common front" of free men' was formed.[30] Having linked worker and intellectual in a common front, Rivet attempts to find a connection between them which goes beyond an abstract appeal to liberty. Of the intellectuals, Rivet notes that their work 'does not finish at the door of the laboratory, studio or lecture hall; they pursue it in their every act and often into their dreams'.[31] Thus the intellectuals 'live from their labour like the most simple craftsmen and the most humble labourers, and this constitutes a link between the groups'.[32] Rivet then continues:

> I do not doubt the strength of this link, but it is also the point at which the similarity between the intellectual worker and the manual worker ends, at least under the social conditions of capitalist regimes. For the manual worker, work is only a means of securing his subsistence and that of his family and, in fact, it is a form of servitude or, if you prefer, a necessity. For the intellectual, work is an end in itself, it is first and foremost a source of pleasure; it is not merely a means of earning a wage.[33]

There is a stumbling here. Rivet, a professor of ethnology, would not use the word 'servitude' lightly, but making a second attempt with 'necessity' does not help his case. For the problem confronting him cannot be conjured away with a change of terminology. The problem is this: in creating a common front of 'free men' Rivet is also forced to acknowledge that freedom is not enjoyed by all in equal measure. The 'intellectual worker' might work and be free, but this privilege is not extended to the 'manual worker'. Here Rivet confronts the contradiction which Marx described, the contradiction between the language of *liberté, egalité, fraternité* and the conditions for the extraction of surplus-value.

One did not need to be either a philosopher or an ethnologist to identify this problem, however. Writing a year after Rivet, and probably with the Le Chapelier law in mind, the seamstress Jeanne Bouvier noted that the liberty won by the Revolution was principally a bourgeois acquisition. 'The bosses are freed. They can set up shop where they wish. They can produce poor quality goods. And, in the name of this holy liberty, they can reduce the wages of their workers and employees.'[34] This freedom won by capital would, in due course, enter into conflict with the freedom of universal suffrage and produce the contradictions of the Republic.

Before February 1934, the position of the revolutionary left was that the contradictions of the Republic would ultimately be overcome by the successful prosecution of the class struggle. This success would be the fruit of working-class unity; in this analysis, the oppression that visited on the working class united it, and its members had only to recognise this to struggle successfully for their freedom. Hence the policy of the united front, the policy pursued in different ways by both the CGT and the PCF. In the immediate aftermath of 6 February 1934, the leadership of the CGT were the first to recognise that the struggle had now to be articulated with a campaign of Republican defence. Yet it was the CVIA which succeeded in developing this articulation. Whilst its terms were unstable, as Rivet was forced to concede, with this articulation the working class became again the bearer of the Jacobin tradition. Even so, for the Popular Front to emerge as a parliamentary coalition, the PCF would also have to embrace this tradition.

Communist and Jacobin

If the members of the working class were restored to a role in 1934, the stage on which they were to act was not thereby transformed. The drama was to be played out on the parliamentary terrain. This is to say that the historical bloc which Gramsci saw established with the Third Republic was not to be transformed; rather, a new political bloc was to be formed which would maintain the overall configuration of the historical bloc.[35] Yet to secure this new formation the PCF had to abandon its policy of fighting 'class against class' and assume a position within the Republican imaginary. Internal and external factors contributed to this process. Bernard Pudal has argued that the various tactics of the Third Period were means of implanting the PCF and securing its reproduction as a proletarian party; this was achieved by the summer of 1930 and it was at this date that Thorez renounced sectarianism.[36] Then, from the early summer of 1934, the worsening of relations between Germany and the Soviet Union created a Franco-Soviet rapprochement.[37] In this situation the French section of the Third International could be viewed more favourably within the Chamber, and Thorez was thus given further encouragement to shift the position of the party.

The process of transforming the party may be traced through the development of the language of its leader. Annie Kriegel has demonstrated that through the spring of 1934 Thorez gradually redefined the meaning of 'unity'.[38] In an article published at the end of May, Thorez designated the united front as an 'antifascist' one.[39] And in an article of 15 June, he emphasised 'unity' rather than the 'united front'.[40] Finally, in a speech of 26 June, Thorez demanded: 'Unity of action at any cost'.[41] The consequence of this shift of position was the pact signed with the Socialists on 27 July, which marked the transition from the united front 'from below' to one organised 'from above'.[42]

The next development was the transformation of the united front of the working classes into a 'Popular Front'. Thorez proposed this in his speech of 9 October. In this speech he certainly retained much of the aggressive tone of his earlier declamations. Yet he also presented the theory of historical materialism as a continuation of the materialism of Diderot and Voltaire. Thorez thereby annexed to Marxism two figures frequently claimed as precursors of Radicalism, in the process offering an instance of that capacity for progress and perfectibility which was a central tenet of Radicalism.[43] This prepared the ground for the proposal to extend the pact with the Socialists. Thorez sought 'to attract new forces' in order 'to seal an alliance between the middle classes and the working class'.[44] If Thorez preserved the terms of struggle by preserving the idea of the front, in extending this front beyond the working classes he exceeded the terms of class struggle in a move analogous to that made by the CVIA. However, this did not amount to a call for an alliance with the Radical party.[45]

Nevertheless it could be said that the Radicals were being prepared for such an alliance. Two weeks after Thorez proposed the Popular Front, Daladier marked his return as a political force with a speech calling for a campaign against 'the 200 families'.[46] These 200 were the largest shareholders of the Banque de France, the only shareholders permitted to choose the bank's twelve governors. For Daladier the 200 families thus represented a new concentration of power and in this perspective the Banque de France was the new Bastille. This rhetoric was, then, a part of the heritage of the Revolution. Although it was first revived in the early Third Republic, in 1934 it was given a new lease of life by Daladier.[47] If the Jacobinism of Thorez gave a new lineage to Marxism, then the Jacobinism of Daladier operated reciprocally to give the Radicals a renewed focus in the struggle against the inequalities of capital.[48]

The final consolidation of the Popular Front was the result of events in the spring and early summer of 1935. On 16 January 1935 the Comintern's political secretariat approved the new French policy. At this moment the PCF attempted to dilute the policies the Socialists were proposing for a Popular Front programme to make that programme more palatable for the Radicals.[49] And now there was a further shift in the language of the French Communists. Perhaps this may be seen most clearly in the use of the term 'Popular Front'. Denis Peschanski has shown that although the term was coined in October 1934, it only came to be fully exploited by the PCF in May 1935.[50] At this point the vocabulary of class was abandoned. As a consequence the party shed part of its image as an insurrectionary agent of the Soviet Union. As the central committee of the PCF noted in June 1935: 'For many peasants and petty bourgeois in the country the bogeyman is no longer the Bolshevik with the knife between his teeth. It is fascism, the men of the Croix-de-Feu, the Camelots du roi and the Solidarité française with their daggers and revolvers'.[51] This situation effectively reversed that of the 'class against class' period. As opposed to the intransigence of this phase, the strategy of the Popular Front enabled the struggles of the Communists to be articulated with those of the petty bourgeoisie and the peasantry. This strategy thus rehearsed that of the Jacobins, as Thorez himself suggested.[52] And thus the 'Jacobinisation' of the PCF in 1935 enabled the party to occupy a terrain previously held by the Radicals.[53]

The tactics of the PCF would not, however, have been successful without certain other factors. The Radical Pierre Laval signed a Franco-Soviet pact on 2 May 1935 and Stalin now declared his approval of policies of national defence. As the PCF quickly adapted itself to this changed situation a further obstacle to an alliance with the Radicals was removed. The second decisive factor was the pattern of the results of the municipal elections of 1935. These elections revealed a marked swing to the left and effectively demonstrated the unpopularity of the Radical policy of concentration, the policy of seeking parliamentary alliances with the centre and right.[54] In the 5th *arrondissement* Rivet stood as a Popular Front candidate against a veteran of 6 February and the success of the antifascist candidate was one of the clearest signs of the transformation of the political landscape. In this situation the Radicals were forced to the left just as the turn of the PCF to the discourse of 'the people' brought the party to the right. With this convergence the force of the Republican imaginary was renewed. And this renewal was confirmed by the process of sealing a Popular Front from above, a process begun when the Radical party agreed to participate in rallies celebrating 14 July 1935.

The call to the people

Already by the early summer of 1935 the mythology of the Popular Front had been established. This mythology traced the origins of the movement to the events of February 1934: the parliamentary capitulation following the violence of the 6th, and the spectacle of popular resistance on the 12th. Within this mythology, 6 February demonstrated the extent of the fascist threat, and 12 February the spontaneous antifascist response. If the Chamber had seemed paralysed by the threat, 'the people' had refused to be cowed by violence. 'The people' would defend the Republic if the elected representatives would not. This mythology served to unite various factions, and was certainly effective in defining the antifascist struggle. Yet on 14 July 1935 this version of the mythology reached the limits of its efficacy. This was the consequence of the Radical participation in the Popular Front demonstrations. For if the antifascist struggle was defined as a defence of the Republic, then the participation of the Radicals was problematic. Was it not this party which had capitulated in February? How then could the other members of the Popular Front countenance collaboration with the Radicals? And yet how could this be avoided? For if the antifascist struggle entailed the defence of the Republic and its institutions, then this struggle had to be carried to the Chamber. And for the antifascist forces to succeed there the participation of the Radicals was required. In short, the mythology of the Popular Front demanded that it be sealed from above, at the level of the political parties, but this also threatened the movement as it had hitherto been defined.

The potential contradiction between an antifascist popular movement and an antifascist parliamentary coalition was registered by a range of protagonists. That the coalition would be a betrayal of the workers was an argument voiced with the most spleen by Trotsky.[55] A more guarded variant of his arguments was made within the SFIO by the group around Marceau Pivert.[56] Within the PCF, the *Que faire?* group mounted an opposition to Jacobinisation based on similar principles.[57] And if the early history of the Second and Third Internationals still exercised an influence on the revolutionary parties, so the electoral abstentionism of early syndicalism had its effect on the CGT. Thus the left-wing unity gradually forged since the summer of 1934 could be undermined in a number of different ways by the sealing of the Popular Front from above.[58] From another perspective, certain members of the Radical party had reason to resist the formation of the coalition precisely because it was an involvement with previously revolutionary factions.[59]

This, then, was the effect of 'fascism' on the French political bloc. The left wing was forced away from its conventional forms of class struggle towards the centre and a defence of the institutions of the bourgeoisie. And the centre was in turn forced out of its habitual parliamentary sphere and into a new engagement with the working classes. For the supporters of the Popular Front, of course, these two trajectories could intersect in a Republican defence. The task confronting the organisers of the 14 July demonstrations was to ensure this intersection.

14 July had been made a national holiday under the Third Republic. Henceforth the storming of the Bastille was celebrated as the moment of popular intervention in the French Revolution. If since 1919 the day had increasingly been appropriated by the right wing as an occasion for military display, it remained, nevertheless, the festival of the Republic.[60] And whilst in the immediate aftermath of 12 February 1934 a Republican language could not be employed equally by all protagonists, such a difficulty did not arise for the commemoration of 14 July 1935. The Radicals could certainly claim an attachment to this language of greater longevity than that of either the Socialists or the Communists, yet the Republican tradition was no longer an exclusive preserve. That this was so reveals the distance travelled by the left. Yet that the reanimation of the symbols of a democratic culture was to take place on the streets indicates the trajectory still to be traced by the Radicals, for taking to the streets was carrying the members of the party beyond their normal sphere of operations.[61] Yet it had to be so. The Radicals had succumbed to the pressure of violence and had destroyed the legitimacy of the Radical Republic. This legitimacy had been destroyed by street violence and it could only be fully restored by further action on the streets.[62] For if the era of violent demonstrations was effectively closed by the events of February 1934, the streets remained the theatre for symbolic confrontations.[63]

Given the potential conflicts arising from the sealing of the Front from above, it is not surprising that the organisation of the events of 14 July was initially undertaken by extra-parliamentary groups. Whilst the first impetus for the 14 July demonstrations came from the pacifist Amsterdam-Pleyel movement, the first meeting to discuss the project was convoked by this group together with the CVIA and the Ligue des droits de l'homme.[64] This meeting was held at the Palais de la Mutualité on 17 June.[65] At this point no representatives of the political parties were involved.[66] The provisional planning committee met at the headquarters of the Ligue, and the president of this committee was Basch, the president of the Ligue.[67] It was Basch and Rivet who approached

Edouard Herriot, the president of the Radical party, to secure the participation of that party.[68] On 19 June Herriot put the proposition to his party committee and gained its approval; five Radicals were to liaise with the provisional committee: Paul Anxionnaz, Raoul Aubaud, Jacques Kayser, Robert Lange and Ernest Perney.[69]

Following the agreement of the Radicals, the full Comité d'organisation met for the first time on 21 June 1935.[70] A programme was now agreed which transformed the conventional celebrations of Bastille day into a means of reviving the Republic. The celebrations of 1935 were closely modelled on the Revolutionary *fêtes des Fédérations*. One of the organisers, Jean Guéhenno, was explicit on this point.[71] Like the Revolutionary festivals, the celebrations of the 14th were to be defensive acts of unity; and like the *Grande Fédération* of 14 July 1790, the events of 14 July 1935 were an attempt to bring a popular movement under official control.[72] The celebrations would begin with a festival of youth on the evening of 13 July.[73] 14 July itself would feature a mass meeting, 'The Assizes of Peace and Liberty', with a keynote speech, supporting declarations and an oath to be sworn by delegates gathered from across France. This meeting would be followed by a march from the Place de la Bastille to the Place de la Nation. In the evening, the oath would be sworn again by the assembled marchers.

The first announcement of the demonstrations of 14 July was a call addressed 'To the People of France'.[74] Whilst this announcement rehearsed the language used by the CGT in calling the strike of 12 February, the two calls were made under quite distinct conditions. The success of the 12th was the result of decisions made by three separate organisations while, in contrast, the call to demonstrate on the 14th was made by a Comité d'organisation acting on behalf of 48 associations. Now the unity at the summit represented by this committee had to be reproduced at the base. This was the purpose of the call to 'the people'.

According to the terms of this address, the French people had revealed liberty to the world on 14 July 1789 and the task now was to consolidate this victory. Thus the 14th became at once 'a day of remembrance' and a 'day of hope', and a continuity was established between the struggles of the past and those of the future.[75] Certainly, this was one more instance of the articulation of antifascist struggles. Yet the articulation was to be of a specific kind, it was to be an articulation of the struggles of 'the People of France', of 'the people' as the sovereign will. This 'popular sovereignty' was to be dressed against the 'vast conspiracy' of the 200 families.[76] The identification of people and nation, first established in 1789 with the National Assembly, was to be reaffirmed in the antifascist struggle. Now 'the people' had to 'liberate the Nation' from the grip of the new feudal overlords.[77]

Such seems to have been the wish of the committee. Offering an interpretation of the 14 July demonstrations Robert Lange confirmed that their purpose was to 'show to the fascists that they have ranged against them the mass of the sovereign people'.[78] This, at least, is what he hoped to show; yet his description of the looked-for crowds as 'the sovereign people' was not a demonstration that they were such. And it could not be. For such a demonstration requires the ritual of the ballot box, and this ritual was not yet available. Nevertheless, an analogous demonstration had to be made if the events of 14 July were to restore the legitimacy of the Republic. Thus the organisers had recourse to the swearing of an oath. If the description of the crowds as sovereign could not be demonstrated as a fact, it could at least be made a self-description: 'the people' could acclaim 'the people'. Thus 14 July would not only be the 'day which revives the first victory of the Republic', as the oath has it, but would also mark the revival of the Republican imaginary.

The oath of 14 July, cited at the beginning of this chapter, was published as the conclusion of the call to 'the People of France'. It was drafted by André Chamson and Jean Guéhenno.[79] The new oath, as an affirmation of unity, recalled the Tennis Court Oath of 20 June 1789, in which the Deputies of the Third Estate swore 'never to separate, and to meet wherever circumstances demand, until the constitution of the kingdom is established and affirmed on solid foundations'.[80] And the new oath was derived from that of the Tennis Court insofar as it was a defence of the liberties which those meeting at the Tennis Court had sought to establish through a constitution. Yet as well as asserting a defence of *liberté*, the oath was also a promise to secure *egalité* and *fraternité* in their modern forms: a promise to give 'bread to the Workers, work to the Young', and 'Peace for humanity to the World'.[81]

However, the oath printed was not the same as the oath taken. An oath has to be sworn before witnesses, otherwise it is merely a statement. The published text was a declaration of intent on the part of the Comité d'organisation. But it was only a declaration; at best, it suggested terms for participation on 14 July. On publication, the printed text simply moved from above to below, from parties, associations and committees to 'the people'. Yet while issuing from above, the oath was to be sworn on the day the Bastille was stormed, the day 'the people' intervened in the Revolution. And it was to be sworn not only by the leaders, but also by the led.

The inauguration of the Popular Front

The call to 'the people' of France was met with a national response; on 14 July 1935 some 500,000 marched through Paris, and many more assembled in towns and villages across the country.[82]

At the mass meeting at the Buffalo stadium in Paris the opening speech was delivered by Basch. He declared that the liberty threatened by the Affair had to be 'secured from attack, once and for all'.[83] I have already discussed how Basch linked 'the people' of 1789 with 'the people' of 1935 and how he linked in his person the struggle of the Dreyfusards with that of the antifascists. Here both Republicans and revolutionaries could recognise their programmes. Thus Perney's speech on behalf of the Radicals opened with the declaration: 'The festival of 14 July is a living symbol which sustains the republican nation.'[84] And in Jacques Duclos's speech for the PCF he noted that the Communists were 'conscious of being the inheritors and upholders of the glorious revolutionary traditions of our country'.[85] For Perney, 14 July brought back to life past struggles and past victories. For Duclos the 14th was an anticipation of triumphs to come. Thus, at the Assizes of Peace and Liberty, the new temporality of struggle was confirmed. 14 July was both commemoration and inauguration; this was the triumph of Jacobinism for the Radicals and the Communists alike. Indeed, sympathetic commentators such as Guéhenno and Chamson saw not Perney but Duclos as the incarnation of the Jacobin spirit.[86] They felt a particular charge in Duclos' rendition of *La Marseillaise*. The strains of this anthem were now reconciled with those of *L'Internationale*. Here, for the first time since 6 February 1934, the signs were in the right order. On that winter night couplets from *La Marseillaise* and *L'Internationale* had competed and this was afterwards taken as a further indication of the confusion reigning that evening.[87] On the 14th, according to Guéhenno, Duclos made each anthem serve as a refrain for the other.[88]

The continuities of struggle figured in different ways by Basch and Duclos were different means of representing the Popular Front. Yet these representations were not the realisation of the Front. That was to be accomplished by the taking of the oath.

At the Buffalo stadium, the swearing of the oath was representative; for the oath was sworn by 10,000 delegates assembled from the regions of France. These delegates could be considered the latter-day counterparts of the Deputies sent to the Estates General. Yet it was no longer a question of remaining united to establish a constitution as that task had been completed in 1875 by the new Jacobins of the Third Republic.

Rather, the task was to defend this achievement. On swearing the oath, the delegates undertook this defence. However, this was not simply the rehabilitation of a discredited Radicalism. For the Jacobinism of 1935 was not that of 1875; with the events of February 1934 the working class had returned to the stage. The protagonist of French history, 'the people-nation', now spoke with a new accent, transforming the Jacobinism previously vaunted by the Radicals. Yet whilst the delegates at the Buffalo stadium spoke with this new accent, it was to be heard much more clearly in the second swearing of the oath, in the evening of 14 July.

In the afternoon of the 14th demonstrators converged on the Place de la Bastille, answering the call to 'the people'. They had come to preserve the Liberty revealed to the world on 14 July 1789 and to storm new Bastilles. Before 14 July 1935 these metaphors of preservation and conquest were largely the property of a political caste. On the 14th the metaphors were made physical: the Bastille column became an actual rallying point. Before the 14th the column was a dead monument, a symbol only in the weakest sense. Yet when the crowds moved on to the Place de la Bastille the symbol was reanimated.[89]

In attempting to secure the hegemony of the Third Republic, the Popular Front proceeded through the articulation of distinct struggles against oppression. This practice of articulation required the construction of nodal points to fix partially the meaning of these struggles in relation to the defence of the Republic. Such nodal points are discursive but at privileged moments the discourse is lifted above the textual. The swearing of the oath of the 14th was such a moment, when the textual became embodied. And the convergence on the Place de la Bastille was another such moment. Now Bastille became a nodal point and the struggles of the Popular Front were given a physical articulation. But this physicality was not that of the street battle, this was not the physicality which had left corpses on the Place de la Concorde on the night of 6 February 1934. The new physicality held to the parameters set by the custodians of public order. For it was to be understood as a defence of this order. And this was made explicit in the trajectory of the march.

From Bastille, the crowds moved up the hill towards the Place de la Nation. The marchers followed a path from the site of popular intervention to a site dedicated to the Republic and ornamented, if that is the word, by Aimé-Jules Dalou's monument, *La Triomphe de la République*.[90] The path was traced not only by a selection of delegates but by the assembled masses. On 12 February 1934, Socialists and Communists had converged at the Place de la Nation and this action was now repeated. But in the repetition – the response to a call – the action was transformed and given a Republican coding. Thus the triumph commemorated by Dalou ceased to be an historical event. Instead, it became the achievement of the day. This achievement was crowned by the second swearing of the oath. Now the oath was sworn by 'the People of France'. So, unlike an oath sworn by a monarch or by mere delegates, here 'the people' declared a popular sovereignty and each individual swearing also acted as witness before the others.[91]

With the second swearing of the oath a new form of Jacobinism became hegemonic. Whatever ambiguities had attended the action of 12 February 1934, and whatever divergence there had been in the coverage of that action, it could now be secured as a first moment of Republican defence. The swearing of the oath was a confirmation of this. The role given to the working class was now clearly scripted; the new form of Jacobinism acknowledged 'the people' as a class whilst defining its action in relation to 'the people' as the sovereign will. Thus the new accent would be heard speaking largely familiar lines. The working class was not about to assume leadership as a class for Jacobinisation had precisely entailed the surrendering of the language of class. Yet the second swearing of the oath should not therefore be seen as some form of entrapment. The importance of the ceremony hardly lies in a legally binding status. The ceremony was significant because it confirmed the intersection of militant and parliamentary spheres. If sections of the working class now committed themselves to defend a Republic previously regarded with suspicion if not outright hostility, by the same token a section of the political caste previously comfortable in the Chamber now acknowledged that its legitimacy derived from the support of the working class. The oath thus established a new set of exchanges between leaders and led.

Such exchanges did not by themselves resolve the contradictions of the bourgeois Republic and for this reason the ceremonies of 14 July met some resistance. A self-consciously proletarian commentator such as Tristan Rémy chose to reject the events of the 14th because he saw the celebration of the tricolour as the celebration of a symbol 'steeped in the wretchedness of the workers' struggles'.[92] Yet at this moment Rémy was effectively isolated in his resistance. Many preferred to follow Basch in seeing an unproblematic kinship between the Revolution and the Republic. And many were willing to see the links between the festivals of 1790 and 1935. To the extent that the latter festival could be the recreation of the former, 'the first victory of the Republic' was revived. With the second acclamation of 'the people' the Republic had triumphed. This acclamation ensured 'the mutual recognition of subjects and

Subject' and 'the subjects' recognition of each other'.[93] It was this success which was soon to be celebrated in a brochure and film commemorating the events of 14 July 1935.

The commemoration of 14 July 1935

The orchestrated history of 14 July 1935 comprises three popular acclamations: that of the representatives on the morning of the 14th, that of 'the people' in the evening and that commemorated in the brochure and film. The oath of the 1935, like that of 1789, was a declaration of commitment. On 14 July, the declaration sufficed. Subsequently, words had to become deeds. For the oath, like the trinity of *liberté, egalité, fraternité,* constituted a programme to be realised. Yet because the events of the 14th had sealed the Popular Front from above, the oath now had to be translated into the formal political language spoken on the parliamentary terrain. Much could be lost in such a translation, including 'the impassioned sentiment' of 'the people'.[94] The oath of 14 July had united 'the intellectuals' and 'the people', it had united the leaders and the led in a common cause and yet the translation of the oath into a political programme threatened to convert this unity into what Gramsci would have termed 'purely bureaucratic, formal relations'.[95] Such a statement should not be taken merely as a cynical judgement on the parliamentary process, as if the Chamber were simply a *marché de dupes*. For the translation to the Chamber repeated the threat which appeared with the sealing of the Front from above on 14 July. Yet the 14th had proved a success and accordingly provided the means to counter the new threat. This threat was to be met by a commemoration of 14 July, one designed to preserve the passions of that day. The ceremonies performed by 10,000 or 500,000 may have involved a measure of bad faith or ambivalence (although of course such matters are largely inaccessible to historical enquiry); the commemoration of these ceremonies was a different matter. The third acclamation was to be exemplary. And it is this which gives the brochure and film their significance. They offer the exemplary image of the Popular Front.

Commemoration is a form of reenactment. The brochure and the film had both to stage this reenactment. The central event to be reenacted was, to be sure, the acclamation of 'the people'. Yet this entailed far more than the mere recycling of texts and symbols, for the oath itself was more than a text and the Bastille column more than a symbol.

The decision to produce a commemorative brochure and film was taken by the Comité national du rassemblement populaire, a body constituted from the Comité d'organisation. This new committee continued to meet throughout the summer of 1935 during which period its activity was effectively identical with that of the Ligue des droits de l'homme.[96] The committee undertook to draft the programme for the Popular Front and also appointed a subcommittee for 'propaganda' which was given responsibility for the brochure and film. This subcommittee comprised Robert Lange and Gabriel Cudenet of the Radical party, Florimond Bonté of the PCF, Rabaté of the Amsterdam-Pleyel movement and the film-maker Jean Epstein.[97]

Whilst the 45-page brochure and the nine-minute film were nominally produced by the same subcommittee, the conditions of their production and circulation clearly differed. The brochure, entitled simply *14 juillet 1935*, was far more widely available than the film. It was published in the last week of August.[98] It reproduces the contents of No. 21 of *Les Cahiers des Droits de l'Homme*.[99] However, unlike the journal, the brochure is illustrated with photomontages. These appear on the outer and inner covers, with a further suite inserted in the centre of the volume. A note on the back cover indicates that Robert Lange was responsible for the design and Marc Réal for the photomontages. Réal worked principally in advertising, directing the Dorland studio of the Walter Seymour Maas agency, yet he also produced cover montages for *Vu*. As such he was one of a number of photographers who translated techniques developed in advertising into the expanding market of the illustrated press.[100] Lange was one of the so-called Young Turks on the left of the Radical party and a supporter of the party's reform; he had been one of the five party members designated to make contact with the organisers of the 14 July celebrations.[101]

The film, *Le Defilé du 14 juillet 1935*, was a co-production which involved the collaboration of the SFIO and the Communist Association des écrivains et artistes révolutionnaires.[102] Unfortunately, but unsurprisingly, the film did not pass the censor and therefore could only be screened privately. The film does not carry a credit for a director, but one has to assume that Epstein played some significant role here. Besides the constraints imposed on its circulation, the film was also constrained in terms of its budget, its footage limited to sequences shot on 14 July. In contrast, the brochure is framed by retrospective accounts. Yet of course both brochure and film were produced retrospectively, and this imposes particular conditions on their interpretation.

The tacit but reasonable assumption is that whoever purchased the brochure or watched the film had participated in one of the day's demonstrations. Thus the brochure and the film had to structure an existing set of perceptions without traducing them. In this respect the brochure and film differ from that conventional reporting in which the reader and viewer have no direct engagement or clear sense of outcome. And the brochure is thus closer to a family album than to a photojournal.

The contents of the brochure are arranged in a broadly chronological order. The volume opens with a reprinting of the call to 'the people' of France. This is followed by the first retrospective account, a series of impressions noted by André Chamson. After these introductory remarks, there are transcripts of the speeches made at the Assizes of Peace and Liberty, the majority of which are by representatives of the various associations involved. Next comes the suite of photomontages. This is followed by the declaration of the Rassemblement read by Rucart and the oath as read by Rabaté. There are then declarations made on behalf not of organisations but of the regions of France. Four further accounts detail the march, the festival of youth, and aspects of the events' organisation. The brochure concludes with a statement on the continuing work of the Comité national du rassemblement populaire.

Chamson's introductory remarks establish the terms of the popular response. His terms have to be mine. Chamson, of course, was a co-author of the oath and his account is structured around the oath-taking. Whilst his principal subject is the Assizes, he begins by noting of the morning: 'At this moment, the resolute and disciplined masses had not taken to the streets in either Paris or the provinces, and no-one was yet able to establish whether popular vigilance would entirely respond to the call of the organising committee.'[103] For Chamson, it was these circumstances which gave meaning to the Assizes. They prefigure 'the engagement of the popular masses'.[104] Thus, according to Chamson, the Assizes should be understood as a faithful image of the nation. In his description, the 10,000 delegates at the Buffalo stadium, 'each being only a representative of hundreds and of thousands of other men, symbolised, therefore, at once the will, the labour, the spirit and the very flesh of the Nation'.[105] The delegates represent the nation and they express its will in the swearing of the oath. Chamson closes his account with a description of the oath-taking. He concludes that the content of the oath was less significant for those participating than 'taking the oath together, whilst feeling themselves borne by one of those events which go beyond mere individuals and fix the march of history'.[106]

Yet even as Chamson describes the first swearing of the oath he notes that 'hundreds of thousands' were to repeat it the same evening.[107] Thus Chamson's account is framed in a specific manner; at both the beginning and the end of the text the delegates at the Buffalo stadium are juxtaposed with 'the people'. And this is because, in swearing, the delegates are made 'responsible to the great movement which the people alone would be able to realise'.[108] After all, the representatives may only represent; it is for 'the people' to realise the Popular Front. The delegates are united in the swearing of the oath but it is only when 'the people' swears that the image of the nation becomes the nation. Now 'the people-nation' stands against the 'factious leagues'. As in Gramsci's account, the national protagonist is defined against sectarian national positions.

The brochure commemorates an enactment of unity; the commemoration is not only of the declaration of commitment but also of the transition from the representative to the popular. Thus the commemoration required not just a national image, an image of unity, but an image of the process of unification. That the technique of photomontage was exploited to this end is not surprising. And this is not merely because montage, as assemblage, may make explicit the process of composition. In designing the brochure, Marc Réal was required not only to furnish an image of 'the people' of France, he also had to show 'the people' discovering a common cause. Réal had not just to represent the nation, he had to show the procedures used to create a national image. These procedures comprised at once a set of figures at least as old as the Republic and a newer set of techniques, refined by the illustrated press.

The exemplary image

National types and photomontage techniques could be combined in various ways as was evident from the imagery circulated in National Socialist Germany and the Soviet Union. The subcommittee for propaganda had naturally to avoid Hitler's imagery but also Stalin's because the antifascist struggle had been defined as a defence of the Republic and not as a struggle to found new soviets. The Popular Front was a mass movement but one which had to be seen to avoid the methods of the one-party states. Accordingly, the subcommittee sought an image of 'the people-nation' which acknowledged the conditions of the mass movement whilst avoiding the totalitarian aspects potential in such an image. The balance required was one which had already been struck by the magazine *Vu* and hence, it seems, the subcommittee's decision to employ Réal, who had worked extensively for that magazine and was well versed in its procedures.[109]

Vu found its readership by applying modern graphic techniques to securely established themes and genres. This editorial policy is perhaps better understood as an attempt to supplant the conservative *L'Illustration* than as an anticipation of the Communist *Regards*. And the image of France presented by *Vu* is better understood as an attempt to renew tradition rather than as an attempt to revolutionise it. This was made explicit in a series of special issues published between the winter of 1931 and the summer of 1932, dealing, respectively, with the Soviet Union, the United States, Germany and France. In the world as seen by the magazine, the Soviet Union and the United States are the two poles of modernity. Their forms of Communism and capitalism clash in a struggle for control of Germany and hence produce the crises threatening to destroy the country. By contrast, the genius of France lies in its traditions of moderation, its ability to steer a course between extremes. The Weimar Republic presents an image of confusion which is the inverse of the stability of the Third Republic. Yet both types of image would be exploited by Réal in his commemoration of 14 July 1935.

In *Vu*, the opposed situations of France and Germany were represented in condensed form on the respective covers of the special issues (Figs. 2 and 3). 'France: A Moderate Country' establishes a set of relations between the particular and the general. The foreground plane of the cover is occupied by a photograph of a peasant, the next plane is

Fig. 2 Anon. 'France: A Moderate Country', *Vu*, No. 220, 1 June 1932, front cover. Photograph: the author. Private Collection.

Fig. 3 Anon. 'The German Enigma', *Vu*, No. 213, 13 April 1932, front cover. Photograph courtesy of Victoria and Albert Museum.

occupied by a silhouette of a spire and weather vane, and the ground bears an outline of the national borders. The three planes of the design serve to correlate three transitions. A transition of scale moves from the human figure to architecture to territorial boundaries. A graphic transition is from the photograph to the intermediate form of the silhouette to the abstraction of the outline. Finally, there is a transition from the peasant as a French type to the outline of the French territory. And if there is an ambiguity in the silhouette of the spire – which some viewers would wish to see as an image of the Catholic Church and others as a simple support for the Gallic cock – then let the absence of a declarative sign be understood as a form of reticence, one example of the vaunted French moderation. This understatement could be said to govern the whole; there is no need for an insistence on the relationship between this physiognomy, this costume and this territory. After all, the cover is speaking to the French of matters French. This discourse may use the elisions common to the vernacular. My exegesis, and perhaps any exegesis, has the unfortunate effect of slowing the discourse, of making the fluent speech halting. Yet if such a stumbling is inappropriate to the French image, it is inevitable in an attempt to describe the German image. The cover of 'The German Enigma' offers only a set of terms, unrelated, without propositional status. Like the French image, this design has three planes, but it has no governing principle of organisation. The foreground plane is occupied by a male and a female athlete, the next plane by the features of President Hindenburg, and the ground is occupied by a large, faceless crowd. Is one to accord priority to the athletes as they occupy a privileged position in the foreground? Or should that priority be accorded to Hindenburg, whose features occupy the largest part of the composition? And what would be the consequence of choosing between these alternatives? Could Hindenburg represent the crowd? Could the athletic types? The caption does not clarify matters, and its partial reprinting in a larger scale is like the insistent repetition of an unanswered question.

The French and German special issues thus provide the type and counter-type of the coherent national image. Yet in designing the commemorative brochure, Réal did not rely solely on the kinds of procedure used to represent the country of moderation. For he had to illustrate the process of cohering rather than an achieved cohesion. And to do this he required the seeming disorganisation of the counter-type as well as the fluency of the type.[110]

Réal's cover for the brochure is both summative and introductory. On this cover a number of the figures who played leading roles in the formation of the Popular Front are juxtaposed with the principal part of the oath of 14 July (Fig. 4). The presence of the leaders indicates that the brochure, like the call, comes from above. Certainly some figures are anonymous, but it is easy to recognise others. Duclos is visible at the upper right, clutching a rope as he rides on the modern equivalent of a triumphal chariot. And Romain Rolland, present as a member of the Amsterdam-Pleyel movement, is visible at the left, smiling broadly as he is enfolded in the banner of the Rassemblement. And in the foreground there are the principal figures of the Radical party, including Perney, Herriot and Daladier. The presence of these latter politicians is, of course, a sign of the participation of the Radical party on the 14th, and thus a sign of the sealing of the Popular Front at the level of the Chamber. The cover is not, however, an image recording the formation of a parliamentary coalition. By their position in the foreground, preceding the oath, the Radical figures are presented as the very leaders of the demonstration, yet these leaders are not separated from their followers. The extreme disjunctions of scale used to present the German enigma are of course avoided, as is the corresponding tension between

Fig. 4 Marc Réal, *14 juillet 1935*, Comité national du rassemblement populaire, Paris 1935, front cover. Photograph: the author. Courtesy of the Bibliothèque de l'Office Universitaire de Recherche Socialiste, Paris.

the leader's face and the faceless masses. Whilst the cover of the brochure shows individuals, and these recognisable as politicians, they are, quite literally, faces in a crowd. On this 14 July politicians cease to be an administrative caste and, going down onto the street, they are reunited with 'the people'. That this is the significance of 14 July is confirmed by the manner in which the politicians are juxtaposed with the oath. The oath is not reproduced merely as a text, printed over the montage. Instead it is incorporated in the montage, for it is included in the version which was mounted on a placard and paraded through the Parisian streets. This version, by its very scale, affirmed the text as an oath, that is, as a public declaration before witnesses. The politicians – those issuing the call to 'the people' – are the first to make this declaration. They are represented making their commitment. This also suggests how the brochure itself is to be understood. For the brochure does not offer a 'propaganda' image designed simply to gain the consent of its audience; rather it offers an image to which the leaders have given their consent. In this manner the cover proposes the terms in which the brochure is to be read. It is exemplary.

The front cover thus prepares the enactment of unity. The second photomontage then establishes the conditions under which the enactment will take place (Fig. 5). This montage, captioned 'Symbols and slogans', is placed inside the front cover. It could be described as prefatory. This description at least suits its position opposite the call to 'the people' of France, that is, opposite the initiating moment. The call was made in the name of the Comité d'organisation on behalf of the member associations and it is these associations which are represented in the montage. Prompted by the caption, a viewer may discern this quickly enough. Réal has selected and cropped photographs which clearly differentiate marchers, the respective banners signalling allegiance to Communism, Socialism and Radicalism. The montage is prefatory, then, in that it does not show 'the people' united, but rather the different groups which will unite.

The photographs in the montage are scattered in a seemingly more or less haphazard fashion around an image of the Bastille column. If the call to 'the people' is the precondition for the unified response then the montage demonstrates the conditions for articulating a unified response: the construction of a nodal point. When 'the people' marched to this column on the 14th this nodal point was made physical. It is this process which Réal's montage figures; the various groups, photographed on different streets, are assembled by Réal at the Place de la Bastille.

Yet for the Place de la Bastille to be a Republican political space, and to function as a nodal point, it was necessary that it be occupied in a particular manner. This occupation is figured by the third element in the montage, the group of spectators in the foreground. The demonstrators on the Place de la Bastille were demonstrating against government policies but, beyond this protest, the more significant aspect of the event was the affirmation of a Republican tradition. What was most important was that 'the people' demonstrated to 'the people'. The role of the spectators in the image is to figure this. Of course, the spectators also figure the viewer of the brochure but that in itself is a form of reenactment and commemoration.

Yet this montage remains a prefatory work; it represents only a first convergence, the means by which the diverse organisations participating in the Popular Front will be brought together. Thus the montage is an anticipation of the events of the 14th. Within the sequence of the brochure, these events are formally introduced by Chamson's text. His introduction turned on the distinction between the formal declarations

Fig. 5 Marc Réal, 'Symbols and slogans', *14 juillet 1935*, Comité national du rassemblement populaire, Paris 1935, inside front cover. Photograph: the author. Courtesy of the Bibliothèque de l'Office Universitaire de Recherche Socialiste, Paris.

of the morning and the truly popular response of the afternoon. This distinction was used by Réal to organise the next sequences of the brochure, the transcripts of the Assizes and the central suite of montages. The montage of symbols and slogans represents different groups rather than 'the people' united, and this differentiation persists in the presentation of the transcripts. Each of the principal organisations of the Rassemblement is represented, the PCF by Duclos, the SFIO by Paul Faure, and so on. This sequence of texts is set against the suite of montages, for the suite is organised not around a succession of political leaders, but around the response of 'the people'.

The suite opens with a summative image, as is emphasised by its caption, 'A day of enthusiasm' (Fig. 6). This summation is concerned less with a sequence of events than with a set of relations, the relations between leaders and led. The party apparatus of politicians and placards displayed on the inner and outer covers is retained in this montage, but

Fig. 6 Marc Réal, 'A day of enthusiasm', *14 juillet 1935*, Comité national du rassemblement populaire, Paris 1935, unpaginated. Photograph: the author. Courtesy of the Bibliothèque de l'Office Universitaire de Recherche Socialiste, Paris.

these figures and motifs are reordered. Thorez and Duclos are clearly visible at the upper left of the image, and Thorez has been caught in a suitably commanding pose, but these figures do not dominate; they are not placed in the foreground, and are not given a scale markedly distinct from that of the militants and demonstrators. Thorez and Duclos, as elected Deputies, are literally representatives. Their form of representation, however, was not yet secure at the end of the summer of 1935 and required the support of other forms.

The Popular Front was realised when its discursive nodal points were made physical and in the first instance this was achieved in the convergence on Bastille. Another physicality is represented in the lower right corner of the montage, by the woman wearing a Phrygian bonnet. She may be defined as Marianne, the embodiment of the Republic. Yet whilst the presentation of this woman in profile with her bonnet marks her as a symbolic figure, she is also simply an individual caught by a camera, part of the staffage of a news photograph. Moreover, the text below the montage prevents the woman from maintaining a completely allegorical function. It reads: 'After the march of 500,000 men, the delegates of the Rassemblement Populaire gather at the Bourse du Travail to count the proceeds from the sale of Phrygian bonnets'. On this occasion the attribute of Liberty is also a commodity, the woman is an individual who has identified herself with the Republic through a simple purchase. This introduces a tension into the image, a tension between Marianne and the individual woman. Thus the woman in the bonnet is a broken allegory because here a tension between the universal concept and the particular body is left unresolved. It is this tension between the universal and the particular which produces a contaminated universality. Both herself *and* Marianne, the woman is a particularity whose body is split; she is the Republic yet she is also an individual member of the population. In this sense the woman in the bonnet enacts the shift from representation to realisation established by Chamson. Thus the woman in the bonnet is to serve as a figure for 'the people-nation', she is to represent at once the popular class and the sovereign will. Yet even as the woman figured this new participation she also figured the contradiction within the Popular Front and the very limits of participation.

The woman may be understood as a live allegory and as such part of a tradition stretching back to the Revolution, to 10 November 1793 when a woman was posed on the altar of Notre Dame as a Goddess of Reason.[111] This practice flourished again in 1848 and also during the Commune.[112] Yet of course whilst the woman represented in the photomontage was able to participate on the 14th as an embodiment of the

Third Republic, she was unable to participate in the political life of that Republic because women were not enfranchised. As Bernadette Cattanéo of the Comité mondiale des femmes made eminently clear in the spring of 1935, ' "universal" suffrage, in these circumstances, is still only "universal" for men'.[113] Given this, the woman in the Phrygian bonnet is a representation but precisely not a realisation. On the 14th the Popular Front attempted to exploit moments when metaphors became physical, and Perney had even spoken of the whole festival as a 'living symbol' of the Republican nation, yet in the figure of the woman these terms could reverse themselves. Tristan Rémy registered this in his denunciation of the Bastille Day celebrations. For if the women present on the 14th could figure Liberty they could also figure the failures of the Republic. Thus Rémy noted one woman in the crowd with a tricolour,

> dragging it along like her regrets ... for all things considered the Republic had not given her much apart from this Liberty and in return for it she was to defend the Republic once again. This woman was the living symbol of the demonstration, far more so than the throng of flags. The flags belonged to the rassemblement. But this woman was the actual proof that – apart from that freedom to which the workers' organisations owe so much – everything else remains to be done.[114]

The convergence on the Place de la Bastille was supposed to be the moment the dead symbols were revived. But for Rémy the living had experiences and regrets that the symbols of the Republic did not; a life was not commensurate with a living symbol. Yet if the figure of the woman could be read in contrary ways, so, inevitably, could the positions of Rémy and Cattanéo. Rémy was present on the 14th and his account appeared in the organ of the CGT, a key organisation within the Rassemblement. Cattanéo's Comité mondiale was also an adherent organisation and a photograph of her colleague Gabrielle Duchêne appears in the brochure. These individuals had to live the contradictions of participation. The success of the Rassemblement exacerbated such contradictions, even as the montage drew together leaders and led, and as Thorez donned his tricolour sash and the women their bonnets. Yet just as the contradiction of 'the people' had been recast and made the horizon of the Republic, so the contradiction of the Popular Front could be projected towards a far horizon, or at least one as distant as the completion of a programme and the fighting of an election campaign.

The brochure could not but figure the contradictions, yet it could give them an acceptable form within the Republican imaginary, a form which the Popular Front from above could sanction. Here the image of the mass demonstration played a central role. In the next image in the suite the actual march through Paris is the principal subject (Fig. 7). Just as this march was prepared by the call and the Assizes, so this montage incorporates motifs that Réal has already presented. Of these the most prominent is, of course, the Bastille column. Yet the placard with the oath may be glimpsed again, under the retouched flag on the left-hand page. And the triumphal chariot bearing Duclos reappears on the right-hand page. The reappearance of these motifs establishes a continuity with the previous montages. And yet in the montage of the march no single motif predominates; the Bastille column does not form a compositional axis, and the text of the oath is barely legible. Nor does the montage present the neat ordering of the earlier one dedicated to symbols and slogans, which had carefully distinguished between marchers and witnesses, and separated both from the public space of the Place de la Bastille. That montage had represented the different political groups converging; the montage of the march represents 'the people' united. In this unity political affiliations seem, for the moment, irrelevant. And political leaders are also subordinated. Such figures are still present of course, including Léon Blum, the man in the panama hat in the photograph set towards the centre of the right-hand page. But Blum has to be glimpsed amongst other members of the crowd; he is not a figure gesturing from a platform.

Thus in the montage of the march the ordering principles used in the previous montages no longer obtain. This montage has something of the happy disorder of memory. Rather than offering a coherent view of the march the montage offers an assemblage of impressions, the experience of the march. And this experience had a twofold significance. First, the presentation of the experience established that the march was not simply a spectacle; it was not to be compared with the military parades taking place the same day on the Champs Elysées. As a form of display, the military parade belonged to the opponents of the Popular Front; it was a preferred form of Colonel de La Roque's Croix-de-Feu, and it found its purest expression in Riefenstahl's *Triumph des Willens*. Such parades established a clear distinction between participants and viewers and it was precisely this distinction which Réal was working to overturn. For what Réal sought to commemorate was not passive spectatorship but what Chamson had described as 'the engagement of the popular masses'. And this is the second significance of the experience of the march. Réal sought

Fig. 7 Marc Réal, 'From Bastille to Nation', *14 juillet 1935*, Comité national du rassemblement populaire, Paris 1935, unpaginated. Photograph: the author. Courtesy of the Bibliothèque de l'Office Universitaire de Recherche Socialiste, Paris.

TÉ DU
LEMEN

to figure this experience because he sought to commemorate the moment the Popular Front was realised, the moment metaphor was made physical.

The montage of the march undid the hierarchy between viewers and viewed; politicians were now faces to be glimpsed in the crowd. This established a new relationship between 'the people' and its representatives. And once this had been established, Réal could offer an image of the Assizes. This next photomontage offers an image in which 'the people' became an audience (Fig. 8). This montage is dominated by photographs of named individuals, significant figures in the formation of the Popular Front. The presence of a variety of political leaders is important to identify the nature of the Popular Front as a coalition of forces massed for the defence of the Republic. Leadership lay nominally with Basch, as President of the Comité national. His image is included of course, and numbered one, a nice indication of his status as *primus inter pares*. But his portrait is not distinguished by any other means. Indeed none of the portraits is privileged either by scale or position. There is no hierarchy or discernible sequence. Even the image of Rabaté reading the oath is not

Fig. 8 Marc Réal, 'The Assizes of Liberty at the Buffalo Stadium', *14 juillet 1935*, Comité national du rassemblement populaire, Paris 1935, unpaginated. Photograph: the author. Courtesy of the Bibliothèque de l'Office Universitaire de Recherche Socialiste, Paris.

given a special treatment.[115] The individuals pictured are thus representatives, just as the delegates at the Assizes were. The transition from these representatives to the realisation of the Front as a national phenomenon would complete the image of the Popular Front. This was the task of the final double-page spread and the last image in the central suite treating the events of 14 July.

This fifth image is captioned, 'Without forgetting the regional Rassemblements ...', (Fig. 9). This image does not represent individuals, but rather a series of gatherings. As with the montage on the inner cover, this montage has the Bastille column at its centre. Yet whereas the earlier montage used a series of Parisian street scenes, this double-page spread contains images of regional cities such as Bordeaux and Marseilles. And whereas the earlier montage presented distinct organisations, this montage presents already united groups: not, say, the Socialists of Bordeaux but the united people of Bordeaux. Thus, in this montage, Paris and the provinces are literally brought together as the call to 'the people' generates a national response.

Paris and the provinces are united at the Bastille and this is confirmed by the figures which frame the composition, at the left a single man and in the lower right a small group of spectators. The single man presides over the image as a generic Frenchman, a symbol of the French people to match the figure of Marianne. The strong backlighting of this photograph makes the figure truly generic, for it is almost silhouetted. Réal used this device to create productive ambiguities, and, as the montage presents the provincial contexts for the Popular Front, this encourages a reading of the figure as one subsuming worker and peasant, just as city and country are united.[116] Moreover, as in the first montage in the brochure, spectators are represented as witnesses. Yet now it is clear that they are witnesses to the unified response of 'the people'. If the Republican imaginary is secured with the oath to defend the Republic, then these spectators are witnesses to the oath. And this is confirmed by the very fact that the spectators in the fifth montage are themselves generic figures: they may be witnesses to rallies in Bordeaux, Nice or Saint-Etienne. Thus the Place de la Bastille is confirmed as a nodal point which is more than a merely physical point of convergence for marchers. It is now explicitly presented as an overdetermined site, a symbolic point of convergence for the nation.

The brochure thus functions, on a national scale, like a family photograph album used to record and solemnise the festivities in which the group affirms its unity.[117] The individual photographs used in the brochure, with their casual compositions and awkward framing, recall

Fig. 9 Marc Réal, 'Without forgetting the regional Rassemblements … ', *14 juillet 1935*, Comité national du rassemblement populaire, Paris 1935, unpaginated. Photograph: the author. Courtesy of the Bibliothèque de l'Office Universitaire de Recherche Socialiste, Paris.

plements Régionaux ... voici quelques
3. Grenoble. 4. Saint-Étienne.
Nice. 8. Dieppe.
FÉDÉRA
RÉSERV
CAFÉ LAURELLI

Fig. 10 Jean Biondi, untitled photograph of the Assizes of Liberty, unpublished, 14 July 1935. Photograph: the author. Courtesy of the Bibliothèque de l'Office Universitaire de Recherche Socialiste, Paris.

the photographs taken on the occasion by amateurs, such as the Socialist militant Jean Biondi (Fig. 10). Taking this photograph was an individual act of commemoration for Biondi's own photograph album. Réal's brochure gave such individual acts a national dimension. Once again the particular was to be universal.[118]

The viewers and the viewed

Turning a page may be like making a cut. Turning from the montage of the Assizes to the montage of the regional demonstrations may be understood in such terms. The editors of the film of 14 July seem to have shared this understanding. In fact, there are two striking parallels between the composition of brochure and film, bearing on the treatment of the speakers at the Assizes and on the relations between the Assizes and the demonstrations of the afternoon.

In the sequence of the 9-minute film dedicated to the Assizes, the close-ups of speakers are taken from almost precisely the same angle and distance as the photographs of individuals montaged in the brochure.[119] Moreover the juxtaposition of speakers and audience in the montage is presented in the film by repeated cuts between the tribune and the crowds. Thus the presentation of the Assizes in both brochure and film emphasises the relationship between viewers and viewed. In both instances this is a visual exchange between leaders and led. Yet of course what takes place within the stadium is only preparatory; for the Front is to be realised on the street, with the response of 'the people'. In the brochure this is confirmed by the sequencing: montages of the street precede and follow the montage of the Assizes. In the film an even more forceful device is used. Following the brief extracts from the morning's speeches, Rabaté, the secretary of the Comité d'organisation, stands to read the oath for the first time. As he reads, shots of the assembled crowd show figures beginning to raise their fists in salute. As he concludes there is a cut to the Parisian streets, whilst the soundtrack continues with the voices of the crowd swearing the oath. In this cut, the film brings together the first and second swearings, the response of the delegates and the response of 'the people'.

Thus the film, like the brochure, employs specific techniques to ensure that the sovereignty of 'the people' is acclaimed by 'the people'. This is what is contained in the cut from stadium to street, and in turning the page from the Assizes to the regional demonstrations. This enactment of unity is one where each individual swears, whilst witnessing others swear. Thus the imaginary is secured.

This is the exemplary image of the Popular Front, an image which is constituted by far more than an iconography. It is constituted in a mode of viewing, a mode described by Benjamin in his celebrated essay on reproducibility, an essay drafted a few months after the brochure and film were circulated. 'In great festival processions, giant rallies, and mass sporting events, and in war, all of which are now fed into the camera, the masses are brought to look themselves in the eye.'[120] Yet what is involved in this encounter? Benjamin offers two answers to this question. His answers depend on the attitude adopted towards the encounter, which may be either progressive or regressive. I shall use these answers to form a first assessment of the image of the Popular Front.

Benjamin defines the progressive and regressive attitudes by considering the nature of the filmed performance. He presents this performance in analogy with the performances given by factory workers in response to the requirements of the production line. Here Benjamin quotes Pirandello to the effect that 'film actors ... feel as if exiled. Exiled not only from the stage but from themselves'.[121] Marx had long ago commented on the exile of the worker. That exile, that alienation, was a direct consequence of the first alienation, the alienation of the worker's labour-power.[122] This alienation undergoes a series of permutations during the era of manufacturing and then during the era of large-scale industry.[123] The result is described by Benjamin when he notes how 'during the working day, the majority of citydwellers in offices and factories have to abdicate their humanity and submit to the control of machines'.[124] As a consequence, 'in the evening, these same masses flock to the cinemas in order to witness the film actor take revenge for them, not only by asserting his humanity (or something like it) against the machine, but by putting the machine in the service of his triumph'.[125] The masses have therefore a great interest in the actor's ability to sustain what they cannot, but this is not only an interest in the illusion created by the cinema.

Benjamin argues that in the representation 'of man's image by the machine, the self-alienation of man becomes highly productive'.[126] For the filmed performance is an assemblage, like any commodity produced under an advanced division of labour, and thus film has the potential to demonstrate the extent to which technology has penetrated everyday life. As a consequence of this penetration, the film actor is alienated not only from himself but also from his audience. 'While he stands before the lens he knows that in the end he stands before the mass of spectators. But he is no more able to present himself to this market constituted by the masses – where he offers not only his labour but also his body – than any other factory product.'[127] Thus the film actor literally acts out the alienation of the wage-labourer, the turning of self into commodity.

Yet to see this is to maintain the analogy between the actor and the worker as producer, and this analogy is not that promoted under capital. For capital, the hidden abode of production is to remain hidden, and this includes the production space of the film studio. The worker is not to identify with the alienation of the film actors' dismembered experience. Rather, the worker is to identify with the projected performance. Benjamin characterises this identification with the film star as a regression to the cultic. It is an identification with 'the false radiance' of the commodity and finds 'its counterpart in the cult of the public, a cult which fosters the corrupt mentality of the masses which authoritarian regimes seek to substitute for class consciousness'.[128] Against this regression, Benjamin poses a dialectical reversal. He notes that 'the newsreel demonstrates quite clearly that any individual can find themselves being filmed. But that possibility is not enough. *Any man today has the right to be filmed.* This right can best be clarified by considering the historical situation of literature today'.[129]

> For centuries it was in the nature of literature that a small number of writers confronted many thousands of readers. This began to change

> at the end of the last century. With the growth and extension of the press, which constantly made new political, religious, scientific, professional, and local organs available to readers, an increasing number of readers turned into writers ... Thus, today, there is hardly a European worker who could not find an opportunity to publish, somewhere or other, his own observations on his work in the form of some kind of report. Thus the distinction between author and public is about to lose its axiomatic character.[130]

Yet this change is most readily apparent in the development of cinema, 'where shifts which in literature took place over centuries have occurred in a decade. In cinematic practice – above all in Russia – this shift has already been partly realised. A certain number of those involved in Soviet films are not actors in our sense but people who portray themselves – and first of all in their own work process.'[131] Here the hidden abode of production is revealed and there is the possibility of an actual exchange between readers and writers, between viewers and viewed. This, for Benjamin, is the progressive aspect of film.

Yet in Western Europe, the 'aspiration of the isolated individual to put themselves in the place of the star, to break free from the mass, is precisely what draws the masses to the film shows. The film industry stakes itself on this quite private interest in order to corrupt the original and justified interest of the masses in film.'[132] Benjamin concludes his account by arguing that this corruption is given its final form in the totalitarian state which tries to organise the proletarianised masses without touching the property relations of capital.[133]

The image of the Popular Front established by the brochure and film of 14 July 1935 may be positioned between Benjamin's progressive and regressive modes of perception. This image is a clear rejection of the authoritarian insofar as it is a rejection of the hierarchy in which the masses are only permitted the worship of the star and the dictator. For the masses do represent themselves. At this point, at least, they appear as a protagonist, rather than as a passive recipient of the spectacle. Yet there are limits to this representation. The masses are not represented as the working class. This class remains in exile. Rather, the masses are represented as 'the people' of France. Certainly, 'the people' may demonstrate that 'great solidarity' which Ernest Renan proposed to define the nation. For Renan, this solidarity is constituted by 'the sentiment of the sacrifices made and of the sacrifices still to come'.[134] These words could serve well enough as a description of the temporality of struggle confirmed on 14 July. Yet Renan was aware that the solidarity of the nation was equivocal. 'Now, the essence of a nation is that all individuals have many things in common, and also that all have forgotten many things.'[135] Donning his tricolour sash, Thorez certainly had much to forget, including the words of *The Communist Manifesto*. The commemoration of 14 July entailed its own special kind of amnesia.

The Rassemblement continues

The task of commemoration was to preserve the passions of 14 July and the stakes involved in this are made explicit in the final montage in the central suite. This image is captioned simply 'The Rassemblement goes on ...' (Fig. 11). The montage is one of continuation, and as such is a specific reworking of the preceding images. Once again, the Bastille column is made central. Yet this image now overlays two further images. In the upper left corner is a photograph of the committee convened on 2 August to begin drafting the programme of the Popular Front. And

Fig. 11 Marc Réal, 'The Rassemblement goes on ... ', *14 juillet 1935*, Comité national du rassemblement populaire, Paris 1935, unpaginated. Photograph: the author. Courtesy of the Bibliothèque de l'Office Universitaire de Recherche Socialiste, Paris.

below is a photograph of public sector workers reaffirming their commitment to the oath at a meeting of 30 July. With such a reenactment, this montage establishes the shape of commemoration. As the prominently displayed dates on the column make clear, Bastille Day was now a commemoration of 1789 and 1935. Thus the symbolism of the column was transformed.

Following 14 July 1935 the Bastille column became not simply a point of convergence, the location of an event, but also a symbol of the 'spirit' of 14 July. To use Guéhenno's terms, the column became a symbol of the 'mystique' of the 14th.[136] The montage of the regional celebrations had established the column as a symbolic point of convergence for the French nation. Thus the genius of Liberty atop the column had presided not just over the Place de la Bastille but also over France. Yet despite this spatial extension, the montage of the regions was temporally limited to the actual celebrations of 14 July. As such it commemorated the conditions of the festival, the moment in time when urban space was made over into festive space. And this was acknowledged by the use of the Place de la Bastille as the ground for the montage. Yet it is precisely this space which is removed from the final montage. The column now occupies the foreground, overlaying the other photographs and distinguished from them by a bold white outline. Moreover, the three photographs are set on a neutral ground, a device Réal did not employ in any of the previous montages. The function of the column as a symbol of 'mystique' now takes precedence over its function in urban space.

This mystique had its own significance. If the cover of the brochure presented the leaders making the call to 'the people', and the sequence of montages showed the national response to this call, how, in turn, were the leaders to respond? This question was posed in the second retrospective account in the brochure, a pendant to Chamson's text dealing with the events of the afternoon and evening. This account closes around midnight on the 14th, with a dialogue between the author, Amedée Dunois, and an anonymous bourgeois colleague. This second individual observes that the actions of 'the people' will necessarily have consequences, for 'this afternoon the Popular Front proposed its candidacy for power'.[137] However, he continues, 'whilst the Popular Front has shown its strength it still lacks a programme'. Dunois is not troubled by this absence. 'One can make a programme from principles. Nothing's easier.'[138] Yet his interlocutor responds: 'Nothing is more easily done. Yet it remains to be done.'[139]

The task remaining was undertaken by the committee shown in the final montage. Yet the task of the committee is presented in a particular light. The committee is juxtaposed with the reenactment, the confirmation of the power of the oath and a continuation of the passions of 14 July. The photograph of the committee shows those who will translate the oath and the passions into a programme and to this extent the montage makes explicit a 'passage from *knowing* to *understanding* to *feeling* and vice versa from feeling to understanding to knowing'.[140] For the montage constructs a passage between 'the popular element' and 'the intellectual element' drafting the programme.[141] However the exchange involved in the mutual acts of swearing and witnessing the oath is here translated to another level. This final montage, and indeed the publication of the brochure, are evidence of the continuing work of the Rassemblement. And the viewer of the montage bears witness to this.

The brochure aided the translation of the Front into a movement of national unity, that is, it served to instantiate the Republican definition of the Popular Front advanced by the Radical party. This definition of the Front was secured with the publication of the final programme of the Popular Front. And Lange, the designer of the brochure, was also the representative of the Radical party on the committee drafting the programme. Brochure and programme may therefore be seen as parallel productions, locating the Front within the parliamentary framework, a framework which the events of 14 July had potentially exceeded.

The success of the Republican definition may be demonstrated by briefly tracing the fortunes of the Popular Front between July 1935 and May 1936. At the annual congress of the Radical party (held on 27 and 28 October 1935), the party noted its collaboration with a 'defensive front' and confirmed a desire 'to contribute ... to seeking bases for action which could be proposed, without prejudice, to all sincere republicans'.[142] This phrasing rendered ambiguous the commitment of the Radicals. Ambiguities persisted in the final form of the programme, published on 11 January 1936. The introduction to the programme presented it as 'directly inspired by the watchwords of 14 July', yet it avoided concrete proposals.[143] For example, it recommended a reduction of the working week without a reduction of the weekly wage, yet failed to specify a precise number of working hours. Nevertheless, this programme led to the election success of the Popular Front in May 1936. This victory was the apotheosis of the Popular Front within the parliamentary regime, the apotheosis of Jacobinism.

Yet whilst the events of 14 July 1935 confirmed the unity of the Front, and the brochure commemorating these events gave a form to this unity by casting 'the people' as 'the nation', this articulation was only partially fixed. Just as the contradiction within the Republic was cast to its horizon as the struggle for *liberté, egalité, fraternité,* so the variant of this contradiction within the Front was not resolved in its programme but cast into the immediate future beyond election victory. Given this, it is not surprising that the moment of the election victory was also the very moment at which the Front was contested. It was at this moment that an audience appeared for the criticisms voiced by figures such as Tristan Rémy. This, in turn, was to demonstrate the limitations of Jacobinism.

3
'Free Men': The Image Contested

> Sometimes, in the midst of work, he paused ... For a few seconds elation made him unaware of his surroundings. Then he went back about his business as if nothing had happened.
> 'You're dreaming mate', Alexis said to him.
> 'Yes', he answered happily, 'I'm dreaming. I'm thinking of the time when we'll be free men.'[1]

This scene is banal, but then I think it is meant to be. The brief respite experienced by the worker – his name is Eugène Picard – is a commonplace. The respite, the moment of reverie, the flight from the realm of unfreedom: these are all staples of the literature addressed to working life. This is not to say that the novelist quoted, Tristan Rémy, lacks imagination, for the repetition of the tropes is part of the point. Rémy's novel, dealing with a strike wave in 1936, tries to hold close to the rhythms of the shop floor. And on the shop floor locution, gesture and execution are all subject to repetition.

Yet the moment of respite could also be central to the strike; one could foreshadow the other. The fleeting happiness of Picard's response to Alexis could be an anticipation of the transient freedom of the strike, which itself anticipated another, more distant, moment of freedom. These freedoms, sometimes only glimpsed, were the prizes at stake in the strikes of 1936. And this struggle towards freedom was also a struggle over the image of the Popular Front. These contests are the subject of this chapter.

The occupation of power

In creating a front of 'free men' Paul Rivet had been forced to acknowledge that freedom was itself divided in the bourgeois republic. The articulation of different struggles which defined the hegemony of the Popular Front produced its own conflicts. No one was more exquisitely sensible to this than Léon Blum. If the conflicts could not be resolved within the framework of parliamentary institutions, Blum did at least work hard to clarify the position of the SFIO within these struggles. He had argued since 1926 that parliamentary victory for the SFIO meant not the conquest of power and the beginning of revolution but only the exercise of power within the existing political institutions. In July 1935, as the Popular Front emerged, Blum refined the relationship between conquest and exercise by adding a third term: the occupation of power, a means of defensive struggle against fascism.[2]

This position had consequences for the programme of the Popular Front. That programme limited itself to immediate measures, yet it also forecast that when 'this joint programme has become a reality, a great change will have taken place. Liberty will be better defended; bread more certainly ensured, peace better guaranteed.'[3] For those drafting the programme the task was to strike a balance between caution and ambition. This was an attempt to reconcile the competing interpretations of the Popular Front as an extension of previous parliamentary coalitions and as a broadening of the united front. It may also be seen as a nice equivocation.[4] However the different interpretations of the Front did not mean that it was placed in a state of conflict. For in the period before the elections, the varying interpretations were not forced into a confrontation. Before the elections the Front existed only potentially and the task for its supporters was to realise it on the parliamentary terrain. After 14 July 1935 this task became hegemonic, in the sense that other tasks and struggles became subordinate to it. Previously, the sacrifices involved in the formation of the Front had been largely self-imposed. At this end of the scale was the seemingly intimate act of drawing a line through text, the example of self-censorship set by the syndicalist Marcel Martinet, who removed certain criticisms of the PCF from the text of *La Culture prolétarienne* because, although he had reservations about the Popular Front, 'one does not have the right to obstruct something which would prove useful for the true unity of the working class'.[5] At the other end of the scale were the larger calculations involved in the drafting of a common programme and the fighting of an electoral campaign. The final sacrifices were those exacted in the second round of voting on 3 May 1936, when certain Popular Front candidates withdrew in each others' favour.[6]

Following this second round the Popular Front emerged with a clear victory. The SFIO won the most seats and on 4 May Blum announced that his party was prepared to lead the new government. Yet in accordance with constitutional convention, Blum waited for a period of a month before taking office. During this month a series of strikes took place, which grew to produce the largest strike movement France had yet seen. The image of the Popular Front as a front of working-class solidarity was now reasserted. Thus the discipline of the pre-election period did not survive the victory to which it had contributed. Before the elections there had been at least a sufficient level of consensus as to the immediate tasks confronting the potential Popular Front. Following the elections, the meaning of the victory had to be decided. It was at this point that the divergent interpretations of the Front confronted each other. Now the Popular Front threatened to break down into its constituent classes.

Thus with the occupation of power the Popular Front was transformed. The hegemony exercised within the ranks of the Front had now to be exercised on a parliamentary terrain which subjected it to quite different demands. Yet for the PCF this was also an opportunity. The Communists attempted to preserve a privileged relation with 'the people' by remaining outside the government whilst pledging to support it. This position was defined by Vaillant-Couturier on 6 May 1936:

> We shall not raise the question of ministerial portfolios with a government which is constituted to defend the people, to defend bread, liberty and peace.
>
> We are resolved to bring to this government the support of the assembled masses, at once the most ardent and the most disciplined in the country.[7]

Thorez elaborated on this point on 25 May when he addressed the central committee of the PCF. He emphasised that the defining feature of the victory was the fact that it was imposed by the masses. For Thorez, this gave his party a central role as the mediator between the masses and the new government.[8] Yet of course 'the ministry of the masses' produced its own problems. Some of these were related to the ambiguous relationship between the PCF and the Chamber. As a revolutionary party the PCF was, in principle, opposed to the Chamber as an instrument of oppression functioning in the interests of the bourgeoisie; nevertheless the Chamber was an important terrain where these interests could be contested.[9] The victory of 1936 gave the Communists more influence in the Chamber, yet the party kept a distance from the government, whilst protesting its loyalty. The significance of this position would become clear as the strike wave unfurled.

If the occupation of power posed the question of the relations between leaders and led at the level of the parties, it also posed it at the level of the party organs. Before the election victory the best description of Blum's professional status was as political editor of *Le Populaire*.[10] After the victory he was president of a cabinet-in-waiting. Such a transformation was not just of Blum's status but also of *Le Populaire*'s. For now the party organ stood in a new relationship to the parliamentary terrain. This is not to say that *Le Temps* immediately lost its status as a semi-official publication but it is to register that the election victory disturbed a previously stable alignment between capital and the press. Whilst the exact relationship between *Le Temps* and the Comité des forges et des houillères was debated, there was no doubt that the paper was backed by conservative financial interests. For most of the Third Republic it had been easy enough to identify these interests with the dominant political interests of the country and *Le Temps* functioned through this identification, as to a lesser extent did papers such as *Le Journal* and *Le Matin*. For the readers of these papers the election victory did not break the identification; it seems it was easier to consider the Popular Front an aberration. And as I shall show, for these readers the aberrant status of the Front was confirmed by the strikes which greeted the election victory.

The occupation of the factories

The first strike took place on 11 May at Le Havre, the second on 13 May at Toulouse.[11] Both strikes began in response to the sacking of workers for May Day absenteeism. Thus the strikes were demonstrations of workers' solidarity, demonstrations which were in part encouraged by the belief that a 'great change' was about to take place. Acting on this belief, the strikers adopted the tactic of occupying their factories. Such a tactic was not unprecedented as a means of preventing employers from hiring an alternative labour force, yet these occupations had a new charge in May 1936 as they foreshadowed Blum's own occupation of power.[12]

By the second week of May Blum was already being criticised by members of his own party for inaction. For example, Marceau Pivert, the leader of the *tendance* at the extreme left of the SFIO, noted that the 'leading bodies of the party are lagging behind the masses'.[13] Such impatience also seems to have been a factor in the first Parisian strikes, which began with a strike at the Bloch factory in Courbevoie on 14 May. This strike was not part of a demonstration of solidarity but instead had a pay increase as its principal goal. Whilst this dispute was quickly resolved, further strikes took place in Paris. By 24 May there had been six factory occupations.

Moreover on this day 600,000 demonstrators marched past the Mur des Fédérés at the Père Lachaise cemetery to commemorate the martyrs of the Commune. The PCF was aware that the size of the demonstration was not simply a sign of support for the government about to take office. On 25 May the party passed a resolution containing the following statement: 'The central committee understands and sympathises with the people's evident desire, given that nothing has been achieved in the three weeks since the Popular Front victory, to see put into practice with the greatest urgency the measures agreed in the joint programme.'[14] Thus the impatience earlier voiced by the left-wing minority of the SFIO was now acknowledged by the central committee of the PCF. The impatience sensed by the party was more forcefully expressed the next day by the true unfurling of the strike wave; now the Nieuport factory at Issy-les-Moulineaux and the Lavalette factory at Saint-Ouen were occupied. Blum himself was later to describe these events as a slap in the face.[15]

The origins and timing of the strikes were the subject of bitter disputes in the press and the contradictions produced by the new government were only too evident in the coverage offered by the organs of the Popular Front parties.[16] Thus in *Le Populaire* the first coverage of the strikes coincided with the publication of a provocative article by Pivert entitled, 'Everything is possible'.

> Everything is possible. Yes, everything is possible for those who dare to act, thanks to the atmosphere of victory, confidence and discipline which is spreading over the country. Let's mobilise the party; let's get others to follow us; let's decide, let's act.[17]

Pivert argued that the party now had a mandate for action and that the burgeoning number of strikes in the wake of the election victory was a demonstration of this.[18] Yet Pivert remained in a minority within the party, and the strikes were presented very differently on the front page of the same issue of *Le Populaire*. This account stressed the congenial, leisurely atmosphere within the occupied factories. The author was happy to note 'the seductive sound of accordions and saxes coming from certain workshops'.[19]

These different accounts of the strike – as a festival and as a revolutionary action – were seized on by the right-wing press.[20] On 28 May, in *Le Jour*, Léon Bailby contrasted Pivert's declaration of ambition with *Le Populaire*'s more lyrical description of the factories and swiftly drew the conclusion that the paper was attempting 'to minimise the operation'.[21] Bailby was greatly alarmed by the occupations and saw them as the beginning of a campaign of expropriation organised by the Communists. Such claims were made by a number of papers hostile to the Popular Front, most forcefully in the avowedly right-wing papers such as *L'Ami du Peuple* and *L'Echo de Paris* but also in publications such as *Le Temps*.[22] These papers presented the strikes as political acts and this description served to deny the status of the strikers' claims. Their demands were represented as part of a conspirators' plot. Now Pivert's exhortations were reproduced as threats. And these accusations of incipient revolution were made in the context of the gains won by the PCF in the elections.[23]

The crucial event of this first period of strike action was the stoppage at the gigantic Renault plant at Boulogne-Billancourt. This action of 28 May involved 35,000 workers and soon prompted strikes at nearby plants. The Renault action was decisive in the spreading of the strikes in the Parisian region for the next day it was estimated that nearly 100,000 engineers had stopped work and occupied their factories.[24]

These first factory occupations were a variant of the tactic which had served to inaugurate the Popular Front. When demonstrators had marched from Bastille to Nation on 14 July 1935, they had occupied the spaces of the Republic. The fiction of the Republic was that these spaces belonged to 'the people' and the supporters of the Front simply took that fiction at face value. Spaces previously occupied for protests, and which had therefore signified exclusion, were occupied on Bastille Day to demonstrate support for the Republic. The intersection of the working classes and the parliamentary sphere was achieved by the occupation of 'public' spaces adorned by the state. Yet the occupation of the factories seemed to usher the protagonist of French history onto a different stage.

The factories occupied in 1936 were not political sites of the same order as the Place de la Nation; they were the sites of capital. As the sites of the valorisation process, the factories were spaces in which the gestures of labour were subject to controlling forces. Yet gestures belong to agents and can never be fully mapped and determined and so capital exercises its control most strongly over sites, which can be locked, barred and policed.[25] The occupations of 1936 overturned this control.

The workers occupied the spaces of capital and redefined them; at this moment the streets within the Renault complex were renamed.[26] The factories were turned into political sites.

None of the above is meant to suggest that the strikes which had taken place in France before 1936 were without political dimensions. Yet the strikes of 1936 established a new conjunction. The last major strike wave in France, that culminating in 1920, may have taken place against the backdrop of revolutions in Russia and Germany, but nationally the strikers had to contend with the conservative retrenchment of the immediate postwar period. By contrast, in 1936, the strikes greeted the first socialist president of cabinet. And although Blum had declared that the Front was a defensive occupation of power, the factory occupations were easily interpreted by the right-wing press as an extension of the political power already won. Thus it is not surprising that the Communists acted quickly to rebut Pivert. On 29 May Marcel Gitton declared in *L'Humanité*: 'Not everything is possible'.[27]

The press sympathetic to the Popular Front now began to emphasise the spontaneous nature of the strikes. This was a rejection of the 'soviet conspiracy' and served to confirm the legitimacy of the strikes as protests against pay and conditions. As the Parisian metalworkers were playing a decisive role in the unfolding of the strike action, Marcel Roy, secretary of the Fédération des métaux, went to some lengths to present the strikes in his industry in terms of such protests. In an article published in *Le Populaire* on 28 May and reprinted in *Le Peuple* the following day, Roy discussed the low pay for metalworkers and the harsh conditions produced by Taylorisation.[28] He then noted how the strikes were enabled by the reunification of the Marxist and non-Marxist elements of the CGT in March 1936, confirming the solidarity of the workers. He argued: 'the metalworkers have again found the path of syndicalist organisation. Unity, [and] the victory of the Popular Front are the driving forces behind the confidence the organisation enjoys.'[29] Roy then went on to dismiss the charge that the strikes were led by the Communists, and part of some ulterior plan of the Popular Front. 'The Popular Front is one part of the social mechanism which can and must serve the interests of our cause, but the chief part is and will remain the struggle of the workers, the Syndicat.'[30]

Such arguments were given a very specific visual form in the first photographs of the strike reproduced by the Popular Front press. On the same page as Roy's article, *Le Populaire* printed a photograph of a large number of strikers grouped behind a syndicat banner in the courtyard of

Dans l'usine Nieuport, une partie des grévistes se sont groupés et ont affirmé devant notre photographe, leur attachement à la C.G.T.

Fig. 12 Anon, 'In the Nieuport factory, a group of strikers have gathered before our photographer and confirmed their allegiance to the CGT', *Le Populaire*, 28 May 1936, p. 6. Photograph: the author. Courtesy of the Bibliothèque de l'Office Universitaire de Recherche Socialiste, Paris.

the Nieuport factory (Fig. 12). And just as Roy's article was reproduced in *Le Peuple*, so was this photograph. The caption for the photograph in *Le Populaire* reads as follows: 'In the Nieuport factory, a group of strikers have gathered before our photographer and confirmed their allegiance to the CGT'. As the caption states, the image shows the solidarity of the workers. The massed group literally presents a united front. The significance of this photograph lies in its specific relationship with the social formation constituted by the striking workers. In this public demonstration of their allegiance to the CGT the strikers are represented as a cohesive and self-directed group rather than as the pawns of a few conspirators. No fists are raised here; the workers do not even present themselves as supporters of the Popular Front. If they declare their autonomy, this is not presented as any claim to sovereignty. The autonomy of the group is articulated in the very organisation of the photograph.

Again as the caption indicates, the group addresses the camera. The figures are not caught unawares as in certain forms of photojournalism or documentary photography, nor are the figures marshalled by the photographer for the camera.[31] Thus the strikers' self-presentation is a visual analogue to their series of demands; both may be considered as interruptions of 'normal' relations.

The strike at the Nieuport factory was a resistance to the prevailing social relations of production and the photograph of the strikers was a resistance to the conventions of photographic reportage which made of the subject a passive object. In this sense, the photograph is a resistance to what Steve Edwards has described as the 'monological' operation in which 'the camera turns the subject of the photographer's fascination into an object which is by definition, dumb'.[32] Now, to argue that a photograph such as the image of the Nieuport strikers offers a form of resistance is not to attribute an agency to the image itself. Nor is it to maintain that its meaning and its function are fixed. Yet it is to argue that the photograph functioned within the altered social relations of the strike. The efficacy of this type of photograph lay in its conjunction with these altered social relations.

As much is confirmed by the limited nature of this photograph's circulation. The image of the Nieuport workers was reproduced at a specific point in the development of the strike movement; at the very end of May the movement remained almost completely confined to the Paris region and had not yet assumed the proportions of a national crisis. During this period, the Popular Front papers were at their most supportive of the strikers, for the action did not yet seem any great threat to the incoming government. Accordingly, sympathetic papers printed a number of photographs similar to that taken at the Nieuport factory. The force and significance of these photographs at this juncture may be demonstrated by the fact that such images are entirely absent from the hostile press. And it is difficult to assume that such images were for some reason unavailable when one recalls the 320 photographs the artistic director of *Vu* saw each day. However, the Popular Front press was not to pursue this type of photographic coverage. The elected parties of the Popular Front were not to maintain their support for the strikes and as the relationship between strikers and the workers' organisations was transformed, so the currency of such photographs changed.[33]

The domestication of the strikes

Le Populaire's early coverage of the strike ranged from Pivert's forecasts of revolution to the peaceful sound of an accordion floating from an

Fig. 13 Anon, 'Perched on the gates, the workers at the Renault factories await the results of negotiations between the employer's and workers' delegations', *Le Populaire*, 30 May 1936, p. 6. Photograph: the author. Courtesy of the Bibliothèque de l'Office Universitaire de Recherche Socialiste, Paris.

occupied factory. At the end of May the coverage had not yet narrowed to the extent that these accounts would be made incompatible. A photograph reproduced on 30 May in *Le Populaire* could sustain a number of different readings (Fig. 13). The photograph was captioned: 'Perched on the gates, the workers at the Renault factories await the results of negotiations between the employer's and workers' delegations.' This image could be read for signs of militancy and signs of festivity, and on 30 May such readings could be supported by reference to events narrated in the paper, although each of course would tell in a different way.

The photograph preserves the confrontation with the camera which had been exploited in the image of the Nieuport strikers. Yet this confrontation is now mediated at a number of levels. Some of the strikers raise their fists and place their struggle in continuity with that of the Popular Front. And the caption emphasises that negotiations are being pursued through the correct channels. Although the fact of occupation is presented clearly enough, the signs of militancy are allowed to blur in this image. Some clenched fists open into waving hands. And if the gates are closed, the barrier between the factory and the street is not insurmountable; the figures in the foreground may be strikers, but their presence on the street means that they are not coded as such. Thus a wider set of codes are brought into play. As the photographer draws back to include the figures on the street, defiance itself is relaxed.

Yet if at the end of May signs of both militancy and festivity circulated, it was the account of the strike as a celebration which came to be developed by the Popular Front press as the magnitude of the strike movement became apparent. This may be understood as a development of the account produced by the Radical paper *L'Oeuvre*. The Radicals did not have an official organ, and *L'Oeuvre* was one of five Parisian papers supporting the party.[34] In the early 1930s the other four papers had moved farther to the right, but *L'Oeuvre* had retained both a position on the left and a healthy circulation.[35] The political editor of the paper, Jean Piot, was on the left wing of the party, yet it seems that Henri Raud, the editor in chief, maintained Piot's position because it in turn maintained the circulation.[36]

On 28 May *L'Oeuvre* had carried this description of the strikers and their entertainments:

> The inner courtyard is very lively. Some are reading the papers. A radio is playing a dance concert.
>
> In quiet moments, romantic songs are sung in chorus, the songs of the minute.
>
> Amateur virtuosi have had violins, mandolins and banjos brought in.[37]

This is a description of the lived experience of the strike. The use of the eye-witness mode stands in contrast to accounts such as that offered by Marcel Roy, which conform to the model of the communiqué. Such accounts were prevalent in *Le Populaire, Le Peuple* and *L'Humanité*; all tended to present the strikes within the context of a set of developing political formations, using lengthy citations from various syndicats and workers' delegations. Yet from the beginning *L'Oeuvre* had adopted a mode in which descriptions of the scenes of the strike played a large part. Here the strikes are presented less as a means of forcing negotiations and more as a series of spontaneous festivals. This perspective was in the first instance a result of *L'Oeuvre*'s position as a Radical paper. Whilst at this date *L'Oeuvre* supported the

Popular Front, it was not an instrument for communicating policy, and, rather the reverse, its coverage was an attempt to track the mood and preferences of one section of the movement. *L'Oeuvre* did not so much present information to those directly involved in the strikes as circulate accounts to spheres beyond that of the immediate struggle. Thus part of the paper's task was to make the strikes intelligible.[38] In *L'Oeuvre* the strikes were not presented as a revolutionising of production in which occupation was preliminary to the workers running the machines themselves, as had happened previously in Italy and Poland.[39] Instead the occupations were shown as a holiday, only a break from work and not a fundamental disruption of the relations of production. The machines were not abandoned but maintained for the moment when work was to be resumed. For these reasons, *L'Oeuvre*'s account of relaxation and celebration could conclude with a tribute to the 'working people who understand perfectly that their cause has nothing to gain from disorder'.[40]

This perspective was supported by the photographic coverage of the paper. On 30 May, *L'Oeuvre* published a photograph of the amateur virtuosi with the caption: 'Le «jazz Farman»'. The photograph shows a massed group of figures but these figures do not address themselves to the camera. Instead they direct their attention to the musicians who occupy the foreground of the image; the workers have become an audience. The implications of this were drawn out in the caption given to the image when it was reproduced by *Le Populaire*: 'At the Farman factories: whilst waiting for the results of negotiations ... workers in the factory courtyard listen to the sounds of an improvised orchestra' (Fig. 14). The caption emphasises that the music is a diversion, a means of passing the time whilst the workers' representatives meet their employers. Once again, as in the Nieuport image, the mass of the workers are positioned in relation to the syndicat. Yet whereas in the Nieuport image the workers presented their allegiance themselves, in the Farman photograph they are no longer protagonists. The image of the musicians and their audience is an image of relative passivity; the workers may be on strike, but the time created by the cessation of work is taken up by entertainments. Unlike the Nieuport photograph, this image presents the mass of workers as distanced from political activity.

This account of the photograph is supported by the pattern of its circulation. Besides appearing in *Le Populaire* and *L'Oeuvre*, the photograph was also reproduced in *Le Petit Journal*, *L'Excelsior* and *Le Jour*, respectively Republican, conservative and far right-wing papers. Thus the photographs of the festive strike were reproduced in the papers

Fig. 14 Anon, 'At the Farman factories: whilst waiting for the results of negotiations ... workers in the factory courtyard listen to the sounds of an improvised orchestra', *Le Populaire*, 30 May 1936, p. 1. Photograph: the author. Courtesy of the Bibliothèque de l'Office Universitaire de Recherche Socialiste, Paris.

which consistently avoided reproducing images of politically active workers. Yet this unequal distribution of the images of the occupations was to be relatively short-lived.

The occupations were of space. The hidden abode of production became inaccessible to the capitalist; the instruments of production were withheld. The actions of the strikers thus seemed to pose the question which Maurice Guérin, writing in the democratic Catholic paper *L'Aube*, phrased as follows:

> It is a matter of knowing to whom the instruments of production legitimately belong. One could answer: to those who paid for them with their money: to the bosses and shareholders, the creditors and sleeping partners. And that still appears simple and unarguable. However, what has given the enterprise a certain surplus-value? Labour![41]

The occupations put property relations in question. Having established this, Guérin concludes:

> What is at issue is the right of labour to possess both a share of the property that it has made thrive and a share of the authority over the enterprise to which it has imparted life. Until now, capital has gathered to itself all property and consequently all authority. The time has come when it must share the one and the other, if it does not want to be forced to abandon them altogether.[42]

For Guérin, the occupations marked an epoch. They demonstrated that the moment had arrived for a transformation of the existing relations of production. If this forecast proved correct, the occupations were, in a sense, to become permanent.

Guérin's article was published on 3 June, at the moment when the strikes had spread beyond Paris and were advancing across France. At this juncture Guérin's forecast seemed credible, and the election of the Popular Front seemed, after all, to be bringing about 'a great change'. Yet the change forecast by Guérin was certainly not what the Radical members of the Front had anticipated when they added their signatures to the joint programme. Thus as the strikes spread, the vaunted unity of the Popular Front was made increasingly vulnerable. Whilst the charges of a Communist conspiracy were an attack on the PCF, the purpose of this attack was to expose the extremism of the latter party to the Radicals. The complaisance of the PCF had been crucial to the formation of the Front yet it was the Radical interpretation of the Front which had prevailed after 14 July 1935. It was this interpretation which was put under pressure by the charges of Soviet plotting. In the first days of June as the strike movement grew, so the attacks on the Communists were increased in an attempt to undermine the coalition.

To preserve the unity of the Front, the strikes had to be redefined. The occupation of space was to be figured not as a permanent condition but a temporary one and the occupations were to be given the temporal limits of the festival. Thus a convergence was to be effected between the coverage offered by the organs of the left wing and the position set out by *L'Oeuvre*.

As the PCF was both the focus of the attacks and the most active supporter of the unity of the Front, so the shift in the coverage of the strikes was most marked in its publications. Thus in the issue of *L'Humanité* of 4 June the eye-witness mode used in *L'Oeuvre* was adopted:

> No smoke issues from the high chimneys. One no longer hears the deafening noise of the machines, but instead snatches of a popular

> song playing on the radio or the joyful cries of young strikers caught up in a football match.[43]

Here the moment of respite experienced by Eugène Picard has been lengthened into a holiday. Yet whilst Picard's reverie lifted him above the din of the shop floor, during the strike the machines really stand silent. This cessation of work enables a particular transition; the roar of the machines is replaced by the sounds of sociability. Stopping the machines permits the formation of a new community.

This sense of a new community was central to the strike coverage in the 4 June issue of *Regards*, the Communist-supported magazine which now presented itself as the illustrated weekly of the Popular Front.[44] The front cover of this issue adapted the photograph first reproduced in *Le Populaire* on 30 May (Fig. 15). Waving and saluting figures are still present but the image has been drastically cropped so that less than half the original photograph is shown. As a result the figures occupy a larger

Fig. 15 Anon, 'In the Renault factories with the striking metalworkers', *Regards*, No. 125, 4 June 1936, cover. Photograph: the author. Courtesy of the Bibliothèque Marxiste de Paris.

proportion of the image and this change in their scale encourages a more anecdotal reading. Faces are now brought into view, and with them a set of personal responses. This has the effect of directing the viewer's attention away from the gestures of greeting and defiance figured in the earlier version of the photograph and towards the potential flirtations between male workers and female pedestrians. This type of coverage marked a shift in the editorial policy of *Regards*. The magazine had been established as an alternative to the perceived decadence of the bourgeois press, and earlier editorials had inveighed against illustrated weeklies such as *Voilà* and *Détective*. In 1933 an editorial had declared: '*Regards* has too much respect for its readers to believe that they are only interested in detectives' reports and society gossip and scandal.'[45] Yet, in the changed climate of 1936, this editorial policy of *Regards* was reviewed.[46]

The cropping of the photograph on the cover of *Regards* reordered its signs, further qualifying its already ambiguous militancy. The full significance of this was established within the magazine by the photographs and text dedicated to the strikes (Figs. 16, 17, 18). These photographs,

Dans les usines
avec les
METALLOS
en
grève

Fig. 16 Anon, 'In the factories with the striking metalworkers', *Regards*, No. 125, 4 June 1936, p. 5. Photograph: the author. Courtesy of the Bibliothèque Marxiste de Paris.

Fig. 17 Anon, 'In the factories with the striking metalworkers', *Regards*, No. 125, 4 June 1936, p. 6. Photograph: the author. Courtesy of the Bibliothèque Marxiste de Paris.

and the accompanying article by Pierre Unik, are spread over three pages.[47] The first page is given over to a sequence of three images of the strikers' general and committee meetings. The first image on this page shows a gesturing figure: Jean-Pierre Timbaud of the Syndicat des métaux. Yet this figure does not dominate the image; the photograph was taken from a very low viewpoint so that the composition is crowned by a range of figures looking down at the speaker from a rooftop. Such a view of the strikers was already a part of the iconography made familiar by *Le Populaire*, a sign for the strikers' control of the factories. Yet just as the cover of *Regards* redirected that image of autonomy, so here the strikers are fitted into a relation with the syndicat. The photograph places the sign of the strikers' control with that of the delegate; thus the strikers attend to the delegate but are not presented as directed or coerced. In turn, the relationship established in this image is confirmed by the two photographs reproduced below it. The second image is of Timbaud's audience in the courtyard, and this photograph is placed directly above another of the strike committee reassembled after the delegate's address. Thus, whilst the presence of the syndicat is established, what is emphasised is the process by which the mass of workers formulate their demands.

Fig. 18 Anon, 'In the factories with the striking metalworkers', *Regards*, No. 125, 4 June 1936, p. 7. Photograph: the author. Courtesy of the Bibliothèque Marxiste de Paris.

The first page of photographs works to contain the strike within the framework of conventional negotiations and an analogous containment and organisation is involved in the following two pages. Of the eleven photographs reproduced only one shows a strike meeting while the remainder develop the themes of sociability implied by the magazine's cover. The first two images on the second page show the organisation of a 'parlour', where strikers may meet privately with wives or girlfriends and below these photographs is an image of a father receiving a visit from his son. These photographs establish the strike as a partial interruption of personal relationships yet the images also show the reconstitution of these relations in the new site of the factory. As in the coverage of *L'Humanité*, this sociability is predicated on the cessation of work. At the foot of the page is a photograph of the stilled machines with the caption, 'In the midst of the temporarily abandoned machines there is conversation, joking, newspaper-reading.' Despite the fact of the occupation, the strike is presented less as an annexation of space than an appropriation of time. To make time for talking and joking is to dismiss the threat of expropriation.

In this manner, the imagery of *Regards* served simultaneously to banish the spectre of 'sovietisation' and to assimilate the strike to existing conventions of illustration. Thus the photographs on the final page of the article conform to already established genres. There is another image of an 'improvised orchestra', a photograph of two 'charming workers', one of whom was a beauty queen of the quarter, and a sequence of photographs showing the provisioning of the workers, with a delivery of beer, the sale of cigarettes, and the distribution of bread. These latter pictures form a corollary to the sequence of images on the second page of the article; they defer to a set of human pleasures and appetites seemingly too commonplace to merit discussion. Here the workers are engaged in a struggle for bread rather than in a revolutionary confrontation with the prevailing relations of production. This struggle is presented simply as one part of the broader struggle for 'bread, peace and freedom'. For the new community formed when the machines are silenced is itself an image of a new freedom. This conformity to the rhetoric of the Popular Front is given in Unik's accompanying presentation of the strikers.

> I don't know what to admire most, the seriousness, the magnificent gravity of these workers who know that a powerful adversary has been confronted, who have confidence in themselves, confidence in the syndicat and its increasing membership, confidence in the elected members of the Popular Front who have actively supported them, and in the committees of the Popular Front which organise the solidarity of the strikers, this seriousness or the good humour, the joy that they know to put into this great, grave affair on which their families' bread depends.[48]

In this account any tension between the images of the strike as revolution and as festival is simply internalised as a mild confusion on the part of the commentator as to what is most impressive. Unik's text does not admit of any conflict between the two modes of description; the different accounts of the strike are held in an equilibrium, sustained by the organisation of the Popular Front.

The coverage in *Regards* ordered the strike into acceptable categories and precisely avoided the disruptions of the earliest reporting. The difference between these two forms of coverage is not simply that between the weekly and the daily press, for a type of imagery analogous to that used in *Regards* was also exploited in the daily papers seeking to maintain the unity of the Popular Front. Thus on 4 June *L'Humanité* reproduced several photographs of dances in the factories. On the same day the militant readership of *Le Peuple* was also offered a new image of the strikers; the direct address of the earlier images of massed workers was now moderated in a photograph showing such a group 'fronted' by a woman turned towards the camera. This woman forms the principal subject of the image, making it distinct from earlier group shots. Moreover, the woman seems to be placed on a step, so that she is level with the viewer and slightly raised above the crowd. Just as the imagery of *Regards* had ordered the strike within the inclusive rhetoric of 'bread, peace and freedom' rather than through an imagery emphasising the identity of a class, so the photograph in *Le Peuple* established the female figure as a mediating term between strikers and viewer. This attempt to establish a new form of relation with the viewer is given in the caption: 'Working men and women guarding the factory ... with a smile.'[49] The phrase 'with a smile' comes from a Maurice Chevalier hit of 1921; it still had sufficient currency in 1936 to become the title of a film starring the singer.[50] Thus the photograph in *Le Peuple* and its caption framed the sociability of the strikes in terms drawn from the entertainment industry, a manner of covering events typical of the photojournal *Voilà*.[51] Indeed, ten days later the same combination of codes was used in *Voilà*'s first coverage of the strikes. This coverage included a photograph of women dancing to an accordion; the image was captioned: 'More than one department store was converted into a dance hall and the little errand boys often revealed themselves as the accordionists of the future.'[52] Here the strike is as much an opportunity to escape the routines of work as it is a resistance to the relations of production.[53]

In this manner the strikes began to be assimilated to what might be termed a Popular Front iconography. This was not an image of the Front as a site of exchange between leaders and led, rather it was an iconography constituted from popular pleasures.

Useful pleasures

On 3 June the Union des syndicats de la région parisienne decided not only to support the strikes but to coordinate, and thus contain, the movement.[54] This marked one sense in which the movement was to be guided from above. On the same day the employers in the key industry of metalworking broke off negotiations; the announcement of the collapse of talks was not made until the following day, however. It was thus made to coincide with the installation of Blum's government. This was part of the employers' effort to put pressure on the government to force the opening of negotiations at a national level.[55] The strategy was successful and this marked a second sense in which the strike movement was to be guided from above.

On the evening of 4 June the representatives of the employers' Confédération générale de la production française (CGPF) met Blum, just after the latter had presented his new government to the President. The meeting with the employers began a series of negotiations which stretched over the next few days and resulted in what were to become known as the Matignon Agreements. Here Blum acted as the liaison between the CGPF and the delegates of the CGT, the latter led by their general secretary Léon Jouhaux. On the night of 7 June the leaders of the CGPF and the CGT put their signatures to a document establishing collective labour contracts, the right of workers to join unions, the election of workers' delegates to conduct negotiations with management, and, finally, a series of pay increases of between 7 and 15 per cent.[56] The document also stipulated that strikers should resume work as soon as the management of their firm had accepted the terms of the general agreement. Whilst it has often been assumed that this agreement and the resulting legislation were simply a rapid fulfillment of the Popular Front programme, this was not in fact the case. Adrian Rossiter has emphasised that the programme of January 1936 made no mention of the measures Blum presented to the Chamber on 9 June that same year concerning collective contracts, paid holidays and the 40-hour week.[57] Rather than considering the Matignon Agreements as a coup against the CGPF, Rossiter demonstrates that the employers were pleasantly surprised to find Blum and Jouhaux sympathetic to their point of view. He also suggests that Blum's role as arbitrator relieved the employers of a degree of responsibility for the consequences of the agreement.[58]

The issue of *L'Humanité* for 8 June carried the first details of the Matignon Agreements and hailed a victory. The editors of the party organ could present the agreements as such because the PCF had suspended its revolutionary demands. Thorez confirmed this once more in a speech reported in the same issue of *L'Humanité*. The existing relations of production were not to be transformed at this moment, the French soviets were projected to the horizon.[59] Yet with the suspension of revolutionary demands came the suspension of critical analysis. Thus, alongside the report of the speech by Thorez, Marcel Cachin offered an account of wage-labour which declined reference to the labour process. As Cachin was attempting to respond to the employers' claim that the occupations were an abuse of property rights, he was compelled to address the questions raised by Maurice Guérin. So Cachin, like Guérin, begins with the capitalist conception of property. 'They evoke the rights of property ... They would probably be quite astonished if the wage earners were to reply to them that they themselves also have a property to defend. *It is that of their life,* the only one they have under the sun.'[60] Cachin acknowledges the status of the worker as the proprietor of labour-power, compelled to put this property at the disposal of the capitalist. Guérin had made the same acknowledgement. But Guérin had also acknowledged labour-power as that agency which imparts life to the lifeless constituents of the product in the labour process. As a consequence, he had acknowledged the 'rights of labour'. Cachin does not enter into any discussion of the labour process nor does he explore the consequences of the sale of labour-power. His analysis is arrested at the threshold of the workshop, where hangs the notice 'No admittance except on business'.[61] And on this occasion Cachin seems to have been happy enough to obey this order of capital. He remains in the sphere of circulation or commodity exchange, 'the exclusive realm of Freedom, Equality, Property and Bentham'.[62] He sees only the exchange of commodities, the sale and purchase of labour-power, and as a consequence only demands that the exchange is fair, and results in the payment of a 'living wage'.[63] The context of Cachin's account does not permit him to raise the question of to whom the instruments of production legitimately belong. But then Cachin did not wish to raise this question, any more than Unik did when he surveyed the striking metalworkers. For Cachin and for Unik the social relations of production were to remain hidden. And of course a photograph of workers talking and laughing by the stilled machines does not show these relations; it only shows one sociality disappearing into another.

If the Communist account of the strike obscured more than it revealed, at least it was not the only account proposed from the left wing. The Communists could pretend to the role of 'the ministry of the masses' but there were other candidates for the portfolio. The group gathered around Pierre Monatte's journal *La Révolution Prolétarienne* offered one alternative. Of the accounts of the strike appearing in that journal perhaps the most sustained was that published by Simone Weil on 10 June.[64] This text is the one most frequently cited by historians rehearsing the tropes of the festival. Yet in Weil's text the lyricism of the descriptions of the strike is a counterpoint to the everyday oppression of the workshop. She attempts to restore the festival to its status as an inversion. Yet her alternative account also serves to reveal the limits of the festival.

Weil opens her essay with a discussion of the public incomprehension of the strike and offers the perspective from the shop floor as a means of explanation. 'When one has certain images driven into the spirit, the heart, the flesh itself, one understands.'[65] The account thus exploits the range of techniques proper to the eye-witness report. Here the author has only to surrender to her memories, the immediacy of her experience mediated, of course, by the present tense: 'Here is my machine.'[66] The narrative begins with the author's first day at a new job and the process of submitting to the dictates of the machine. The piecework demands concentration but the repeated gestures are also tiring. 'Little by little the monotony of the task lulls me into a dream.'[67] Weil, like Picard, succumbs to reverie. But the logic of piecework maintains its own remorseless discipline. And payment for this work is presented as an extension of the discipline. 'To count penny for penny. During eight hours of work, one counts every penny. How much are these pieces going to bring? How much have I earned this hour? And the hour after? On leaving the factory, again one counts each penny.'[68] Weil asserts, as Rivet did not, that this situation is one of slavery. This condition of slavery is the root cause of the strike and the election victory of the Popular Front simply provided the occasion to react against the condition.[69] 'One bends beneath the yoke. As soon as the yoke is lifted, one raises one's head again.'[70] The strike is then described as a reversal of the everyday situation:

> The joy of entering a factory by the smiling consent of a worker guarding the gates. The joy of finding so many smiles, so many words of fraternal welcome. How it feels to be amongst comrades, in these workshops where, when I was working, each one of us felt so alone at our machine! The joy of moving freely through the workshops where each used to be riveted to their machine, [now] forming groups, chatting, having a bite to eat. The joy of hearing music, song and laughter instead of the pitiless din of the machines, the powerful symbol of the harsh necessity to which we submitted.[71]

Weil employs many of the devices that Unik and other correspondents used to describe the liberty given by the strike. Yet her account is distinguished by its tightly held tension between constraint and freedom. The virtue of this account remained the manner in which it asserted the non-political origins of the strike through the perspective of lived experience. However this virtue was achieved at a cost. The narration of experience imposed limits on Weil's account. For the experience of conditions is not their explanation. To argue that the oppression of the workplace is the cause of the strike only begs the question of what causes the oppression.

And this question cannot be answered from the shop floor. Precisely in its immediacy, Weil's account is a product of the mystification of capital. In the developed form of the capitalist mode of production it is not only the labour-power of individual workers which objectifies itself in the product and appears as the property of the capitalist. This is also the case for the social configuration in which the workers exist. In this mystification, Marx notes,

> the *social character of the conditions of labour* – and this includes machinery and *capitale fixe* of every kind – appears to be entirely autonomous and independent of the worker. It appears to be a *mode of existence of capital* itself, and therefore ordered by *capitalists* without reference to the workers. Like the *social character* of their labour, but to a far greater extent, the *social character* with which the conditions of production are endowed, as the conditions of production of the combined labour of the *community*, appears as *capitalistic*, as something independent of the workers and intrinsic to the conditions of production themselves.[72]

The machines and the other paraphernalia of the shop floor have their own reality, but this obdurate reality cannot yield the social character of the conditions of labour, any more than a photograph of the stilled machines can. As Benjamin noted, citing Brecht: 'A photograph of the Krupp works or the AEG tells us next to nothing about these institutions. Actual reality has slipped into the functional. The reification of human relations – the factory, say – means that they are no longer explicit.'[73] Yet as Weil adopts an analogous perspective it cannot be reconciled with an analysis of negotiations. Weil offers a narrative of the experience of the workplace, a narrative which may only be unfolded within strict limits. However, these limits are then expressed as the limits of that experience. 'The habit of passivity acquired over years will not be shaken off in a few days, even such glorious days. And then it is not at the point when for a few days one has finally escaped slavery that one can find it in oneself to study the conditions of constraint to which one will submit again.'[74] Here, the very harshness of life in the factory precludes the consideration of the economic relations creating such conditions. The strike is precisely defined as an escape from these conditions, rather than an attempt to redress them.

Yet the account of the strike as festival increasingly stood in a tension with the behaviour of the strikers. The day on which Weil's text was published was also the day on which representatives of the CGT were called by Blum to a further meeting with the CGPF. For the signing of the Matignon Agreements had not secured a return to work. On the contrary, in most industries strikes had continued to spread. And as the strikes spread so there was a growth in street activity on the part of the strikers, a visible militancy which alarmed both the right-wing press and the government. On 10 June *L'Echo de Paris* reproduced a photograph of demonstrators with the caption:

> Yesterday strikers carrying the red flag led several processions through the streets of Paris. Our photograph shows one of these processions on the Rue de Rivoli. The strikers have raised fists. One easily imagines the effect produced on the Parisian public by this revolutionary spectacle, authorised by the public authorities.[75]

The authorities responded to demonstrations of this kind with counsels of moderation. Of these counsels, that issued by 'the ministry of the masses' was the most significant. In a widely reported statement of 11 June, Thorez insisted:

> In certain cases it is even possible that we run the risk of alienating ourselves from sections of the petty-bourgeoisie and the peasantry. So what next? ... So, we must know how to end a strike when satisfaction has been obtained. We must even know how to accept a compromise when all demands have not yet been met but victory on the essential points has been achieved.[76]

This explicit statement of a desire to curtail the strike movement for the sake of maintaining a broad class alliance was matched with a policy of organising ever more elaborate entertainments for the strikers, which served in part to keep them occupied within the factory walls.

These entertainments were illustrated on the front page of *L'Humanité* of 11 June, and in the issue of *Regards* of the same date. Whereas earlier photographs had 'caught' seemingly improvised concerts, the photographs in *Regards* show more carefully staged events. An image of the Jacquemet et Mesnet factory shows three figures in drag, posing before a crowd of workers (Fig. 19). The costume of the foreground figures indicates a self-conscious artifice and this is emphasised by the manner in which the figures perform for the camera, addressing their mime to the photographer. In this photograph the symbolic gender inversion of the performers belongs to the logic of carnival, the logic of temporary inversion. The reproduction of photographs such as this in *Regards* confirmed the definition of the strike as a controlled and temporary

Fig. 19 Anon. [David Seymour], 'A theatrical revue in the courtyard of the Jacquemet et Mesnet factory, Rue de la Convention', *Regards*, No. 126, 11 June 1936, p. 1. Photograph: the author. Copyright: Magnum Photos, New York. Collection: Bibliothèque Marxiste de Paris.

inversion of the conditions of work.[77] Nevertheless, precisely because such images were marked by artifice in their content and composition they could be dismissed by the right-wing press as part of a facade concealing revolution. In *L'Echo de Paris* of 12 June it was argued: 'At the beginning, the strikers wanted to pretend that the strike was conducted with good humour, amidst songs and innocent entertainments. All revolutions begin in this way.'[78] In one respect this is merely a rehearsal of familiar lines about the attempt to 'minimise the operation'. Yet whilst before 11 June the tension between festival and revolution was part of the arsenal used to attack the Popular Front, after this date this tension was increasingly exploited by the press supporting the Front.

The end of the strikes

After 11 June the strikes were increasingly assimilated to existing forms of representation. As this happened the strikes were largely made to work for the mythologies of the Popular Front, and so the tension between militancy and the warmth of song given in *L'Echo de Paris* was recast. In *Marianne*, a weekly with a shifting measure of support for the Popular Front, the 'innocent entertainments' were not presented as a deception, but rather as an alternative to the workers' activism.[79] An article of 17 June entitled 'Souvenirs de «l'occupation». Chansons sur le tas', describes a visit to a little bar frequented by *artistes* on the Boulevard de Strasbourg. A few performers are having a drink before going to entertain the strikers:

> Outside, for the first time, there is a tense atmosphere on the street. Groups are forming, people are active. Processions go by with placards, shouts, slogans, dummies hung from gallows. The strike has spilled out onto the street. There is less good humour, less calm discipline. On the boulevards, these long processions of workers with raised fists give Paris a fevered, troubled air which one would be sure to feel oneself if an effort wasn't made to drive it out like an evil thought.
>
> But straightaway, in the comfortable atmosphere of the little bar, I'm reacquainted with the warmth which gives comfort to good people, the sight of men helping one another.[80]

This account is in effect the reverse of the image of the Nieuport factory, its negative. On 28 May the militancy of workers was presented as solidarity, as comradeship. By 17 June the images of harmony and comradeship had been disassociated from the strikers, and lay outside the description of the strike itself.

This is not to say that the militancy of May was presented as an aberration. If after 11 June the Communists would no longer directly support such militancy, they could not directly condemn it either. Instead, it was to be circumscribed. By the third week of June it was to belong to the past. That past might be glorious but it was, nevertheless, the past. The Communists had to know how to end the struggle. And so did the Communist-inspired Comité mondiale des femmes.

This knowledge was presented in a special issue of *Les Femmes dans l'Action Mondiale* dedicated to the strikes. This magazine provided an ending to the narrative begun in *Regards*. What Unik had pictured in the occupied factory was a series of partially interrupted relations; the occupation involved a separation from home and family, yet it also involved the discovery of a new sociability within the factory. After the Matignon Agreements were hailed as a victory, *Les Femmes dans l'Action Mondiale* could present the restoration of the familial bond. A double-page spread

Fig. 20 Anon, 'The strike has spread across all of France and has effected all industries', *Les Femmes dans l'Action Mondiale*, Special issue, 1936, pp. 5–6. Photograph courtesy of the Bibliothèque nationale de France, Paris.

in the magazine did so by arraying four images of strikers around an image of a mother and child (Fig. 20). The images of strikers are drawn from the Parisian region but also from Dijon and Gironde. The images are generic in their composition and their content. But the captions insist on naming factories and naming towns. Réal had used a similar montage of the typical and the specific in his representation of the regional demonstrations of 14 July 1935. Ideally, such a montage was to be taken as an image of the nation. The title of the pages in the special issue asserts: 'The strike has spread across all of France and has effected all industries.'[81] Yet this does not mean that the strike is directly presented as a national struggle. For the central image of the mother and child is closer to Our Lady than Marianne. The virtues presented are maternal rather than Republican. Here the national slides towards the universal.[82] And this slide towards the universal is confirmed in the caption to the image. 'The Mother, happy and proud, embraces her baby. Not only has she brought him into the world; she has also fought for him, taking part in the sit-down strikes in order to assure everything necessary for this sweet, beautiful child to grow into a strong, happy man.'[83] The fight has entailed a separation, but its pain is now effaced: 'What joy shines from baby's face. He has waited long days for his mother ... and never was her kiss as sweet as it is today.'[84] And so the narrative of *Regards* is brought to its resolution.

Yet this resolution, this maternal embrace, threatened the articulation of feminism and antifascism which the Comité mondiale des femmes had worked to maintain. Previously, the struggle against chauvinism had been inseparable from the struggle against capitalism. And for this reason the Comité mondiale had resisted those feminists who asserted the rights of women without reference to class; Bernardette Cattanéo had explicitly rejected the idea of a simple community of interests shared by all women.[85] Yet now that the struggle against capital was concluded the image of the striking woman was permitted to slide towards a universal category; for the embrace celebrated in *Les Femmes dans l'Action Mondiale* could certainly be read as a sign that the woman belonged to a simple community of maternal interests. Of course, one could still read the double-page spread in *Les Femmes dans l'Action Mondiale* in terms of a contaminated universality. One could still see an articulation of the struggle in the workplace and the struggle in the home, the struggle over pay and conditions and the struggle to bring up the child. Such an articulation was still visible and a measure of visibility was still desirable. For this articulation was one component of the hegemony of the Popular Front. But it is in the nature of the hegemonic articulation, as a construction from dissimilar elements, to be unstable, even reversible. And June 1936 was certainly a moment marked by instability. Hence the Communist desire to circumscribe militancy, to make of it a memory.

This desire was announced in *Les Femmes dans l'Action Mondiale* in the spread following that with the mother and child. Here a dense montage of various groups is captioned: 'Hey ... that's me' (Fig. 21). The pages present a competition in which any woman identifying herself amongst the images may claim a photograph of herself and her comrades. Again, this could be read as a variant on that form of identification encouraged by Réal. But, again, the identification is limited. The photographs to be claimed are defined as souvenirs. This is the final operation of the logic of the festival; the festival is a temporally limited activity and the souvenir may mark that limit. Here the strikes are sent into folk memory.

This operation was made explicit in *Le Populaire*, where the strikes took their place in the accounts which were to settle down into folklore and the privileged folklore which designates itself history. This lengthy process was anticipated on 22 June, when André Varagnac celebrated the sociability of the strikes as part of an authentic working-class culture. Varagnac called for a record of the strikes, replete with descriptions of decorations and a careful documenting of neologisms. Here photographs of the strikes were endowed with new functions. Varagnac's call would be repeated in the *Revue de Folklore Français et Folklore Colonial*, and again in Arnold van Gennep's *Manuel de folklore français contemporain*.[86] Now the occupation of the factories was converted from a militant manoeuvre into an isolation from corrupting influence; living conditions passed over into an ideal set of investigative conditions.

Yet despite these more or less official attempts to fix the strikes within the limits of memory, the terms established by the Popular Front press were not maintained by the strikers themselves. Certain workers produced their own photographs of the strike, and some of these were reproduced in *La Vie ouvrière* and *Regards*. The latter printed a page of such images in the issue of 18 June (Fig. 22). These images do not depend on the tropes of the festival or dwell on picturesque detail. Instead, they return to another form of presentation, that used in the photograph of the Nieuport factory. The workers themselves continued to confront the camera and this marked a refusal of the iconography of the Popular Front. Thus in the Communist press a continuity was established with the earlier strike imagery. This was a necessary accommodation. For whilst attempting to curb the strikes the PCF also wished to preserve 'the ministry of the masses' and to claim a privileged link with the popular base.

However, the continuity established in the Communist press was something of an anomaly. In an attempt to maintain the unity of the Popular Front against what was perceived as the increasing threat represented by the strike movement, the press sympathetic to the new government had come to redefine the objectives of the strike and the very terms in which it was to be conceived. Thus the tactics which emerged to defend the first strikers against accusations of revolutionary intent were gradually adapted and finally directed against the strikers. And so the contradictions in the Popular Front project were played out in the press coverage of the strikes. The election victory of the Popular Front had certainly permitted 'the people' to emerge with a new political profile. But this emergence was incomplete. And this was not simply because the languages and representations of 'the people' as a class were not adapted to the protocols of government but also because the new government was pledged to an occupation of power which limited the scope for adaptation.

Fig. 21 Anon, 'Hey ... that's me', *Les Femmes dans l'Action Mondiale,* Special issue, 1936, pp. 7–8. Photograph courtesy of the Bibliothèque nationale de France, Paris.

... c'est moi »
Chaque lectrice qui se retrouvera sur ces pages aura droit à une photo originale du groupe dont elle fait partie, avec l'autographe du Comité National des Femmes.
Envoyez à l'administration de « FEMMES » (1, Cité Paradis, Paris 10e), la page où se trouve votre photo, et joignez-y le bon de participation ci-dessous

Fig. 22 Anon. 'Workers on strike send their photos to *Regards*', *Regards*, No. 127, 18 June 1936, p. 2. Photograph: the author. Courtesy of the Bibliothèque Marxiste de Paris.

Knowing how to end

The consequences of the strikers' negotiation of the iconography of the Popular Front was dramatised – in contrasting ways – in two novels published in 1937. In *Pain de brique*, the Communist Jean Fréville attempted to present the strike wave through the lens of socialist realism, as a moment in the process of revolutionary development.[87] Thus the strikers at Mignard, Lambert et Cie. are liberated by their actions. They hold improvised dances, then more elaborate masked balls; they have time to reflect on history, on the other June, of 1848, and on the fate of the Commune. A former student from Warsaw working at the factory delivers speeches on the collectivity of workers. This student, Svoboda, declares that whilst waiting for the moment of world Communism 'we must prepare ourselves by educating the masses, making them conscious of their historic mission and arming them for the struggle'.[88] Fréville would exercise similar ventriloquist skills whilst ghosting the autobiography of Maurice Thorez.[89] Thus, like

Varagnac, Fréville wants to make the strikers into a stable category. Whilst Varagnac hoped to achieve this through the isolation of the strikers as a new popular culture, Fréville imagined a perfect allegiance to the Comintern.

In *Pain de brique* the experience of the strikes is filtered through the language available to a given set of social types. In the other novel of the strikes, Tristan Rémy's *La Grande Lutte*, a similar process is at work. Yet whereas Fréville presents only the smooth functioning of the filter, Rémy is as interested in its clogging and blockage. Rémy's earliest novels were set in the *zone militaire*, in the shantytowns and wasteland beyond the Parisian fortifications. These novels were marked by the experience and, to a lesser extent, by the language of the *zoniers*. This experience and language are removed from that of the organised working class. For example, in *Porte de Clignancourt* a child encounters *L'Humanité* as part of another world.[90] Yet Rémy began to approach this other world in the spring of 1936, when he published *Faubourg Saint-Antoine*, a novel with characters drawn from the artisanal class of the old revolutionary quarter. This novel was itself fed through the mill of socialist realism in Louis Aragon's critical reception and in a photographic feature in *Regards*.[91] The experience of having his novel reprocessed was perhaps a factor encouraging Rémy to reflect on the dynamics of the Popular Front. In any case his next novel, that concerning the strike, is set amongst factory workers who have an uneasy relationship with the language of *L'Humanité* and *Le Populaire*.

The central character of *La Grande Lutte* is Picard, an older worker who had taken an active part in the strikes of 1920. He remembers that most workers had simply witnessed that débâcle 'as spectators'.[92] However, the election victory of 1936 encourages a new level of participation. On the train journey into work Picard overhears various debates, one worker commenting that since 'the elections are won, we're worried that the government has forgotten us'.[93] Nevertheless the strike permits Rémy's workers to 'raise their heads' just as those in Weil's factory had raised theirs.[94]

Yet if Rémy's strikers go on to rehearse debates about property and discipline, they do so in the knowledge that the terms of the debate are established by others. The occupied factory is not as isolated as Varagnac would wish; the strikers respond to the hostile coverage of the occupations and in turn their actions are converted into copy and recirculated.

> News vendors pushed into the factory. They ran from workshop to workshop.
> – Ask for *Regards*. Photos of the strikes in progress.

– *L'Humanité*, central organ of the Communist party.
– *Le Populaire*, comrades. Léon Blum's government takes shape.[95]

And as the strike wears on the strikers come to repeat official lines: 'We've got to hold on. If not everything is possible, too bad'.[96] A harassed CGT secretary is even moved to repeat: 'We must know how to end a strike.'[97]

The strike does end, and both Fréville's novel and Rémy's conclude with departures for new struggles. At the close of *La Grande Lutte*, the Communist Simonin, disillusioned with the French Popular Front, decides to join another fight. This is his final speech, delivered to his friend Picard:

> I voted so that things would change, because everyone said with the Popular Front things must change. If they have changed, you can hardly tell. They fired us up before the elections. And now our enthusiasm is just too much for them. Yet fascism will not be destroyed by injunctions, war will not be controlled simply by pacts, and prosperity cannot be introduced by decree. I speak well, don't I? Comrade Pivert wrote that himself. Yet in order to triumph, the workers must fight. He said that too. But it reminds me of the crippled and the lame who sing the Marseillaise. They write like that in the papers, but you don't see them fighting.[98]

Pivert's language cannot be Simonin's; terms lifted from *Le Populaire* sound too much like quotations.[99] Whereas Fréville's Svoboda is word-perfect, Rémy's Simonin does not want to mimic even Pivert. He does not want simply to read out a set speech but he cannot quite find other terms. He seems to feel that after the election victory 'the people' should be able to speak without a script. The workers should be able to become readers and writers. They should be able to become the viewers and the viewed, as they were in photographs such as that of the Nieuport factory.

Coming as it does at the end of the novel, Simonin's broken speech is not simply an attempt to preserve the rhetorical purity of the Second International. It is also a means of registering how a worker becomes estranged from the language of the Popular Front. This estrangement has increased over the length of the novel. It is a means of pointing to the problem of Blum's occupation of power. For this occupation was ultimately an interpretation of the Popular Front which was congruent with the Radical interpretation. Thus it came into conflict with the

Front defined as a movement of working-class solidarity. But this is not to say that the Popular Front was destroyed with the strikes. For at the moment when militancy was circumscribed in France it was reasserted in another place, the place to which the both Simonin and Svoboda depart at the end of the strikes: Spain.

4
'The Apocalypse of Fraternity': The Image Destroyed

> Once more the nightlong rumour of Madrid, the anthem welling up from all the radios, snatches of song and cries of *Salud!*, shrill in nearness or low-pitched in the distance, like careless notes jangled across a keyboard – sounds of hope and exultation spanned once more the silence. [...]
>
> Garcia pointed his pipe-stem, like a revolver, at each man in turn.
>
> 'I've seen the democracies come in against pretty well everything – except fascism. Apart from Mexico the only country which might help us is Russia. And Russia's too far away ... As to those sounds coming in through the window, Monsieur Magnin – I might define them as an Apocalypse of fraternity. They work on your emotions, I can well understand it; they stand for one of the most moving things on earth, and one of the rarest. But all that's got to be transformed – or perish!'[1]

The sounds of hope which had floated across French factory yards now fill the Spanish night. This scene is from *L'Espoir*, André Malraux's novel of the Spanish Civil War, first published in 1937. Here Major Garcia of the Spanish Intelligence Service is addressing Magnin, a French volunteer in the International Air Force. Garcia is reflecting on the earliest phase of the war and the careless rapture with which the Spanish people resisted General Franco's insurrection. For Garcia this Apocalypse is, precisely, a revelation. He acknowledges the great strength of the Spanish people and yet he concludes that the apocalyptic fervour 'spells certain defeat, after a relatively short period, and for a very simple reason: it's in the very nature of an Apocalypse to have no future'.[2] There is an Apocalypse of fraternity, but this fraternity, to pursue Garcia's Biblical turn of phrase, is a blessing and a curse. And this was, in different ways, the case in both France and Spain.

On 16 February 1936, the Spanish Popular Front had won a narrow election victory. Manuel Azaña had formed a moderate coalition government of the Unión Republicana, the Izquierda Republicana and the Esquerra Republicana de Catalunya. Despite the moderation of this government, the victory of the Popular Front confirmed the right-wing rejection of the parliamentary process. Army officers pursued their preparations for a coup. This coup was precipitated on 17 July, when the conspiracy was uncovered. Risings in Spanish Morocco were followed by risings on the mainland but despite the government's initial reluctance to arm the workers, the insurrection was suppressed in Madrid and Barcelona. Thus in Spain, as in France, the forces of reaction met with popular resistance.

On the front page of *L'Humanité* of 19 July 1936 news of Franco's insurrection in Morocco competed with coverage of Hitler's annexation of Danzig. On the same page Jacques Duclos provided the first leader comment on events in Spain. Duclos had been foremost in establishing the Jacobin character of the 14 July celebrations in 1935, and for Duclos, events

> have demonstrated the necessity of an ever greater unity amongst the organisations composing the Popular Front, beginning with the Socialist party.
>
> We believe we are expressing the unanimous opinion of the French Popular Front in wishing that the Spanish Popular Front remain united, maintaining this vital unity in its ranks and among its organisations.[3]

This first commentary already labours the theme of unity, the theme which was to become central to the coverage of the civil war. Yet Duclos left implicit the international dimension of this unity, the unity of the French and Spanish Popular Fronts. However the next day in *L'Humanité* Paul Nizan developed the connection between France and Spain. Nizan concluded: 'Above all, the Spanish Popular Front must break fascism, its organisation and its allies. That is tomorrow's task in Madrid. And let it be said – because this warning must be heeded – it is today's task in Paris.'[4] At first glance Nizan's priorities seem reversed. How could the task be more pressing in Paris than in Madrid under arms? In its perversity, the statement reveals the extent to which *L'Humanité*'s coverage of the civil war was not simply directed towards a French audience but also participated in a French struggle.

The remarks made by Duclos and Nizan in a daily paper may seem to be of limited significance, yet together they establish the terrain on which the conflict within the Popular Fronts would be fought out. In sum, the two texts establish three forms of unity: within the Spanish Front, within the French Front, and between these Fronts. On 20 July these unities were compatible as the governments of France and Spain had a set of shared aims. This situation would not endure.

Those opposed to the Popular Front in France quickly declared their sympathy for the Spanish insurrection. Sharing the front page of *L'Humanité* with Nizan's article was a commentary on these French supporters, those who took desires for realities when they hailed Franco as the man to deliver Spain from the Popular Front.[5] The coverage of *Le Temps* was the first target of *L'Humanité*. If the election victory of the Popular Front had threatened the traditional identification of *Le Temps* and the ruling bloc and introduced a cleavage in the French public sphere, then this cleavage was to widen into a chasm as the Spanish conflict developed. Disputes over misrepresentation of the civil war were to reach extremes. By April 1937 Gérôme of the CVIA had concluded of the right-wing press:

> Behind each old slogan of yours one may discern another which contradicts you. Behind the word HONOUR, one may read: TREASON. Behind the word UNION: CIVIL WAR. And when you say ORDER, one understands: OPPRESSION AND SLAUGHTER.[6]

The collapse of the parliamentary process in Spain and the ensuing civil war thus produced a collapse of language in France, which, in turn, hastened the destruction of the French parliamentary process. This much has to be registered here but my concern in what follows is with another destruction, that of the image of the Popular Front. The hostility of the right was of course central to this process but as damaging was the conflict which developed within the Popular Front.[7] This conflict, the French Apocalypse of fraternity, is the principal subject of this chapter. It is the revelation of the Communist and Socialist press between 19 July and 5 December 1936, when the conflict finally emerged on the parliamentary stage with the abstention of the PCF in a vote of confidence on foreign policy.[8]

French and Spanish struggles

In the first days of the civil war, the French press sympathetic to the Popular Front sought to articulate the Spanish Republican struggle with that of the French workers. It was the success of this articulation which was ultimately to destroy the image of the Popular Front.

On 20 July Blum had received a request for arms from José Giral, the new president of the Spanish Republic. He immediately gave his assent. However, the Spanish military attaché in Paris, Antonio Barraso, revealed the aid arrangement to Henri de Kérillis, a staunch opponent of the Popular Front. De Kérillis then launched a campaign against French aid through *L'Echo de Paris*. On 23 July Blum travelled to London for talks with the British government and on his return the following evening Camille Chautemps warned him of growing unease over his support for Republican Spain. After a cabinet meeting held on 25 July it was announced that the French government had decided not to intervene in the Spanish conflict.[9] The French foreign minister Yvon Delbos then confirmed that this decision embraced both state intervention and private arms sales.[10]

On 30 July Delbos was informed that two Italian military aircraft had crashed in north Africa *en route* to Spanish Morocco, confirming suspicions that Mussolini was actively supporting Franco's rebellion. Nevertheless on 1 August the French cabinet reiterated support for the policy of non-intervention and called for other countries to adopt parallel policies. Yet if the first flurry of diplomatic activity concluded in the policy of non-intervention, simultaneously the Popular Front press established a contrary position, vaunting the unity of France and Spain.

In the issue of *L'Humanité* for 23 July Paul Vaillant-Couturier declared that whilst the rebels were 'men who traditionally present themselves as the guardians of order they can create only anarchy. Their "order" is injustice. They have become arsonists and assassins fighting against their own country and its legitimately expressed will.'[11] One sees already the inversion of vocabulary Gérôme would describe. Such inversions would serve to organise the account of the civil war offered by the Popular Front press in France, for this account had constantly to assert the legitimacy of the Republican cause against that of the pretended guardians of order. Those fighting the rebels were simply defending the popular will. In this context, the duty of France was clear. Vaillant-Couturier asserted: 'France knows who her friends are, and loves them. In Spain, they are those who wish to have the will of the people respected.'[12]

A photograph of workers and civil guards in Barcelona accompanied Vaillant-Couturier's article (Fig. 23). The staffage of the photograph makes it an image of the unity between workers and the true forces of order. Each group confers a legitimacy on the other under the

Fig. 23 Anon. 'Workers and civil guards fraternise in Barcelona', *L'Humanité*, 23 July 1936, p. 1. Photograph courtesy of the Musée Social, Paris.

transformed conditions of the civil war; five workers figure the democratic will and four guards the legitimate authority of the state. In the fraternity of these groups anarchy and oppression cancel each other. This fraternity is carried before the camera by the nine figures. Thus the stance adopted at the Nieuport factory, the stance which recurred in the photographs that striking workers sent to *Regards*, now appears on the street in Barcelona. The revolutionary image of those united in their struggle now appears in a new context.

The coverage of the civil war in *Le Populaire* was at first congruent with that of *L'Humanité*. On 24 July 1936 the Socialist organ printed its first eye-witness accounts from its own correspondents. Robert Fuzier and Jean-Maurice Herrmann sent reports, and both began in the same manner, with a narrative of crossing the border.[13] And in both cases it is the affiliation of the reporters to the Socialist press which eases their passage. These narratives are derived from the coverage of the strikes and specifically from those concerning entry to the occupied Renault plant.[14] Just as the photographic coverage of the civil war was transposed from the context of the strikes, so was the reporting.[15] Whilst in June the workers had controlled French factories, in July they controlled Spanish towns. In June they had protected the machinery, in July they protected churches and works of art. And the example of the Popular Front in France was not lost on Ventura Gassol, the Minister of Public Instruction of the Generalidad, who stated to Fuzier: 'We Catalans remember our brothers at Verdun during the Great War, those who fell with these words on their lips: "They shall not pass". We are happy to take up these words of the French Popular Front: "Here fascism shall not pass".'[16] The coverage in *L'Humanité* struck a similar tone, also emphasising the continuity between the French and Spanish struggles. 'To aid and defend the Spanish people against the organisers of civil war is to defend the French people, it is to work for the security of the country! It is to discharge the duty of the Popular Front, to act in conformity with the interests of France.'[17] That languages are transposed from French to Spanish situations is not any evidence of a paucity of imagination. Rather, it should be seen as an attempt on the part of journalists and photographers sympathetic to the Popular Front to extend that front across the Pyrenees.

The image of the militia

The eye-witness coverage of the Spanish conflict was adopted in *L'Humanité* for the issue of 25 July. These first accounts were furnished by workers who had travelled to Barcelona to compete in an alternative to the Berlin Olympic Games. These athletes had driven straight into the midst of the insurrection but according to *L'Humanité* they were unwavering in their commitment to the Republican cause and were maddened by the impossibility of joining the struggle.[18]

The new mode of coverage adopted was accompanied by a new presentation of the combatants. The first photographs shown in *L'Humanité*, such as that of the 23rd, had shown full-length figures. Now, as French workers offered their personal allegiance to the Spanish cause, the militia were photographed as individual members of a group (Fig. 24). Such images cannot easily be fixed in a genre. They are not comparable to titled portraits, such as those published of Giral and Franco. But nor are such images comparable to wide-angle photographs in which individuals are more emphatically submerged in their actions and interactions. The implied proximity of the viewer and the viewed slows narrative. Here each viewer is brought to look the militiamen and women in the eye.[19]

The contact suggested by the photograph in *L'Humanité* had a particular charge due to the nature of the Spanish struggle. Any militiaman or woman, in taking up arms to defend the Republican government, was confirming their support for this government. The votes of 16 February were constantly recast, the democratic mandate constantly renewed. Yet this renewal was not simply the repetition of a gesture.

In France, on 14 July 1935, the wearing of a Phrygian bonnet had been a gesture of support for the Popular Front; by donning a costume individuals became allegories of the Republic. But this happened on a stage,

Fig. 24 Anon. 'A group of militiamen', *L'Humanité*, 25 July 1936, p. 7. Photograph courtesy of the Musée Social, Paris.

the stage constructed by the time of the festival and the designated routes of the marches. And as staged, the gestures remained only gestures; for the demonstrations held in France were symbolic confrontations. Even the raising of a fist passed conflict into representation. Of course the failure in Spain was that the conflict could not be arrested at this level of representation. But, once the conflict had become physical, this transformed the conditions of representation. Or rather, it dissolved them. Now, when fists were raised for the camera in Barcelona, the gestures were matched not to meetings or demonstrations, but to actions at barricades. The militia, then, were not simply allegories of legitimacy, they were full embodiments of it.

This legitimacy has a particular valence within the Republican imaginary and the embodiment a particular significance. The sovereign will of 'the people' is expressed through universal suffrage and the expression of this sovereign will – as opposed to the expression of the arbitrary will of a monarch – is an affirmation of the liberty of 'the people'. This feature of the Republican imaginary distinguishes it from the monarchist. The monarch is an individual body and the body of the state; yet whilst the monarchy may be incarnated only in a single individual, 'the people' may be incarnated by any individual. Within the Republican imaginary, the individual constantly passes into the universal. In 1935 wearing the Phrygian bonnet was an individual gesture which made the female body an allegory of the Republic. In 1936 those wearing the insignia of the militia became embodiments of the Republic. This is a highly specific version of contaminated universality; it is a pure form of contamination. In contrast to the regular army used by the rebels, the militia presented individuals who have transformed themselves, by their own volition. Such transformations were a feature of the coverage; articles celebrated the courage of ordinary Spaniards, such as the metalworker Larranada, or Fabra, the son of a peasant.[20] This is the first meaning of the Apocalypse of fraternity, its revelation.

However, this moment of revelation was countered by the first announcement of the policy of non-intervention. This profoundly threatened the articulation of the Popular Front in France. The Popular Front had come to power through the articulation of antifascism which had offered a new role for 'the people-nation'. The popular class was to be the guardian of the sovereign will yet could 'the people' also be the guardian of a policy of non-intervention? Was such a policy the expression of its sovereign will?

The announcement of Blum's policy of non-intervention did not immediately transform the character of the coverage in *Le Populaire*, for the newspaper was not simply an organ for the transmission of policy. It had also to address the expectations of its readers and many of these were extremely sympathetic to the Spanish cause. Moreover Blum's decision not to intervene did not win the unanimous support of his party, even if unanimity had been achieved in the cabinet. Thus the editors of *Le Populaire* had to negotiate a particularly fraught path. And it seems that they did not want this path made more tortuous by the adoption of the photographic modes used in *L'Humanité*. The editors of the Socialist organ could not bring themselves to look the militia in the eye.

By contrast, the task of *L'Humanité* was facilitated by the distance which the PCF had maintained from the cabinet, for as a result of this distance 'the ministry of the masses' was not directly implicated in the policy of non-intervention. Nevertheless, *L'Humanité* had also to negotiate with its readership and so, in reporting Blum's policy, the Communist editors confined themselves to denouncing the press campaign launched against the Popular Front in an attempt to divide the government.[21]

Despite this cautious attitude, the image of the militia was increasingly exploited in *L'Humanité*. The issue of 27 July carried on its front page a large photograph of three members of the militia. The image was captioned: 'Young men and women have taken up arms to defend liberty' (Fig. 25). Whilst the figures are shown full length, the size of the image prevents it from being a mere genre piece. For the scale of the photograph in relation to the page is that conventionally reserved for portraiture; the three members of the militia are the scale of, say, Blum on the steps of the Hôtel Matignon. And given this scale it is not too much to see the three figures as analogues of such a leader, a further indication of the legitimacy of the Spanish people's struggle. Yet the figures are anonymous, and so remain instantiations of the popular struggle. The members of the militia are at once themselves and also 'the people' of Spain. And this passage from the individual to the universal is given in the title placed below the photograph, which converts Spain into a figure: 'Hail our sister Spain!'[22] Now the photographed militia-woman is the embodiment of the nation.

This image of the militia is distinct from that formulated for the presentation of the militant group during the strikes. The photograph of the

Fig. 25 Anon. 'Young men and women have taken up arms to defend liberty', *L'Humanité*, 27 July 1936, p. 1. Photograph courtesy of the Musée Social, Paris.

three members of the militia seems closer to the imagery developed to represent the picturesque detail of the strikes. Yet it must be registered that the opposition which developed between the two accounts of the strike, festive and militant, did not appear in the coverage of the civil war. In France the image of the joyous strike could be used to submerge the militant in the domestic and to present the strike within existing genres; the perceived threat to the Popular Front was thus contained. However, in Spain militancy and festivity could not be so readily uncoupled. For the men and women of the militia were embodiments of legitimacy. Their struggle was not a threat to the Popular Front but a defence of it.[23]

The members of the militia were, then, part of a front which could potentially stretch across the Pyrenees. And Vaillant-Couturier sought to demonstrate as much in the article accompanying the photograph of the three members of the militia. Here he related his own journey to San Sebastián and the freedom he found there. The atmosphere and activities Weil described in the factories are now to be encountered on the Spanish streets. 'Everywhere, in the villages, the same spectacle. That of perfectly calm people, breathing the night air with joy, and saluting us with enthusiasm.'[24] As with the strikes, such an atmosphere was a refutation of the accounts of anarchy and violence which circulated through the right-wing press. And as with the coverage of the strikes, the eye-witness mode served to counter such allegations. But whereas in France the imagery of joy came to be opposed to the imagery of struggle, the careless rapture in Spain united the two. At the Deputacion Vaillant-Couturier announces himself:

> Word quickly spreads. A Frenchman! Faces light up. France is here, the France of the Popular Front, the sister of Liberty! Against whom Hitler tries to build a Nazi front in Spain!
>
> And we embraced these shocktroops, militia, and irregulars in red berets, these weary militants. A symbol of our unity, and of our certainty of victory.[25]

This text performs a task analogous to that of the photograph it accompanies, transforming individuals into national symbols. Vaillant-Couturier represents France and when he embraces the militia France and Spain stand together. And with the embrace the eye-witness mode itself comes to perform a new task; the bodily presence implicit in the mode passes over into solidarity. As the situation deteriorated in Spain the authority of this mode was increasingly invoked.[26]

Yet the solidarity of France and Spain was to compromise the solidarity of the Popular Front in France. The day after Vaillant-Couturier's first report from Spain, *L'Humanité* issued its first call for the arming of the Spanish Republicans. This call was relayed by Vaillant-Couturier from the San Sebastián headquarters of the Unión General de Trabajadores rather than appearing as a direct appeal of the PCF, but it nevertheless marked a first rupturing of the relations between the SFIO and the PCF.[27]

Disarticulation

The tensions within the Popular Front became increasingly evident as the divergence between *Le Populaire* and *L'Humanité* grew during the first days of August.

The issue of *L'Humanité* for 3 August published a declaration on the Spanish situation which formally set out the position of the party. If the policy of non-intervention operated through the fiction of the civil war as an internal matter, then the thrust of the Communist declaration was to position the Spanish conflict in the European theatre. This extended the Popular Front in France in two directions; the Republicans of France were linked fraternally to the Republicans of Spain and these legitimate governments were ranged against traitors in Spain, linked in turn with the fascists of Germany and Italy.[28] Yet the Communist calls for solidarity were not yet explicit calls for an end to the embargo. However the attitude of the PCF had hardened by 6 August. On this day Thorez made a direct appeal for the lifting of the blockade:

> Now solidarity must become effective. In order to defeat the rebels who are so well armed by Hitler and Mussolini our people demand – in their own interest – that those who fight in Spain on the front of Liberty are able to obtain all that they need for their struggle ... Any other attitude would be a break with the glorious traditions of the workers and the people of France.[29]

Here Thorez ranges 'the people-nation' – its interests, its traditions – against the policy decided by the cabinet.[30] Nevertheless, at a cabinet meeting of 8 August a unilateral policy of non-intervention was adopted. The frontier with Spain was closed.

The ever-widening faultlines running through the Popular Front were exposed in the coverage of a peace demonstration held at Saint-Cloud on 9 August. This day was organised by Robert Lange, one of the Radicals most closely involved in the organisation and promotion of the events of 14 July 1935.[31] And on 9 August an oath was taken as on 14 July. Yet the image of unity produced on the 14th was not recaptured on the 9th. There were a number of reasons for this, but the principal one was a disagreement over means and ends. Different interpretations of the Popular Front may have animated the crowd on 14 July 1935, but nevertheless the principle of unity was accepted. By contrast on 9 August 1936 although the principle of peace was accepted there was disagreement as to how this end was to be achieved. Thus although a very large crowd made the journey to Saint-Cloud they did not travel with a common purpose. Some doubtless came to support Blum's stated policy: that peace had to be universal. But *Le Populaire* also recorded the cries of those demanding that Republican Spain be armed.[32]

In 1936 there had once again been celebrations on Bastille Day. These were celebrations of the Popular Front in power; they were demonstrations of sovereignty and therefore quite distinct from the earlier demonstrations of protest.[33] Blum's image was now carried through the streets of Paris. The leader was distinguished from the led. And the policy of non-intervention served to convert this distinction into estrangement. Thus although Marianne was present again on 9 August, she was now too much an image of the state, a figurehead rather than an identity to be assumed through the purchase of a Phrygian bonnet. On the 9th Marianne was a single figure, presiding over a living flag of costumed men and women. This flag was a display produced for an audience, and thus quite distinct from the forms of participation represented in the brochure commemorating 14 July 1935. To be part of such an orchestrated display, dressed uniformly in blue, white or red, was to present oneself to viewers in a manner which ran counter to the dialectic of seeing and being seen played out in 1935. Thus on the 9th there was no longer the exchange between leaders and led which had characterised the earlier phases of the Popular Front. By August 1936 this relationship had been transformed.

That the true exchanges between leaders and led now took place in Spain was the stated belief of the Communists. On 9 August Duclos spoke on behalf of his party, demanding: 'What worth do declarations of peace have, if they are not followed by actions?'[34] For Duclos, those acting were the militia defending the Republic and for many the militiawomen were more convincing figures for liberty than Marianne. This much was made clear in the coverage of the demonstration in *L'Humanité*. This coverage was prefaced by an article by Louis de Brouckère, president of the Second International, of which Blum's party formed the French section. The Communist organ reprinted De Brouckère's text from *Le Populaire*, yet this seemingly impeccable gesture of solidarity was an action directed against the SFIO. De Brouckère had declared that certain achievements of the militia, 'the retaking of Barcelona and the attack on the Montaña Barracks in Madrid, are as astonishing as the storming of the Bastille'.[35] For the president of the

Second International the revolutionary tradition is now renewed in Spain rather than France.[36]

The Apocalypse of fraternity had unfolded in Spain as revelation and in France it now began to unfold as destruction.

Eye to eye

The adherence of the Soviet Union to the policy of non-intervention was reported in the issue of *L'Humanité* of 11 August.[37] However, the newspaper continued to inveigh against both the intervention of Germany and Italy and the embargo which prevented the Republican purchase of arms.[38] Now 'the ministry of the masses' had to steer between Stalin's designs and the demands of one section of the French working class. This course carried the PCF ever farther from the position adopted by the cabinet.

Following the announcement of the Soviet Union, the PCF made a formal communication to the SFIO concerning the intervention of Germany and Italy.[39] Over the next two weeks the fascist powers would move slowly towards adherence to the non-intervention pact, whilst continuing to supply Franco's rebels.[40] Yet following adherence the fascists soon broke the pact and on 4 September the French newspapers revealed that Mussolini had delivered 24 aeroplanes to Franco and Hitler 12. This news prompted a further letter from the PCF to the SFIO; in this letter, which was reprinted on the front page of *L'Humanité,* Thorez proposed to Paul Faure that the Communists and Socialists should send a joint deputation to Blum to demand that the blockade be lifted. In short, Thorez now proposed dressing Blum's own party against him.[41]

The letter of 4 September to Faure was a formal expression of protest. Its physical expression was a demonstration at the Place de la République held on the same day, ostensibly to celebrate the sixty-sixth anniversary of the declaration of the Third Republic. With this demonstration the sovereignty of the Popular Front government was contested; the space dedicated to the Republic was occupied to challenge the policy of the Republican government.[42] *Le Populaire* presented the demonstration of the 4th as a response to the appeal of the Comité national du rassemblement populaire, that is to say as a demonstration of loyalty to the Republic. Yet *L'Humanité* presented the event as a protest. 'Tens of thousands of men and women, Communists, Socialists, Democrats and Republicans, marched until nightfall, clearing their way through the crowds, chanting 'Planes! Weapons for Spain! Lift the blockade killing our Spanish brothers!'[43] On 12 February 1934 Communists and Socialists had met at the Place de la Nation and protested against the failure of the government to resist fascism. Now, on 4 September 1936, they met again to make what was in effect the same protest.

Instead of a response to the Comité national, *L'Humanité* presented the chants of the crowd as a direct response to the killing of refugees from Irun. Marcel Gitton's commentary establishes this by citing the account of events given in *L'Information*:

> The inhabitants who had not yet left the town had wanted to take refuge in France; a rebel column on the banks of the Bidossa opened fire on them. Sadly, among the victims were women and children. This fact and the carnage which ensued on the entry of the rebels into Irun has provoked the indignation of the English.
>
> Inside Irun itself the rebels refuse to take prisoners and kill the defenders of the town without mercy.[44]

For Gitton, these actions provoked not only the English but also the French; thus the cry of arms for Spain was redoubled. Gitton demands: 'Let the voice of the people be heard!'[45]

Gitton's rallying cry was supplemented by a detailed account of the demonstration. 'A single thought and a single passion were to be read on the faces and heard on the lips of the immense crowd which came yesterday to the Place de la République. A single thought and a single passion were to be found in the eyes and found in the hearts of the crowd come to declare its settled will.'[46] In emphasising the will of 'the people', Gitton's commentary is in accord with familiar accounts of Popular Front demonstrations. However, Gitton presents a popular will set against government policy. The demonstration is therefore disruptive. And accordingly it is not simply an occupation of space but a transformation of it, one which defies description. 'How to portray the thousand different aspects of the Place de la République, these streets and avenues deprived of their usual appearance to become the frame for a living, breathing mass, bloody from the blows received by unarmed brothers, succumbing at that instant, as Irun burns.'[47] The streets of Paris are transformed by the violence in Irun. When Vaillant-Couturier embraced members of the militia, the solidarity of France and Spain was embodied; when the crowds at République are described as bloodied from the fighting in Irun the same solidarity is invoked.

This embodied solidarity was akin to that created when the supporters of the Popular Front swore the oath of 14 July. And whether describing Paris or San Sebastián, the task of *L'Humanité* was to insist on this solidarity at every turn. Yet appeals to the embodied were increasingly absent from the pages of *Le Populaire*. The Socialist organ had not exploited the photographs of the militia which brought the Spanish and French eye to eye. And after 4 September eye-witness reporting in *Le Populaire* was largely abandoned. Jean-Maurice Herrmann, *Le Populaire*'s principal journalist in Spain, and one opposed to the arms blockade, returned to France a few days after 5 September.[48]

By contrast, in the Communist press the attempt to bring the Spanish and French eye to eye involved pushing photography beyond its own conventions. In an article in *Regards* – pointedly titled 'Visages d'Espagne' – the Russian writer Ilya Ehrenburg explicitly brought the reader eye to eye with the militia. He describes a series of snapshots as follows:

> In the militia barracks, I saw, on a board, family photographs. A young woman, smiling, by a clump of trees. Two little boys playing with a wooden donkey. A woman with a little girl on her lap. 38 photographs from a time of peace, of love. Above them, this inscription: "Look after them! They are our women and children!"[49]

Here personal images are given a public function precisely because of the intimate associations they hold. Just as the figure of the militia transcended an opposition between the militant and joyous, so these photographs were made to transcend a distinction between the private and public. Once again, the particular is made universal. And the universality derives from the particularity.[50] The display of images Ehrenburg describes is clearly intended as an inspiration for the militia, yet when photographed and reproduced in *Regards* the meaning shifts. Here solidarity is to be established not according to principles or ideologies but according to 'common' humanity. This link is sustained at a profound level. Ehrenburg's camera occupies the place of the militia and occupies their gaze. The viewer of Ehrenburg's photograph sees private objects become public, as the private individuals themselves became militia and assumed public roles. And the duties of care implied in familial relations are themselves universalised here. The militia in previous photographs had been objects and embodiments. Here the viewer is offered their subjectivity, both their interiority and their gaze. But this is not to be alienating. We are to see that their subjectivity is our own. And this in turn was to be embodied in the volunteers who left France to fight in Spain.

The International Brigades

During the first months of the civil war, Jean-Richard Bloch, a fairly well-behaved fellow traveller, wrote a series of articles on Spain. These were gathered together in October 1936 to form the book *Espagne, Espagne!* For Bloch:

> President Azaña has clearly shown that the frontier of France, *as a democracy and as a nation*, runs along the Guadarrama front, and that the people of Republican Spain, fighting and dying, thereby defend the independence and the destiny of France [...]. The fate of the mass of the Spanish people is now inseparable from the fate of the French nation. Seen from a certain distance – and such will be the vantage point of posterity – the two nations at this moment form one people, united in a common struggle.[51]

Thus the role of the International Brigades was prepared. France, as a democratic nation, was defended in Spain. If the French policy of non-intervention was scant reward for this defence, the French volunteers to the International Brigades pledged a level of commitment to the Spanish Republic which stood in direct contrast to cabinet policy.

The national-popular articulation of the Popular Front had constituted a frontier of those struggling for their emancipation through the institutions of the Republic. Yet a price had to be paid for this articulation, for as its critics had observed, it was made at the expense of internationalism.[52] However, from one perspective, the volunteers' departure for Spain could seem to mark a return to internationalism. For if the French struggle now took place on the Guadarrama front the popular struggle could no longer be contained by national boundaries. Yet of course this compromised the articulation of the national and the popular. Thus President Azaña's relocation of the French frontier was also a dislocation. However this dislocation did not restore revolutionary internationalism; this was precisely what was downplayed in the Spanish conflict. French and Spanish communists insisted they were simply defending the Spanish Republic, and Stalin's decision to aid Spain coincided with Largo Caballero's formation of a government which included liberals as well as revolutionaries. This is the paradox attendant on the formation of the International Brigades.[53]

Although foreign volunteers were present almost from the beginning of the Spanish conflict, and volunteer groups were organised at the beginning of August, the decision to form the International Brigades was not taken until 18 September 1936. The decision was taken in Moscow but when the official foundation of the Brigades was announced a month later, on 22 October, the initiative appeared to come from Spain.[54]

On 23 October the Soviet Union declared that it would not be bound by the non-intervention pact to any greater extent than the other signatories.[55] This announcement threatened the Popular Front in France from two directions. First, it set the PCF directly against Blum's policy, as was soon made clear in *L'Humanité*.[56] Second, the announcement coincided with the Radical party congress in Biarritz. This congress marked the first plenary meeting of the party since the election victory and the strikes and it saw the beginning of an organised opposition to the Popular Front. It was a member of this opposition, Jean Mistler, who delivered the report on foreign policy; Mistler supported the policy of non-intervention and warned against what he saw as the ideological crusade pursued by the Communists.[57]

Yet the PCF did, in effect, launch a crusade. The policy of non-intervention would now be described as a policy of intervention against the Spanish Republican government.[58] And thus 'the ministry of the masses' came to represent itself as the true guardian of the ideals of the Popular Front; it claimed the legitimacy which the elected government now seemed to lack. Vaillant-Couturier presented the Communist position as a sincere attempt to maintain the unity of the Front without 'sacrificing the interests of the masses'.[59] And he asked whether this was not, after all, the pledge given by the government. Was not this government one 'which has set out to be different "from the others", one which has set out to apply the will of the people, in collaboration with them?'[60]

The formal opposition to government policy was registered on 5 December 1936, when the Communists in the Chamber abstained in a vote of confidence on foreign policy. This was the first rupturing of the parliamentary coalition and as such it marked the beginning of the end of the Popular Front. On this occasion, Duclos once again spoke on behalf of his party. In a reprimand to the government, he sent 'a fraternal greeting to the international volunteers who are fighting at the gates of Madrid and who offer proof of great courage and sacrifice at a moment when many wish to describe lack of foresight as prudence'.[61]

Two days later, Duclos' terms were translated into an eye-witness account for *L'Humanité* penned by Tristan Tzara, the erstwhile Dadaist. Tzara explicitly contrasted the atmosphere of Madrid with that of Paris. 'Despite the debris of bombed houses and gutted palaces, despite the holes reaching down to the *métro* made by the aerial bombardment, Madrid has a tragic, inexpressible beauty.'[62] And in the Spanish capital, Tzara sees the 'conscience of a new humanity, in the process of being created from the ashes'.[63] This he sets against the shabby methods employed in Paris to 'pervert the purest instincts of the masses'.[64] And yet Tzara is able to confirm the resilience of these instincts by offering the case of a 58-year-old peasant and war veteran who has 'closed up his house, sent his daughter to Paris, and has come to enroll himself in the International Brigade'.[65]

Both Tzara and Duclos compared the actions of the International Brigade with the inaction of the Popular Front government. The volunteers in Madrid and Barcelona are presented as pursuing an antifascist struggle from which the French government has abdicated. Popular sovereignty is embattled in Spain but there has not been an abdication. And it is this tension which defines the image of the international brigades as circulated in the French press. For the image of the brigades – as an image of popular intervention – maintained the popular sovereignty defined in France in July 1935. The images from Spain did not derive their force from a simple analogy with the imagery of the strikes – although such analogies in the presentation of defiance and victory do exist and were exploited. Rather, the image of the brigades derived its force from the fact that it was inseparable from the imagery which first defined the legitimacy of the Popular Front.

Tzara made this clear in an article published in *Regards* in the wake of the Communist abstention:

> The same socialists, communists and Radicals ... who on 14 July took part in demonstrations across France, and who refused to believe that words could not also be deeds, these people march today against Franco, and the death which he represents. They struggle for the Spanish people; they offer their bodies in place of the weapons that France refuses to sell to the legitimate government of a friendly country.[66]

Here the national and the popular are placed in conflict and the body of any volunteer could figure that conflict. It was this conflict which destroyed the exchange between leaders and led, and destroyed the image of the Popular Front.

The Apocalypse of fraternity

The policy of non-intervention came to be countermanded by the direct participation of volunteers in the International Brigades. Thus the Popular Front went into exile. Now the conditions for the reproduction of its image only existed in fiction, in works such as Malraux's *L'Espoir*.

Malraux's novel of the civil war opens on the evening of 18 July, the first full day of Franco's rebellion. In the first scene, railway workers in Madrid telephone stations on their network to establish which towns have remained loyal to the Republic. Through a series of terse conversations the map of Spain is redrawn and as the old order collapses Malraux presents the improvised formation of the militias. The first phase of fighting in Madrid culminates in the Republican seizure of the Montaña Barracks on 20 July. Madrid is secured for the Republic, and the new order in the city produces new representations. Here is how Malraux describes the morning of 21 July:

> All the cars in the city, commandeered for the war or for the service of a dream, were roaring down the street amid fraternal shouts. The photographs taken at the Montaña Barracks by photographers formerly employed by the fascist press – which had been nationalised that morning – were passing from hand to hand along the café tables. Militiamen were examining them eagerly. 'That's me!' 'That's us!'[67]

As the militia take control of the city – its barracks, its cars – so they also take control of technologies of reproduction. The press is nationalised. And as this happens, the participants in the storming of the barracks find themselves reproduced, transported before the public. Here the masses are brought to look themselves in the eye. The strikers in France had already had this experience. And the strikers in *Les Femmes dans l'Action Mondiale* had anticipated the reaction of the militia: 'That's me!' Yet the shift from witness to participant, from reader to writer, was blocked in France; the transformation described by Benjamin in the artwork essay could not be completed. Spain presented a different case, one in which Malraux could put Benjamin's arguments to work.

Malraux was certainly familiar with Benjamin's essay; he cited it in a speech on cultural heritage first delivered in London in June 1936.[68] However, when he came to draft *L'Espoir* in May 1937 his concern was neither with cultural heritage nor avant-garde technique but with the changes wrought by the civil war. Malraux suggests that what Benjamin imagined in Moscow was now to be realised in another revolutionary context, that of Madrid. In Madrid readers were to become writers and previously passive viewers were now to be photographed. For war, like the great festival processions, was 'now fed into the camera'.[69]

Benjamin had argued that everyone has the right to be filmed. This right is based on the activity of workers, on their own forms of knowledge and experience. Yet this right is frustrated under the present conditions of capital. However, Malraux saw that an alternative to these conditions could be found on the streets of Madrid. Here, as indicated by the nationalisation of the press, property relations were to be overturned. If previously the masses had been prevented from recognising themselves, such a recognition was now available to the militia. They were able to look themselves in the eye. And as they looked, so a legitimacy was confirmed, just as the legitimacy of the Popular Front in France was confirmed in July 1935. Indeed Malraux makes Garcia, the observer of Apocalypse, draw a parallel between France and Spain. Describing the fraternity of the Spanish volunteers, the officer comments: 'I found just the same spirit in Russia in 1917; and, less than six months ago, in France'.[70] Such sentiments were repeated many times in the Communist press during the first months of the war.[71] Yet it was in the nature of this fraternity to have no future. The fervour of which Garcia spoke would realise itself in a fraternity of the dead.

On the morning of 21 July, the militia could recognise themselves in the newspapers, amidst fraternal shouts. Here, the camera confirmed a fraternity and with it a legitimacy. Yet soon the camera was to be pushed back into its older role, its most banal role, as an instrument of mortification. Malraux concludes the second part of his novel with the fall of Toledo and the execution of Republican prisoners. As Franco's troops try to organise the victims, the Republican Captain Hernandez wonders: 'Would they *never* manage to get the prisoners facing the rifles like a wedding group facing the camera, into the correct pose?'[72] However at last 'the three had taken the right pose; yes, all was ready for the camera'.[73] Ehrenburg had made the camera congruent with the gaze of the militia. Now it becomes congruent with the gaze of their executioners.

There is one final reversal. On 3 November 1937, the Communist-supported evening paper *Ce Soir* began a serialisation of *L'Espoir*. Jean-Richard Bloch and Aragon were the editors of *Ce Soir* and guessing at their reasons for choosing this serialisation is not too difficult. In January 1937, less than two months before their editorial collaboration began, Aragon had reviewed Bloch's book on Spain. He contrasted the urgency of Bloch's writing with the flat quality of newspaper prose:

> With tragic indifference, the opened newspaper parades trivia, ephemera, war communiqués, pared accounts of disasters, the impassive duels of the diplomats. The day's pages fall from heedless hands, in apartments where the aroma of the morning's coffee lingers, in the quiet streets where the wind blows into the gutter: 'General Franco announces a new offensive ... ' Banalities, you will turn to dust. People of France, when will you open your eyes, and your hearts? Can you not hear the terrible cries from Spain, the cannon drowning the sound of the human voice?[74]

Depuis un an, la mort plane sur les Madrilènes...

Il y a un an...

Il y a aujourd'hui un an, dans les tranchées, devant Huesca, des hommes écoutaient avec angoisse les nouvelles que la T.S.F. apportait du front de Madrid.

Getafe était pris. Les Marocains menaçaient Carabanchel. L'ennemi fasciste attaquait la Casa del Campo. La voix empâtée de Queipo de Llano annonçait la prise totale de la capitale pour le lendemain.

Dans un combat particulièrement meurtrier, la colonne « Culture et Action » venait d'arracher aux factieux les passes d'Estrecho-Quinto et elle avait pu progresser ensuite de vingt-cinq kilomètres. Des contre-attaques l'avaient fixée devant Chimillas. Ses fusils tiraient déjà dans les premières maisons de la capitale du Haut-Aragon. Douze cents hommes tenaient le front des villages Argüis, Nueno, Arascues, Apies, Igriès, Banastas. Rien qu'à Bolea, en face, les rebelles avaient 2.000 « guardia civil » en réserve.

Mathieu CORMAN.

Lire la suite dans la 3e page

L'ESPOIR

par ANDRÉ MALRAUX

Cette femme douloureuse n'est-elle pas le symbole de l'Espagne martyre ?

Lire dans la page magazine l'émouvant récit de Malraux

Fig. 26 Anon. 'Is not this suffering woman the symbol of martyred Spain?', *Ce Soir*, 7 November 1937, p. 1. Photograph: Max Adcock. Private Collection.

Proust had already noted how fresh atrocities accompanied fresh coffee, but whereas the the narrator of *Sentiments filiaux d'un parricide* is exemplary in his indifference, Aragon is not. When he and Bloch came to edit *Ce Soir*, the engagement of the eye witness played a key role. And Malraux, as a squadron leader in the Republican air force, was exemplary in his engagement, as was emphasised in the introduction to the first extract from his novel.[75] The serialisation of *L'Espoir* does not present the entirety of the novel but rather a series of non-consecutive extracts. Thus *L'Espoir* is fitted to its new context as its serialisation approximates journalism rather than the integrated narrative of a conventional novel. The mode of witnessing which dominated the accounts of the civil war is here given a final realisation.

The serialisation was illustrated, yet not with sketches but with photographs of actual incidents and actual victims of the war. Thus a photograph of the taking of the Hotel Colon during the first day of fighting in Barcelona accompanies Malraux's fictional account of the same events. Such a form of coverage recognised and exploited a truth of the work of the reporter-photographer: that photographs are instantiations, symbols in which joy, or suffering, are at once specific and generic. To say this is not to diminish suffering but it is to recognise the task the images are made to perform. This was made clear on the fifth day of serialisation. On the front page of *Ce Soir* of 7 November 1937 an

..Et les femmes suivaient avec le désir brouillon d'être utiles.

Fig. 27 Anon. [Robert Capa] ' ... And the women followed with the burning desire to be useful.', *Ce Soir*, 7 November 1937, p. 8. Photograph: Max Adcock. Copyright: Magnum Photos, New York. Private Collection.

article recalled the attack on Madrid of Mola, Varela and Yagüe, launched exactly a year before.[76] This article is accompanied by a photograph of a woman captioned: 'Is not this suffering woman the symbol of martyred Spain?' And next to this image was placed an insert for that day's instalment of *L'Espoir* (Fig. 26). This instalment, from close to the end of the novel, details the aftermath of a plane crash and the peasants' rescue of the wounded airmen. A photograph accompanying the text shows another suffering woman, her pain now to be read in the context of the airmens' plight (Fig. 27). Her pain is transformed, and put to work, just as that of the woman on the front page is.

This is a reversal of Benjamin's imagining of readers becoming writers. This imagining had been prompted by the transformation of the press, in which the newspaper offered the model for a new literature. In this context an older division of labour was to be overturned and those reading would assume their rights, and they would write. Malraux had suggested that this could be realised in Madrid and Barcelona. But in *Ce Soir* an old order is reasserted. The newspaper does not become a new literature, rather literature, Malraux's novel, becomes news. So, in the end, even under the Popular Front, the masses were not able to portray themselves.

A Paris, dans les écoles, toutes les classes ont été assurées. Voici en particulier la sortie des enfants à l'école

Fig. 28 Anon. 'In the Parisian schools no classes were disrupted. This was the scene as the children left school', *Le Matin*, 1 December 1938, p. 1. Photograph: Max Adcock. Private Collection.

Epilogue: 30 November 1938

On 1 December 1938 the front page of *Le Matin* carried a single photograph, a photograph of children leaving school (Fig. 28). The event shown is not distinctive; it is entirely banal. The school is unimportant; it is not even identified, although one can make out that it is in the second *arrondissement*. The photograph itself is unremarkable; it does not isolate a dramatic exchange, or reveal a telling detail. The composition has a studied neutrality, approximating the glance of a passer-by on the other side of the street. Yet the editors of *Le Matin* were not alone in adopting this form of coverage on 1 December. Similar photographs – of different subjects but equal banality – appeared in a number of newspapers. These papers included *Le Figaro, Le Journal* and *Le Jour-L'Echo de Paris*.[1]

Writing of the Spanish Civil War, Simone Weil had argued that 'a social transformation can only be correctly judged in terms of its effect on the everyday life of the people'.[2] What many editors wished to show on 1 December 1938 was that no social transformation had taken place, that everyday life continued undisturbed. On 1 December the unremarkable was, for once, remarkable. This was because of the general strike of 30 November. In showing an open school, an open *métro* station, or a busy department store, the newspapers were not simply marking the absence of strikers. They marked a disappearance. If in the aftermath of 6 February 1934 'the people-nation' had emerged as the protagonist of French antifascism, then this protagonist was forced to make a final exit on 30 November 1938.

The immediate, declared reason for the CGT to call a general strike had been to protest against the decree-laws promulgated by Paul Reynaud on 13 November in fulfilment of a policy announced by Daladier on 21 August. Reynaud's measures included adjustments to the legislation for the 40-hour week and were thus a direct challenge to the now mythologised conquests of June 1936. This was a challenge which the CGT had to meet in some form, but the form of the general strike was imposed on the leadership by the rank and file. According to André Delmas, increased agitation in the autumn had led a number of local officials to fear that the CGT would lose control of its base. The general strike was therefore called as a means of reasserting the authority of the Confédération whilst containing the agitation by giving it a focus.[3] A constant refrain of the CGT was that the general strike was to repeat the success of 12 February 1934, the occasion on which French workers came to the defence of 'the people' of France.[4] With such claims a whole history was evoked, the history of the Popular Front, the history of the exchanges between the leaders and the led. It was the very possibility of such exchanges which was destroyed on 30 November and this is why my account of the image of the Popular Front has to conclude on this day.

This is not to suggest that the Popular Front was destroyed in one day, as the result of an unforeseen crisis. Quite to the contrary, the process of destruction took two and a half years.

The strikes of June 1936 increased the flight of capital from France which had begun with the election victory of May. If the abstention of the PCF in the vote on foreign policy of 5 December 1936 was the first formal rupturing of the Popular Front, it was this flight of capital which caused the first formal curtailment of the Popular Front project. To halt the flight Blum announced a 'pause' in reforms on 13 February 1937. Nevertheless, he resigned on 21 June after the Senate refused to vote him the decree powers necessary to resolve the financial crisis. Blum was succeeded by Camille Chautemps, who formed a government with Socialist participation. Yet on 15 January 1938 this cabinet resigned after a rupture with the Communist deputies, who had announced their intention of abstaining in a vote of confidence. On 18 January 1938 Chautemps formed a government without Socialist participation. Nevertheless, when the Socialists refused to support this government, Chautemps again resigned. Blum then returned to power for 26 days between 13 March and 10 April; his resignation was once again the result of the Senate's opposition to his financial policies. This marked the end of the Popular Front at the parliamentary level. Blum was now succeeded by Daladier, who was to remain president of cabinet until 20 March 1940.[5]

Yet the destruction of the Popular Front was not simply a matter of its collapse as a parliamentary project. For the contradictions within the Front became increasingly evident within the organisations comprising it. Opposition to Blum's policies within the SFIO led to a split within the party at its congress of June 1938; as a result Pivert formed the Parti socialiste ouvrier et paysan.[6] The contradiction within the PCF would be termed a conflict of loyalties if such an expression were not so inappropriate. The party continued to vaunt its commitment to the unity of the Popular Front. This commitment nevertheless had to be set against both the party's subordination to Stalin's foreign policy and its attempt to maintain a privileged relationship with the working class. As a result, in the autumn of 1938 the PCF was brought into direct conflict with the Radicals. In respect of foreign policy the conflict was over Daladier's signing of the Munich Agreement of 30 September. In respect of economic policy the conflict was over the proposed adjustments to the 40-hour week. These conflicts were also signs that the Radical party had adopted a new direction. At the party congresses of 1936 and 1937 Radical opposition to the Popular Front had taken the form of opposition to collaboration with the Communists, although general support for the Front was maintained. Yet the perceived effects of the strikes of June 1936 and the Communist opposition to non-intervention coalesced in a Radical anticommunism which Daladier exploited at the party congress of October 1938. Here he denounced the PCF for breaking the solidarity of the Rassemblement populaire. Then, on 10 November, the Radicals formally withdrew from the Rassemblement.[7]

The divisions within and between the parties ensured that the Popular Front from above was destroyed. Yet there remained the Popular Front from below. Daladier's challenge to the conquests of June 1936 was a direct challenge to this Front and the militancy of its members. For the receding of the strike wave of June had not marked the end of strike activity. On the contrary the Matignon Agreements had been interpreted at the base as a sign of the political efficacy of striking. Thus there were a number of strikes in protest against the policy of non-intervention. On 15 October 1936 the general secretary of the CGT was forced to make a public appeal for an end to the incessant striking. Nevertheless 1937 saw an exceptional level of strike activity.[8] There was a major strike wave in the Parisian region in September and a strike of the Parisian public services in December. Finally, in August 1938, a dockers' strike spread from Marseilles along the Mediterranean coast and prompted Daladier's challenge of 21 August. This challenge in turn provoked the agitation of the autumn and resulted in the calling of the general strike. Thus the hegemony of the Popular Front collapsed into a 'trial of strength' between the workers and the government.[9]

The conditions for the strike of 30 November 1938 were distinct from those of 1936 in that the government was no longer seeking to arbitrate between the workers and capital but was clearly allied with the latter. Given this, the announcement of the strike five days in advance of the event was a tactical error, as it provided Daladier with the opportunity to introduce a series of countermeasures which undermined the efficacy and impact of the strike.[10]

Despite the fact that as many stopped work on 30 November 1938 as on 12 February 1934, the strike was widely regarded as a failure. It was this failure which was celebrated in the right-wing press. This was a celebration of the destruction of the image of the Popular Front.

In this book, my argument has been that the image of the Popular Front was one which served to renegotiate the contradiction within the bourgeois constitutional state, the contradiction between two roles for 'the people': as politically free and as socially enslaved. The Republic held out the promise that 'the people' as an oppressed class could be emancipated by 'the people' as the sovereign will of the nation. Realising this programme of *liberté, egalité, fraternité* was the declared aim of the new Jacobins and the means of exercising hegemony during the Third Republic. To be sure, this hegemony was that of the bourgeoisie but it was to be exercised in the name of 'the people'. Thus the Republican programme ensured exchanges between rulers and ruled, a relationship between leaders and led.

It was this relationship which was threatened in February 1934 and it was this relationship that the Popular Front was to secure. I have argued that the image of the Popular Front was a means of doing so precisely because it operated as a site for exchange. The exchange between leaders and led was established with the celebrations of 14 July 1935 and the commemoration of these events provided the exemplary image of the Popular Front. The image constructed by Robert Lange and Marc Réal was exemplary because it was not simply an iconography but the site at which an iconography was recognised and affirmed as legitimate. Such an image could not be imposed by leaders but only proposed; the exchanges depended on the agency of the audience. And in the summer of 1935 maintaining exchanges between leaders and led was crucial. For on 14 July the Popular Front was sealed from above, at the level of the political parties, and at this moment the Front was redefined. To defend the Republic, the Front had to prevail in the Chamber of Deputies, yet moving onto this parliamentary terrain threatened to collapse the Front into a set of bureaucratic, formal relations. In 1935, the image of the Popular Front was to prevent such a collapse.

In 1936, the image of the Front was to play a different role. With the election victory of May, the Popular Front parties came to 'occupy' power. It now seemed that the programme of the Front could be realised and that, in the words of the programme, a 'great change' could take place. Yet this change could be imagined in sharply divergent ways. Whilst Léon Blum imagined a defensive occupation of power, many of those striking imagined the final emancipation of 'the people' as an oppressed class. Such divergence threatened the unity of the Popular Front and a new image of the Front was pressed into service to transform the strikes into a series of festivals. Now the exchanges between viewers and viewed were largely transformed into the more conventional relationship between audience and performers.

With the outbreak of the Spanish Civil War, the possibility of a more dynamic exchange was reasserted. Those who had been prevented from playing an active role in France could now do so in Spain. Now the militia and the International Brigades could be presented as the true defenders of the Republic. Yet this popular intervention in the Republican struggle could not be reconciled with the French government's policy of non-intervention and, ultimately, this destroyed the possibility of exchanges between leaders and led.

Summarised in this fashion, the history of the image of the Popular Front may be understood as a history of contingency. By this I mean more than that the image operated through the agency of its viewers. What I have sought to emphasise is that each successful transformation of the image was also potentially the moment of its failure. In 1935 the image worked to secure the Popular Front from above but this was at the expense of the Front from below. In 1936 this image contributed to election victory but the transformation of the Front from potential to actual government resulted in a further curtailment of its popular base. And finally, when the image of the Popular Front succeeded in mobilising support for the cause of the Spanish Republic, this success resulted in the destruction of the image. In each case, the success of the image as a site of exchange required more than the renewal of a mandate. For in each case the success transformed the very terms of the exchange. Perhaps this should be understood as a condition of hegemony. If hegemony is defined as the articulation of distinct struggles then the successful conclusion of any individual campaign will require a process of rearticulation.

The history I have offered here is one of rearticulation, a history of the ways in which the struggle against capital could be linked with the defence of the Republic. These articulations were necessarily unstable and tracing the contests over the image of the Popular Front reveals this instability with a particular clarity. Thus what the history of the image reveals is the complexity of the interaction between the Front from above and the Front from below. These interactions were crucial to the Front as a popular movement, yet they cannot be recovered from histories narrowly defined by the actions of policymakers. Instead of such conventional histories, which adopt the purview of the hegemonic class, I have tried to demonstrate how the relations between classes are maintained. This has required not only a reexamination of press photography but also a broader reassessment of the political uses of the image. In turn, I hope this has clarified the project of a Gramscian art history.

Finally, I hope to have opened a new perspective onto the extraordinary period of the Popular Front. For it certainly was extraordinary when 'the people' stepped once more to the front of the stage. The impact of this may be measured by the extremity of the reaction the Popular Front provoked. Something of this reaction can be seen in the exultation of papers such as *Le Temps* on 1 December 1938. For *Le Temps*, a period of revolutionary disturbances had been drawn to a close and the Republic had been restored.[11] The Popular Front was now revealed as an aberration, a momentary lapse from the true republican tradition. And for *L'Excelsior* the true Republic was not that of *liberté, egalité, fraternité* but that of *loi, travail, patrie*, this definition foreshadowing the trinity of Vichy: *Travail-Famille-Patrie*.[12] Thus a return to normality was celebrated with descriptions of the Parisian streets; journalists noted with satisfaction the invisibility of the strike. The signs of restored order were everywhere to be seen, evident in the uninterrupted rituals of everyday life. Paris was bustling, but the streets claimed for the Popular Front had been emptied.

Notes

Introduction: 6 February 1934

Sources for introits: Karl Marx and Friedrich Engels, *The Communist Manifesto*, Trans. Samuel Moore, Oxford University Press, Oxford and New York 1992, p. 23; Maurice Thorez cited in Jacques Duclos, *Le Triomphe du Front populaire. De la Conférence Communiste d'Ivry (Juin 1934) aux Assises de la Paix et de la Liberté du 14 Juillet 1935*, Les Publications révolutionnaires, Paris 1935, p. 20, ellipsis added; Simone Weil, 'Expérience de la vie d'usine', *La Condition ouvrière*, Gallimard, Paris 1951, pp. 241–59, p. 241. Translations are my own unless otherwise noted.

1. Carlo Rim, 'Grandeur et servitude du reporter photographe', *Marianne*, No. 70, 21 February 1934, p. 8, ellipsis added.
2. André Delmas, *Mémoires d'un instituteur syndicaliste*, Editions Albatros, Paris 1979, p. 225.
3. See Daniel Guérin, *Front populaire: Révolution manquée*, Actes sud, Arles 1997, p. 105 ff.
4. Marcel Aymé, 'Les Signes extérieurs', *Marianne*, No. 70, 21 February 1934, p. 8.
5. Rim, 1934, p. 8.
6. Karl Marx, 'The Class Struggles in France: 1848–1850', *Surveys from Exile: Political Writings*, Vol. 2, Ed. David Fernbach, Trans. Paul Jackson, Penguin Books, Harmondsworth 1992(a), pp. 35–142, p. 71.
7. Antonio Gramsci, *Prison Notebooks*, Vol. 2, Ed. and Trans. Joseph A. Buttigieg, Columbia University Press, New York 1996, pp. 179–80.
8. See, of course, Jürgen Habermas, *The Structural Transformation of the Public Sphere: An Inquiry into a Category of Bourgeois Society*, Trans. Thomas Burger and Frederick Lawrence, Polity Press, Cambridge 1996, especially p. 159 ff.
9. Of these technical histories perhaps the most systematic is Helmut Gernsheim with Alison Gernsheim, *The History of Photography: From the Earliest Use of the Camera Obscura in the Eleventh Century up to 1914*, Oxford University Press, London 1955. On the history and limitations of this model see Anne McCauley 'Writing Photography's History before Newhall', *History of Photography*, Vol. 21, No. 2, Summer 1997, pp. 87–101, and Douglas R. Nickel 'History of Photography: The State of Research', *Art Bulletin*, Vol. 83, No. 3, September 2001, pp. 548–58.
10. The most significant of the more recent works presents the technical history of photography in an appendix whilst relying on a technical definition: see Ian Jeffrey, *Photography: A Concise History*, Thames and Hudson, London 1981. Jeffrey was certainly aware of the difficulties of a 'history of photography' and chose to complicate the conventional narratives by producing a new technical history: *Revisions: An Alternative History of Photography*, National Museum of Photography, Film and Television, Bradford 1999.
11. The key sociological text is Pierre Bourdieu *et al.*, *Photography: A Middle-brow Art*, Trans. Shaun Whiteside, Polity Press, Cambridge 1990. On the implications of the use of photography in art practice see Abigail Solomon-Godeau,

'Photography after Art Photography', *Photography at the Dock: Essays on Photographic History, Institutions, and Practices*, University of Minnesota Press, Minneapolis 1991, pp. 103–23. For a history and survey of these practices see Douglas Fogle, *The Last Picture Show: Artists using Photography, 1960–1982*, Walker Art Center, Minneapolis 2003. For one assessment of the impact of 'sociological critique' and 'critical deconstructionism' see John Roberts, *The Art of Interruption: Realism, Photography and the Everyday*, Manchester University Press, Manchester and New York 1998, p. 4.

12. For example see Abigail Solomon-Godeau, 'Who is speaking thus? Some questions about documentary photography', Solomon-Godeau, 1991, pp. 169–83. Significantly, this essay ends in the same fashion as Solomon-Godeau's essay on art practice, with a reference to Martha Rosler's photowork of 1981, *The Bowery in Two Inadequate Descriptive Systems*.
13. Of the histories written via the photograph the most important remains Alan Trachtenberg, *Reading American Photographs: Images as History, Matthew Brady to Walker Evans*, Hill and Wang, New York 1989. For the present book the most important works derive from the Spanish Civil War: see Caroline Brothers, *War and Photography: A Cultural History*, Routledge, London and New York 1997 and François Fontaine, *La Guerre d'Espagne: Un deluge de feu et d'images*, BDIC-Berg International, Paris 2003.
14. An important precedent for this method of enquiry is the brief essay on the political functions of photography by Umberto Eco: 'A Photograph', *Faith in Fakes: Essays*, Trans. William Weaver, Secker and Warburg, London 1986, pp. 213–17.
15. Julian Jackson, *The Popular Front in France: Defending Democracy, 1934-38*, Cambridge University Press, Cambridge 1988, p. xi.
16. The two most significant recent treatments of the Popular Front are to be found in Gerd Rainer Horn, *European Socialists Respond to Fascism: Ideology, Activism and Contingency in the 1930s*, Oxford University Press, Oxford 1996 and the relevant chapters of Danielle Tartakowsky, *Les Manifestations de rue en France: 1918–1968*, Publications de la Sorbonne, Paris 1997.

1 The Republican Imaginary: Hegemony and its Reproduction

1. Louis Althusser, 'Ideology and Ideological State Apparatuses (Notes towards an Investigation)', *Lenin and Philosophy and Other Essays*, Trans. Ben Brewster, New Left Books, London 1971, pp. 121–73, p. 168.
2. Althusser, 1971, p. 168.
3. Althusser, 1971, p. 168.
4. For a full exploration of Republicanism and its sacred dimensions see Claude Nicolet, *L'Idée républicaine en France (1789–1924): Essai d'histoire critique*, Gallimard, Paris 1982, especially pp. 497–507.
5. Althusser, 1971, p. 171.
6. Comité national du rassemblement populaire, *14 juillet 1935*, Comité national du rassemblement populaire, Paris 1935, p. 3.
7. Karl Marx, 'The Class Struggles in France: 1848–1850', *Surveys from Exile: Political Writings*, Vol. 2, Ed. David Fernbach, Trans. Paul Jackson, Pengiun Books, Harmondsworth 1992(a), p. 43.

8. Marx, 1992(a), p. 47.
9. Marx, 1992(a), p. 109.
10. Marx, 1992(a), p. 71.
11. Marx, 1992(a), p. 71. However, Marx's account of the contradiction does reveal the manner in which he registered the interaction of the political and economic in the constitution of classes. The relationship between individual protagonists and class identity is extremely complex and Marx approaches this relationship in different ways in his political and economic writings. Thus the account of the class struggles in France has to be supplemented by the account given in *Capital*. The early chapters of the latter volume contain a series of reflections on characters as personifications and bearers of economic relations. For a discussion of these aspects of *Capital* see Jacques Rancière, 'The Concept of 'Critique' and the 'Critique of Political Economy'', *Ideology, Method and Marx: Essay from Economy and Society*, Ed. Ali Rattansi, Routledge, London and New York 1989, pp. 74–180, especially p. 159 ff.
12. Marx, 1992(a), p. 46.
13. Karl Marx, *Capital: A Critique of Political Economy*, Vol. 1, Trans. Ben Fowkes, Penguin Books, Harmondsworth 1990, p. 170.
14. Marx, 1990, p. 274.
15. Marx, 1990, p. 280, ellipsis added.
16. Marx, 1990, p. 280.
17. Marx, 1990, p. 301.
18. Marx, 1990, p. 300.
19. Marx, 1990, p. 302.
20. These two paragraphs are a highly condensed summary of Chapters 6 and 7 of the first volume of *Capital*: Marx, 1990, pp. 272–306. These chapters are central to Marx's argument as they form a hinge between the account of the transformation of money into capital and the account of the production of absolute surplus-value. My summary necessarily and problematically excludes a full discussion of the circulation of commodities treated by Marx in the first chapters of the first volume.
21. For an overview of the French case see Jacques Juillard, 'Le Peuple', *Les Lieux de mémoire*, Vol. 3, Ed. Pierre Nora, Gallimard, Paris 1992, pp. 184–229. Juillard's account has been particularly important for my own argument. The complexities of *le populaire* are explored in Adrian Rifkin, *Street Noises: Parisian Pleasures, 1900–1940*, Manchester University Press, Manchester and New York 1993.
22. Karl Marx, 'The Eighteenth Brumaire of Louis Bonaparte', *Surveys from Exile: Political Writings*, Vol. 2, Ed. David Fernbach, Trans. Paul Jackson, Penguin Books, Harmondsworth 1992(a), pp. 143–249, p. 175 and pp. 222–5.
23. The programme is reproduced in Pierre Barral, *Les Fondateurs de la troisième République*, Colin, Paris 1968, pp. 66–9. For the importance of this programme see François Furet, *Revolutionary France: 1770–1880*, Trans. Antonia Nevill, Blackwell, Oxford 1992, p. 522. For the place of the programme in 1934 see Jammy-Schmidt, *Idées et images radicales*, Excelsior, Paris 1934, p. 24 ff. Jammy-Schmidt was a deputy on the left of the Radical party and his text offers a mythology of the party from the perspective of 1934. Thus the Second Empire is described as 'Napoleonic fascism', p. 25.
24. Marx, 1992(a), p. 176.

25. Marx, 1992(a), p. 176.
26. Much has been written about the contrast Gramsci draws between the course of the Russian Revolution and the struggle for socialism in the West. Perry Anderson has stressed that Gramsci's application of Lenin's concept of hegemony to the structures of bourgeois power in the West was 'a new and decisive step': 'The Antinomies of Antonio Gramsci', *Antonio Gramsci: Critical Assessments of Leading Political Philosophers,* Vol. 2, Ed. James Martin, Routledge, London and New York 2002, pp. 339–410, p. 353. Yet it should be noted that this extension of the concept makes the contrast between East and West less important than the contrast between Western European powers. It is for this reason that Gramsci develops an account of the French case.
27. Antonio Gramsci, *Prison Notebooks,* Vol. 2, Ed. and Trans. Joseph A. Buttigieg, Columbia University Press, New York 1996, p. 178.
28. Gramsci, 1996, p. 178.
29. Gramsci, 1996, p. 178.
30. Gramsci, 1996, p. 178.
31. Antonio Gramsci, *Prison Notebooks,* Vol. 1, Ed. and Trans. Joseph A. Buttigieg, Columbia University Press, New York 1992, p. 155.
32. Gramsci, 1992, p. 148.
33. Gramsci, 1992, p. 139. There are numerous comments on the Jacobins in the notebooks but see especially the first notebook, note 44: Gramsci, 1992, pp. 136–151.
34. Gramsci, 1992, p. 215.
35. Gramsci, 1992, p. 215.
36. Gramsci, 1992, pp. 216. The material in square brackets is Gramsci's own marginal addition.
37. Gramsci, 1996, p. 169.
38. Gramsci, 1992, pp. 215–16.
39. The above, of course, is only a sketched outline. For a fuller account developed from the Gramscian perspective see Eric Hobsbawm, *The Age of Capital: 1848–1875,* Weidenfeld and Nicolson, London 1995, especially pp. 98–115. For an account which has striking parallels with Gramsci's whilst nevertheless reaching largely contrary conclusions see Furet, 1992.
40. Marx, 1992(a), p. 176.
41. Marx, 1992(a), p. 47.
42. This is Gramsci's formulation of a passage from the preface to *A Contribution to the Critique of Political Economy*. Gramsci, 1996, p. 157.
43. Gramsci, 1996, p. 157.
44. Gramsci, 1996, p. 157.
45. Gramsci, 1996, p. 157.
46. The above paragraph and those below are based on a reading of the fourth notebook, which contains Gramsci's first extended discussion of the concept of hegemony. This discussion is the centrepiece of a series of remarks headed: 'Notes on Philosophy. Materialism and Idealism. First Series'. Gramsci probably began this series, which opens the fourth notebook, in early 1930 soon after he had completed the first notebook and around the same time that he began a third and fifth notebook. Yet the fourth notebook is of a different character to these other volumes. Whilst the early volumes may fairly be described as miscellanies, the series of remarks in the fourth notebook is a

first attempt at a systematic organisation of material. For Buttigieg's dating of the notebooks and an assessment of their contents see Gramsci, 1992, pp. 22–41 and Gramsci, 1996, pp. ix–xi and pp. 523–7.

47. Gramsci, 1996, p. 179.
48. Gramsci, 1996, p. 179.
49. Gramsci, 1996, pp. 179–80.
50. Gramsci, 1992, p. 148.
51. Gramsci, 1996, p. 183.
52. Gramsci, 1996, p. 180.
53. Gramsci, 1996, p. 180.
54. Gramsci, 1996, p. 152.
55. For one assessment of the 'official' tradition see Gramsci, 1996, p. 140 ff. And for the failures of 'economism' and 'ideologism' see pp. 177–78. The question of Gramsci's position within the Marxist tradition is extremely complex. It is striking that Gramsci rarely uses the term class; this may in part be a matter of avoiding censorship but it has also to be understood as an aspect of Gramsci's rejection of economism. For one concise discussion of these matters see Thomas Nemeth, *Gramsci's Philosophy: A Critical Study*, The Harvester Press, Brighton 1980, pp. 86–8.
56. Marx, 1992(a), p. 56.
57. That an account of the intellectuals is integral to an account of hegemony is clear from the ordering of the fourth notebook. A general description of the interdependence of 'the people' and 'the intellectuals' precedes the discussion of the operation of hegemony and that discussion is itself extended into a cluster of notes dedicated to the function of the intellectual. This cluster was begun in November 1930. For the dating of these notes and their relationship to the rest of the fourth notebook, see Gramsci, 1996, pp. 524–7.
58. Gramsci, 1996, pp. 173–4, ellipses added. The material in square brackets is Gramsci's own marginal addition.
59. Gramsci, 1996, p. 179 and p. 180.
60. Gramsci, 1996, p. 200.
61. Gramsci, 1996, p. 201.
62. Gramsci, 1996, p. 201.
63. Gramsci, 1996, p. 201.
64. Gramsci, 1996, p. 201.
65. Gramsci, 1996, p. 202.
66. Gramsci, 1996, p. 202.
67. Gramsci, 1996, p. 203.
68. Gramsci, 1996, p. 203.
69. Gramsci, 1996, p. 207.
70. For details of Basch's career see Françoise Basch, *Victor Basch ou la passion de la justice: De l'affaire Dreyfus au crime de la milice*, Plon, Paris 1994.
71. Gramsci, 1996, p. 52.
72. Gramsci, 1996, p. 52.
73. Gramsci, 1996, p. 52 and p. 53.
74. Gramsci, 1996, p. 153.
75. For the development of the party as a bureaucratic apparatus organised supralocally see Jürgen Habermas, *The Structural Transformation of the Public Sphere: An Inquiry into a Category of Bourgeois Society*, Trans. Thomas Burger

and Frederick Lawrence, Polity Press, Cambridge 1996, p. 201 ff. For the French case see Raymond Huard, *La Naissance du parti politique en France*, Presses de la Fondation nationale des sciences politiques, Paris 1996. Huard argues that there are two conditions for the development of the modern party. First, a partisan grouping must be understood to hold a legitimate position rather than merely occupying a position of dissent. Second, this grouping must extend beyond an affiliation of politicians to find extra-parliamentary support (p. 154). Huard argues that these conditions emerged in France around 1870, in part as a result of universal suffrage (p. 154 and p. 316). The legalisation of political associations in 1901 – itself a consequence of the Waldeck–Rousseau law of 1884 – sealed the development of the modern party (pp. 312–16).

76. For the relationship between parties and the press see Claude Bellanger *et al.*, *Histoire générale de la Presse francaise*, Vol. 3, Presses universitaires de France, Paris 1972, pp. 137–45 and Raymond Manevy, *La Presse de la IIIe République*. J. Foret, Paris, 1955, pp. 21–2 and pp. 159–60 and p. 190. In Paris the number of dailies fell from 82 in 1919 to 50 in 1937: see Bernard Boilloz, *Les Périodiques français édités à Paris de 1919–1939: Classification, description bibliographique et évolution*, Doctorat de troisième cycle, Université de Paris VIII, 1978, p. 556
77. See Bellanger *et al.*, 1972, p. 477 ff., Boilloz, 1978, p. 359 ff. and Pascal Ory, *La Belle Illusion: Culture et Politique sous le signe du Front populaire, 1934–1938*, Plon, Paris 1994, p. 550 ff.
78. The weekly press dramatically expanded its market share in the interwar period. For example, in Paris its share rose from 42% in 1919 to 62% in 1937: see Boilloz, p. 360.
79. *Paris-Soir*, 1,800,000; *Le Petit Parisien*, 1,100,000; *L'Humanité*, 375,000; *Le Populaire*, 250,000. Circulation figures vary, of course. Those referred to here are for 1937 and are taken from David Wingeate Pike, *Conjecture, Propaganda, and Deceit and the Spanish Civil War: The International Crisis over Spain, 1936–1939, as seen in the French Press*, California Institute of International Studies, Stanford 1968, p. 4.
80. This is a matter of considerable complexity. For a succinct overview of the various interests at stake see Pike, 1968, pp. 3–14. For a full assessment of the Popular Front period see Ory, 1994, pp. 515–611. Ory's work is indispensable for the study of the Popular Front. Yet his account of the press during this period should be supplemented by the long-term view which suggests that the move to the right of the mainstream papers was in part a response to the formation of the PCF: see Bellanger *et al.*, 1972, p. 484.
81. For example Emile Lohner helped to establish the weekly *Vendredi* after having worked for *Le Temps* and experienced the extent of that newspaper's corruption: see André Chamson, Jean Guéhenno, Andrée Viollis 'Histoire de 'Vendredi'', *Vendredi*, No. 29, 22 May 1936, p. 1.
82. Ory, 1994, p. 519.
83. Pierre Gérôme was particularly active in this cause: see his *La Presse et Franco*, Comité de vigilance des intellectuels antifascistes, Paris 1937.
84. For an account of the project see Ory, 1994, pp. 534–40.
85. For the cultural policy of the PCF see Ory, 1994, p. 57 ff. and for the attitude to the press see pp. 548–50. The attitude of the Communists stands in contrast to that of the Socialists. For the latter's difficult relationship with

modern techniques of communication see Eric Nadaud, 'Le Renouvellement des pratiques militantes de la SFIO au début du Front populaire (1934–1936)', *Le Mouvement Social*, No. 153, October–December 1990, pp. 9–32.

86. *Regards* began publication as the monthly *Regards sur le monde du travail* in 1932. *Ce Soir* began publication in March 1937.
87. These remarks are directed to the large circulation portfolio of the PCF. This was not of course the complete range of party publications. The PCF also supported smaller circulation literary and theoretical journals which did go some way to addressing the different tendencies within the party.
88. For a discussion of the political context of this shift and the resistance to its consequences see Bernard Pudal, *Prendre parti: Pour une sociologie historique du PCF*, Presses de la Fondation nationale des sciences politiques, Paris 1989, p. 168.
89. Anon, 'Un journal du soir doit être un journal de loisirs, nous dit Jean-Richard Bloch', *Presse Publicité*, No. 10, 16 May 1937, pp. 1–2 and 26.
90. On leisure policies see Ory, 1994, p. 714 ff.
91. On this transformation of *Paris-Soir* and its significance see Françoise Denoyelle, *La Lumière de Paris: Les Usages de la photographie, 1919–1939*, L'Harmattan, Paris 1997, p. 97 ff. Denoyelle's work is crucial for an understanding of the development of press photography in France.
92. From 134,059 to 260,619: see Denoyelle, 1997, p. 102.
93. Denoyelle, 1997, p. 21.
94. See René Duval, *Histoire de la radio en France*, Alain Moreau, Paris 1979, p. 32 ff. and Alan Williams, *Republic of Images: A History of French Filmmaking*, Harvard University Press, Cambridge, Mass. and London 1992, p. 157 ff. *The Jazz Singer* was produced in 1927 but not screened in France until January 1929.
95. Anon. 'La presse de demain sera une combinaison du journalisme politique et du journalisme d'information', *Presse Publicité*, No. 9, 9 May 1937, p. 3.
96. For the full programme of 10 films see Williams, 1992, p. 27.
97. Richard Abel, *The Ciné Goes to Town: French Cinema, 1896–1914*, University of California Press, Berkeley, Los Angeles and London 1994, p. 23.
98. Richard Abel makes precisely this comparison, see Abel, 1994, p. 91. Here I should explain that I have not included an examination of the newsreel in my analysis of the image of the Popular Front. There are several reasons for this omission, not the least of which is the question of my own competence. However, the principal reason for excluding a discussion of the newsreel lies in the circumstances of its production. For the supporters of the Popular Front were largely denied access to this medium: all six major companies involved with the production of newsreels were privately owned and all six were more or less hostile to the Popular Front: see Ory, 1994, p. 559. Indeed perceived bias in the newsreels frequently provoked complaints and even projects for reform, although none came to fruition. For one protest against the newsreels see Andrée Viollis, 'Cinéma-Actualités', *Vendredi*, No. 29, 22 May 1936, p. 3. For a further protest and a discussion of reform see Germaine Decaris, 'Le Gouvernement et le cinéma', *La Lumière*, No. 482, 1 August 1936, p. 5. For a discussion of an attempt to develop a Socialist newsreel see Nadaud, 1990, p. 20 ff.
99. Duval, 1979, p. 42.
100. Duval, 1979, p. 50.

101. This information is drawn from the radio listings in *Le Populaire*, 7 February 1934, p. 5. However, these broadcasts should not be confused with radio news broadcasting as it currently exists. For an overview of programming during the years of the Popular Front see Cécile Méadel, 'Programme en masse, programme de masse? La Diffusion de la radio en France pendant les années trente', *Masses et culture de masse dans les années trente*, Ed. Régine Robin, Les Editions ouvrières, Paris 1991, pp. 51–68.
102. Marcel Proust, 'Sentiments filiaux d'un parricide', *Contre Sainte-Beuve*, précédé de *Pastiches et mélanges* et suivi de *Essais et articles*, Bibliothèque de la Pléiade, Gallimard, Paris 1971, pp. 150–9, p. 154.
103. See Denoyelle, 1997, p. 23 ff.
104. Walter Benjamin, 'The Newspaper', *Selected Writings*, Vol. 2, Eds. Howard Eiland, Michael W. Jennings and Gary Smith, Trans. Rodney Livingstone and others, Belknap Press of Harvard University Press, Cambridge, Mass. and London 1999, pp. 741–2. René Crevel also made the observation that the novel was moving ever closer to journalism: see his 'Individu et société', *Commune*, No. 23, July 1935, pp. 1204–11, p. 1207.
105. This summary skates rather lightly over a number of complexities. For observations on the narrative forms of newspaper reports see Habermas, 1996, pp. 169–170. And Benedict Anderson has argued that the newspaper is profoundly fictive due to the editorial policies which imagine connections between disparate events: see *Imagined Communities: On the Origins and Spread of Nationalism*, Verso, London and New York 1993, p. 33 ff.
106. I prefer this transliteration to the term 'photojournalist' as it preserves in its clumsiness the sense of an emergent hybrid practice which the more familiar term does not.
107. Carlo Rim, 'Grandeur et servitude du reporter photographe', *Marianne*, No. 70, 21 February, 1934, p. 8.
108. This discussion of the anonymous image is in part connected to Molly Nesbit's discussion of the photographic document as a 'detailed blank' able to serve a variety of uses: see *Atget's Seven Albums*, Yale University Press, New Haven and London 1992, pp. 14–18, quotation p. 16. Yet in the prewar period, with which Nesbit is largely concerned, the photographic document was not fully exploited for publication. Instead, it was largely addressed to professional uses. The 'unprofessional, general viewer' emerged only in the interwar period: see Nesbit, 1992, p. 79.
109. For details of this period of expansion see Boilloz, 1978, p. 491 ff.
110. For these journals see Dominique Baqué, *Les Documents de la modernité: Anthologie de textes sur la photographie de 1919 à 1939*, Jacqueline Chambon, Nîmes 1993, p. 292 ff. and p. 311 ff.
111. Alexandre Libermann, 'La première qualité d'une photo d'actualité c'est la sincérité', *Presse Publicité*, No. 9, 9 May 1937, p. 14.
112. See Pierre Albert and Gilles Feyel, 'Photography and the Media: Changes in the Illustrated Press', *A New History of Photography*, Ed. Michel Frizot, Könemann, Cologne 1998, pp. 359–69.
113. On, *Excelsior* as a precursor see Denoyelle, 1997, p. 48 ff.
114. Of the early agencies, the four most important were Manuel (founded 1900), Rol (1904), Meurisse (1904), and Trampus (1905): see Denoyelle, 1997, pp. 68–86.
115. The term *reportage photographique* is potentially misleading as it does not simply refer to the work of the *reporter photographe* but also to the work of

the *illustrateur*. For a characterisation of this latter type see P.L. 'Jean Roubier', *Le Photographe*, No. 462, 20 July 1938, pp. 215–16.

116. *Photo Annuaire*, Publications photographiques et cinématographiques Paul Montel, Paris 1922, p. 285.
117. *Photo Annuaire*, Publications photographiques et cinématographiques Paul Montel, Paris 1928, p. 395.
118. See *Annuaire de la Presse*, Annuaire International de la Presse, Paris 1929, p. 890.
119. Thus for 1928 the directory for the Paris region has eight agencies providing *reportages photographiques*, of which half are cross-listed as providing studio work: see *Annuaire de Commerce Didot-Bottin*, Didot-Bottin, Paris 1928, p. 3245 and p. 3585. By 1938 the figures are 18 and 2 respectively: see *Annuaire de Commerce Didot-Bottin*, Didot-Bottin, Paris 1938, p. 2145 and pp. 2370–1. Whilst there are certainly ambiguities in the listings, and in the title of the rubric, it is clear that the principal growth in this area is due to the expansion of the market for *actualités*.
120. For an important account of the issues raised by the classification of photography see Steve Edwards, 'Photography, Allegory, and Labor', *Art Journal*, Vol. 55, No. 2, Summer 1996, pp. 38–44.
121. Walter Benjamin, 'L'Oeuvre d'art à l'époque de sa reproduction mécanisée', Trans. Pierre Klossowski, *Zeitschrift für Sozialforschung*, Vol. 5, 1936, pp. 40–68, p. 48.
122. For negotiations over contracts and rights see anon. 'Il est temps pour les journalistes photographes de travailler à leur propre contrat', *Le Journaliste*, No. 101, August–September 1934, p. 7.
123. On the formation of this section see anon. 'Les Journalistes de l'objectif au Syndicat National', *Le Journaliste*, No. 93, October–November 1933, p. 12.
124. Maurice Boiry, 'Nous ... les reporters photographes', *Presse Publicité*, No. 2, 21 March 1937, p. 13.
125. The struggle to defend the reporter-photographer as such may be followed through the pages of the organ of the Syndicat national des journalistes, *Le Journaliste*: see anon. 'Les reporters photographes sont des reporters', *Le Journaliste*, No. 91, May 1933, p. 8.
126. See Henri Guernut *et al.*, 'Proposition de loi relative au Statut Professionnel des Journalistes', *Le Journaliste*, No. 90, April 1933, pp. 3–6.
127. See anon. 'Barême des traitments minimum des Journalistes professionnels du département de la Seine pour l'année 1936', *Le Journaliste*, No. 110, February 1936, p. 5. The difficulty of defining the various types of labour is noted in anon. 'Chez les Reporters-Photographes', *Le Journaliste*, No. 112, April 1936, p. 7.
128. Boiry, 1937, p. 13. These figures are a little low and it has been plausibly suggested that Boiry is describing only those who were members of his association: see Denoyelle, 1997, p. 59. For a comparison, Manevy gives the following for *Paris-Soir* in 1939: 10 reporter-photographers and 216 photographic correspondents. Of course it is very difficult to know what status the latter had. Manevy, 1955, p. 175.
129. Anon. *Le Journaliste*, August–September 1934, p. 7.
130. For extracts from the statutes and other details concerning the Syndicat, see *Annuaire de la Presse*, Annuaire International de la Presse, Paris 1935, p. 232.

131. See Denoyelle, 1997, p. 56, and for a full discussion F. de Lanot, 'La Photographie et la presse', *Bulletin de la Société Française de la Photographie et de Cinématographie*, Vol. 21, No. 2, February 1934, pp. 41–8, and No. 3, March 1934, pp. 63–8.
132. Denoyelle, 1997, pp. 53–6.
133. For the history of the Confédération nationale see A. Rambaud, 'Congrès National', *La Photographie Professionnelle*, No. 6, July 1936, pp. 3–31. For Belin's proposal and the response of the Confédération see A. Rambaud, 'Parlons clair', *Le Photographe*, No. 425, 5 January 1937, pp. 10–11.

2 'People of France': The Image Created

1. Comité national du rassemblement populaire, *14 juillet 1935*, Comité national du rassemblement populaire, Paris 1935, p. 1.
2. This important point is made in Danielle Tartakowsky, *Les Manifestations de rue en France: 1918–1968*, Publications de la Sorbonne, Paris 1997, p. 349.
3. This summary is indebted to the work of Serge Berstein. For the significance of the violence see his *Le 6 février 1934*, Gallimard, Paris 1975. For the wider consequences of the 6th for the Radical party see his *Histoire du Parti Radical: Crise du Radicalisme 1926–1939*, Presses de la Fondation nationale des sciences politiques, Paris 1982, p. 284 ff.
4. Again, this is a point made in Berstein, 1975, p. 219. It is also emphasised in Peter J. Larmour, *The French Radical Party in the 1930s*, Stanford University Press, Stanford 1964, p. 144.
5. Antonio Gramsci, *Prison Notebooks*, Vol. 2, Ed. and Trans. Joseph A. Buttigieg, Columbia University Press, New York 1996, p. 173.
6. Confédération générale du travail, 'Au peuple! Aux travailleurs!', *Le Peuple*, 9 February 1934, p. 1. See also Antoine Prost, 'Les Manifestations du 12 février 1934 en province', *La France en mouvement: 1934-1938*, Ed. Jean Bouvier, Champ Vallon, Seyssel 1986, pp. 12–30. Prost attends to both the role of the CGT on the 12th and to the importance of this day for the formation of the Popular Front.
7. André Marty, 'Une grève générale sans précédent', *L'Humanité*, 13 February 1934, p. 1.
8. Marty, 1934, p. 1, ellipsis added.
9. Anon. 'Ce que fut la journée', *Le Populaire*, 13 February 1934, pp. 2–3, p. 2, ellipsis added.
10. Anon. *Le Populaire*, 13 February 1934, p. 3, ellipsis added.
11. Cited in anon. *Le Populaire*, 13 February 1934, p. 3.
12. Anon. *Le Populaire*, 13 February 1934, p. 3. For the importance of the distinction between the Front 'from above' and 'from below' see Gerd Rainer Horn, *European Socialists Respond to Fascism: Ideology, Activism and Contingency in the 1930s*, Oxford University Press, Oxford and New York 1996, p. 27 ff.
13. For this claim see Pierre Gérôme, 'Le Front populaire', *Vigilance*, No. 25, 1 July 1935, p. 3.
14. Alain, Paul Langevin and Paul Rivet, 'Aux Travailleurs', *Commune*, Nos. 7–8, March–April 1934, pp. 859–864, p. 859. The title of the manifesto was a partial echo of the call made by the CGT on 9 February.

15. Alain, Langevin and Rivet, 1934, p. 859.
16. Alain, Langevin and Rivet, 1934, p. 859.
17. The founder members of the CVIA were sincere in their belief that the events of February revealed the fascist threat to France; however, Robert Soucy has argued that fascism was not a direct threat at this date and that it was the growth of the Popular Front which increased the appeal of fascism for certain fractions of the right wing: see *French Fascism: The Second Wave 1933–1939*, Yale University Press, New Haven and London 1995, pp. 30–6. This argument is a contribution to a complex debate over the nature and extent of French fascism. For Soucy's overview of the debate see pp. 1–12.
18. Gramsci, 1996, pp. 80–1, ellipses added. The material in the first set of square brackets is Gramsci's own marginal addition.
19. Ernesto Laclau and Chantal Mouffe, *Hegemony and Socialist Strategy: Towards a Radical Democratic Politics*, Verso, London and New York 2001, p. 85.
20. Laclau and Mouffe, 2001, p. xiii.
21. Laclau and Mouffe, 2001, p. xiii.
22. Laclau and Mouffe, 2001, p. xiii.
23. Laclau and Mouffe, 2001, p. 113. Needless to say, the arguments proposed by Laclau and Mouffe have generated some controversy, not least over the question of the extent to which their project is '*post*-Marxist' and 'post-*Marxist*', as they acknowledge: Laclau and Mouffe, 2001, p. 4. For their account of hegemony as articulation is an attempt to move beyond the category of hegemonic classes. Thus they attribute an autonomy to the political sphere which is incompatible with Gramsci's sense of hegemony as 'political but also and above all economic', Gramsci, 1996, p. 183. Nevertheless, their account clearly does not preclude the articulation of 'class' struggle, even if it does preclude its privileging. For one overview of the questions raised here see Michèle Barrett, 'Ideology, Politics, Hegemony: From Gramsci to Laclau and Mouffe', *Mapping Ideology*, Ed. Slavoj Žižek, Verso, London and New York 1994, pp. 235–64.
24. Etienne Constant, 'Le Droit au travail et le droit à la vie ...', *Les Femmes dans l'Action Mondiale*, No. 8, 15 April–15 May 1935, pp. 4–5, p. 4.
25. Gabrielle Duchêne, 'Pourquoi ce mouvement', *Les Femmes dans l'Action Mondiale*, No. 1, undated [1934], pp. 1–2, p. 1, ellipsis added. Duchêne, the leader of the movement, was a fellow traveller, and the inspiration for the committee was Communist: see Christine Bard, *Les Filles de Marianne: Histoire des féminismes, 1914–1940*, Fayard, Paris 1995, p. 297.
26. Gramsci, 1996, p. 202.
27. Bernadette Cattanéo, 'Travailleuses des villes et des champs contre la misère, le fascisme, la guerre. Debout! Organisez-vous!', *Les Femmes dans l'Action Mondiale*, No. 1, undated [1934], p. 6.
28. For the Comité mondiale des femmes, see Bard, 1995, p. 297. For the SFIO see Julian Jackson, *The Popular Front in France: Defending Democracy, 1934–38*, Cambridge University Press, Cambridge 1988, pp. 219–20. In an article of October 1934, Cattanéo complained that the Comité was receiving little attention: see 'Les Socialistes avec nous!', *Les Femmes dans l'Action Mondiale*, No. 2, October 1934, n. p. The complaint was prescient for despite its success the Comité has not entered the histories of the Popular Front. The Comité is not discussed in any of the four standard accounts of the Front: Jackson,

1988; Jacques Kergoat, *La France du Front populaire*, Editions La Découverte, Paris 1986; Georges Lefranc, *Histoire du Front populaire, 1934–1938*, Payot, Paris 1965; Pascal Ory, *La Belle Illusion: Culture et Politique sous le signe du Front Populaire, 1934–1938*, Plon, Paris 1994. Ory mentions the group once (p. 950) and Lefranc once – with Duchêne as its representative – in connection with the preparations for 14 July 1935 (p. 77). Of those involved in the Comité, Andrée Viollis is mentioned by all authors but in her capacity as an editor of *Vendredi*. Only Lefranc and Ory make reference to her other activities: Lefranc, p. 302; Ory, pp. 88, 189, 585. Ory makes one reference to Duchêne (p. 58).

29. Paul Rivet, 'Les Intellectuels', *Vigilance*, No. 18, 10 March 1935, p. 3.
30. Rivet, 1935, p. 3.
31. Rivet, 1935, p. 3.
32. Rivet, 1935, p. 3.
33. Rivet, 1935, p. 3.
34. Jeanne Bouvier, *Mes mémoires, ou 59 années d'activité industrielle, sociale et intellectuelle d'une ouvrière*, L'Action intellectuelle, Poitiers 1936, pp. 174–5.
35. Gramsci used the term 'political bloc' relatively rarely. For an elaboration of the concept see Anne Showstack Sassoon, *Gramsci's Politics*, University of Minnesota Press, Minneapolis 1987, especially p. 121 ff.
36. Bernard Pudal, *Prendre parti: Pour une sociologie historique du PCF*, Presses de la Fondation nationale des sciences politiques, Paris 1989, pp. 144–58. Pudal's work is of great importance for the study of the PCF during this period.
37. On the international context of the PCF turn see Denis Peschanski, *Et pourtant ils tournent: Vocabulaire et strategie du PCF, 1934–1936*, Klincksieck, Paris 1988, p. 38 ff.
38. Annie Kriegel, 'Langage et stratégie: L'exemple du Front populaire', *Communismes au miroir français: Temps, cultures et sociétés en France devant le communisme*, Gallimard, Paris 1974, pp. 95–114, p. 108 ff.
39. Kriegel, 1974, p. 111.
40. Kriegel, 1974, p. 111.
41. Kriegel, 1974, p. 114.
42. Needless to say, these developments were not universally welcomed. The contradictions within the Popular Front were most forcibly denounced by Léon Trotsky: see 'Whither France' and 'Once Again, Whither France', *On France*, Ed. David Salner, Pathfinder, New York 1979, pp. 29–62 and pp. 67–128.
43. Maurice Thorez, 'A tout prix, battre le fascisme. Pour un large Front populaire antifasciste', *L'Humanité*, 12 October 1934, p. 4. For the Radical cult of the Encyclopedists and the party's doctrines of progress see Jammy-Schmidt, *Idées et images radicales*, Excelsior, Paris 1934, p. 5 and p. 12, respectively.
44. Thorez, 1934, p. 4.
45. See Horn, 1996, p. 28.
46. For an account of the speech and its positive reception see anon. 'Le Congrès de Nantes, unanime, fait confiance aux ministres radicaux pour défendre les libertés démocratiques', *L'Oeuvre*, 28 October 1934, p. 1 and p. 4.
47. See Pierre Birnbaum, *Le Peuple et les gros: Histoire d'un mythe*, Grasset, Paris 1979, p. 16 and p. 27 ff.
48. For the significance of Daladier's speech see Berstein, 1982, p. 636, note 29.

49. Berstein, 1982, p. 365.
50. Peschanski, 1988, pp. 101–02 and p. 106.
51. Cited in Jacques Duclos, *Le Triomphe du Front populaire. De la Conférence Communiste d'Ivry (Juin 1934) aux Assises de la Paix et de la Liberté du 14 Julliet 1935*, Les Publications révolutionnaires, Paris 1935, pp. 37–8.
52. From October 1934 Thorez invoked the Jacobins with increasing frequency. See in particular 'Interpellation', *Journal Officiel: Débats Parlementaires, Chambre des Députés*, Session of 13 November 1934, pp. 2294–8. The importance of this speech is discussed in Nicole Racine and Louis Bodin, Eds. *Le Parti communiste français pendant l'entre-deux-guerres*, Presses de la Fondation nationale des sciences politiques, Paris 1982, p. 225.
53. The term 'Jacobinisation' is used in Kriegel, 1974, p. 104. Jacobinisation entailed a shift in the attitudes of the PCF towards the nation; on this shift see Serge Wolikow, 'Le PCF et la nation au temps du Front populaire', *Antifascisme et nation: Les Gauches européennes au temps du Front populaire*, Eds. Serge Wolikow and Annie Bleton-Ruget, Editions universitaires de Dijon, Dijon 1998, pp. 129–40.
54. For the significance of these elections see Yvan Combeau, 'Les Elections municipales de 1935. Acte de naissance électoral du Front populaire', *L'Information Historique*, No. 56, 1994, pp. 195–200.
55. See Trotsky, 1979, especially p. 40 ff. and p. 98.
56. See Daniel Guérin, *Front populaire: Révolution manquée*, Actes sud, Arles 1997 p. 125 ff. The group around Pivert would become La Gauche révolutionnaire in the autumn of 1935: on this formation see Guérin, 1997, p. 146 ff.
57. See for example Marcel Bréval 'Le Parti et les "classes moyennes" ', *Que faire?*, Nos. 1–2, November–December 1934, pp. 16–24.
58. For a survey of these issues see Pierre Broué and Nicole Dorey, 'Critiques de gauche et opposition révolutionnaire au Front populaire (1936–1938)', *Le Mouvement Social*, No. 54, January–March 1966, pp. 91–133.
59. See Berstein, 1982, pp. 369–71.
60. On this history see Christian Amalui, 'Le 14-juillet: Du Dies irae à jour de fête', Nora, 1992, pp. 421–72.
61. See Jacques Kayser, 'Le Parti radical-socialiste et le rassemblement populaire 1935–1938', *Société d'Histoire de la Troisième République*, New Series, No. 14, April–July 1955, pp. 271–84, p. 272. Taking to the streets was not necessarily a welcome development for all members of the SFIO either: see Eric Nadaud, 'Le Renouvellement des pratiques militantes de la SFIO au début du Front populaire (1934–1936)' *Le Mouvement Social*, No. 153, October–December, 1990, p. 24 ff.
62. See Tartakowsky, 1997, pp. 344–9 and Ory, 1994, p. 789 ff.
63. This important argument is made in Tartakowsky, 1997, p. 329.
64. See Victor Basch, 'Le Front populaire', *Les Cahiers des Droits de l'Homme*, New Series, No. 28, 10 November 1935, pp. 695–6.
65. Comité national du rassemblement populaire, 1935, p. 29.
66. Kayser, 1955, p. 271. That the political parties were absent is contested in Lefranc, 1965, p. 77. However, the account provided by the organisers in 1935 also suggests the absence of the political parties: see Comité national du rassemblement populaire, 1935, p. 29.
67. See Ligue des droits de l'homme: Comité central, 'Séance du 27 juin 1935', *Les Cahiers des Droits de l'Homme*, New Series, No. 23, 10 August 1935, pp. 593–6.

68. Kayser, 1955, p. 271.
69. Berstein, 1982, p. 367.
70. Kayser, 1955, pp. 272–3.
71. Jean Guéhenno, 'Valeur d'une fête', *Europe*, No. 152, 15 August 1935, pp. 601–4, p. 603.
72. My account of the Revolutionary festivals is reliant on Mona Ozouf, *Festivals and the French Revolution*, Trans. Alan Sheridan, Harvard University Press, Cambridge, Mass. and London 1988, p. 32 ff.
73. Comité central, 10 August 1935, pp. 594–5. The festival of youth was originally planned for 14 July and then moved forward.
74. The announcement is reprinted in Comité national du rassemblement populaire, 1935, p. 1.
75. Comité national du rassemblement populaire, 1935, p. 1.
76. Comité national du rassemblement populaire, 1935, p. 1.
77. Comité national du rassemblement populaire, 1935, p. 1.
78. Cited in anon. 'Unanime, le Comité exécutif radical approuve la participation aux manifestations du Front populaire du 14 juillet', *L'Humanité*, 4 July 1935, pp. 1–2, p. 2.
79. Lefranc, 1965, p. 82 proposes Jacques Kayser as a co-author, and cites Chamson as the authority for this. Chamson's wife also suggests this: see Lucie Mazauric, *Avec André Chamson*, Vol. 2, Plon, Paris 1976, p. 103. However, Kayser himself explicitly attributes the oath to Chamson and Guéhenno, Kayser, 1955, p. 275.
80. Cited from François Furet, *The French Revolution: 1770–1814*, Trans. Antonia Nevill, Blackwell, Oxford 1996, p. 64.
81. Comité national du rassemblement populaire, 1935, p. 1.
82. All the figures were contested by the right, of course. For the organisers' account see Comité national du rassemblement populaire, 1935, pp. 25–7.
83. Comité national du rassemblement populaire, 1935, p. 3.
84. Comité national du rassemblement populaire, 1935, p. 11.
85. Comité national du rassemblement populaire, 1935, p. 11.
86. See André Chamson in Comité national du rassemblement populaire, 1935, p. 2, Guéhenno, 1935, p. 603.
87. For the sound of the anthems, see Berstein, 1975, p. 164. For this sound as a sign of confusion see the account in *Les Cahiers des Droits de l'Homme*, cited in Berstein, 1975, p. 177.
88. Guéhenno, 1935, p. 603–4. The significance of this reconciliation is discussed in Ory, 1994, p. 71 ff.
89. This reanimation was in response to a crisis; one could say that in such moments of crisis the imagined community of the nation requires a more powerful presentation, that it requires staging. For a full discussion of these imagined communities see Anderson, *Imagined Communities: On the Origins and Spread of Nationalism*, Verso, London and New York, 1993.
90. The significance of this trajectory is discussed in Rosemonde Sanson, *Les 14 juillet (1789–1975): Fête et conscience nationale*, Flammarion, Paris 1976, p. 118. Eric Hobsbawm has made the point that the Place de la Nation was a privileged site for the enactment of the national rituals of the Republic because the work of Dalou was the 'ultimate version' of the statuary of Marianne to be found in every Republican commune. See 'Mass-Producing Traditions: Europe, 1870–1914', *The Invention of Tradition*, Eds. Eric

Hobsbawm and Terence Ranger, Cambridge University Press, Cambridge and New York 1992, pp. 263–307, quotation p. 272.

91. This ordering of the two oaths exploited the traditional progress of events on 14 July, which habitually moved from official to popular celebration. On this ordering see Amalui, 1992, p. 440 ff.
92. Tristan Rémy, 'Une grande journée populaire', *Le Peuple*, 19 July 1935, pp. 1–2, p. 2. On this article see Tartakowsky, 1997, p. 347. For a discussion of the complexity of Rémy's position see Simon Dell, 'On the Metaphor and Practice of Photography: Socialist Realism, the Popular Front in France and the Dynamics of Cultural Unity', *History of Photography*, Vol. 25, No. 1, Spring 2001, pp. 52–60. From a different perspective Trotsky also denounced such demonstrations, seeing them as a means of curbing the masses: see 'France at the Turning Point', Trotsky, 1979, pp. 135–50, p. 143.
93. Louis Althusser, 'Ideology and Ideological State Apparatuses (Notes towards an Investigation)', *Lenin and Philosophy and other Essays*, Trans. Ben Brewster, New Left Books, London 1971, p. 168.
94. Gramsci, 1996, p. 173.
95. Gramsci, 1996, p. 173.
96. See Ligue des droits de l'homme: Comité central, 'La Lutte contre le fascisme et la guerre: Séances du 13 octobre 1935', *Les Cahiers des Droits de l'Homme*, New Series, No. 29, 20 November 1935, pp. 726–30.
97. Comité national du rassemblement populaire, 1935, p. 31.
98. This period is suggested by notices in *Les Cahiers des Droits de l'Homme* announcing the imminent publication and then confirming its appearance: see New Series No. 22, 20 August 1935, p. 559 and New Series No. 23, 30 August 1935, p. 585.
99. See *Les Cahiers des Droits de l'Homme*, New Series, No. 21, 10 August 1935. It is clear that the printing plates used for the journal – with the exception of those for the covers – were reused for the brochure, which explains the anomaly of the latter carrying an advertisement for itself.
100. On Réal, see Christian Bouqueret, *Des années folles aux années noires: La nouvelle vision photographique en France, 1920–1940*, Marval, Paris 1997, p. 18, p. 56 and p. 156, and Alain Fleig, *Etant donné l'âge de la lumière: Naissance de la photographie comme média en France dans les années trente*, Editions Ides et Calendes, Neuchâtel 1997, p. 80 and p. 179. On the importance of the advertising studios see Natalie Cattaruzza, *Le Rôle des patrons, rédacteurs en chef, directeurs artistiques de la presse illustrée dans le développement de certains tendances photographiques, en France des années 1920 aux années 1960 (reportage, photojournalisme, mode, publicité, illustration)*, Allocation de formation et de recherche, Mission de patrimoine photographique, Paris 1995, p. 25 ff.
101. For details of Lange's career, see Berstein, 1982, especially pp. 299–300 and p. 217.
102. Comité national d'organisation du rassemblement populaire du 14 juillet 1935, *Le Defilé du 14 juillet 1935*, Film, Paris 15 September 1935, Vidéothèque de Paris, VDP1224. An opening title indicates the collaborators.
103. Comité national du rassemblement populaire, 1935, p. 2.
104. Comité national du rassemblement populaire, 1935, p. 2.

105. Comité national du rassemblement populaire, 1935, p. 2.
106. Comité national du rassemblement populaire, 1935, p. 2.
107. Comité national du rassemblement populaire, 1935, p. 2.
108. Comité national du rassemblement populaire, 1935, p. 2.
109. Réal provided both photographs and designs for *Vu*. His Dorland studio handled advertising for the magazine and studio and magazine in fact shared an address on the Champs-Elysées, as is indicated by the magazine's colophon.
110. Whilst uncredited, the two cover montages are probably by Réal. The photograph used on the cover of the French issue was certainly used by Réal in the design of another special issue of *Vu* in 1932, *Tout est foutu*. Even the anonymity of the covers may be an indication of authorship, for covers designed by Alexandre Libermann were sometimes credited.
111. Maurice Agulhon, *Marianne into Battle: Republican Imagery and Symbolism in France, 1789–1880*, Trans. Janet Lloyd, Cambridge University Press, Cambridge and New York 1981, p. 27.
112. Agulhon, 1981, p. 65 and p. 140.
113. Bernadette Cattanéo, 'Les Comités féminins se présentent aux élections avec leurs programmes', *Les Femmes dans l'Action Mondiale*, No. 8, 15 April–15 May 1935, pp. 8–9, p. 8.
114. Rémy, 1935, p. 2, ellipsis added.
115. Réal went to some trouble to avoid sequencing; the numbering of the images does not conform with the order in which the speeches were delivered, and nor does the rubric provide any path through the scattered photographs.
116. The silhouetting of the head permits the man's hat to be read either as a cap or a beret, either the attribute of the industrial worker or that of the peasant; this is another moment of reticence.
117. On the photograph as solemnising see Pierre Bourdieu *et al.*, *Photography: A Middle-brow Art*, Trans. Shaun Whiteside, Polity Press, Cambridge 1990, pp. 20–1.
118. As Tartakowsky has pointed out, the act of producing a mass-circulation brochure for national distribution in itself served to nationalise the image of the Popular Front: see Tartakowsky, 1997, p. 359.
119. The obvious exception is the photograph of Perrin, Duchêne, Fonteny, Raynaud and Aubaud at the bottom of the right-hand page of the spread.
120. Walter Benjamin, 'L'Oeuvre d'art á l'époque de sa reproduction mécanisée', Trans. Pierre Klossowki, *Zeitschrift für Sozialforschung*, Vol. 5, 1936, p. 65. The first version of this essay was drafted in the autumn of 1935, the second version between December 1935 and early February 1936. This latter version of the essay served as the basis for the French publication which appeared in May 1936.
121. Benjamin, 1936, p. 53, ellipsis added.
122. See Karl Marx, *Capital: A Critique of Political Economy*, Vol. 1, Trans. Ben Fowkes, Penguin Books, Harmondsworth, 1990, p. 270 ff.
123. See Part 4 of the first volume of *Capital*, Marx, 1990, pp. 429–639.
124. Benjamin, 1936, p. 52.
125. Benjamin, 1936, p. 52.
126. Benjamin, 1936, p. 54.
127. Benjamin, 1936, p. 55.
128. Benjamin, 1936, p. 55.

129. Benjamin, 1936, p. 55.
130. Benjamin, 1936, p. 55–6, ellipsis added.
131. Benjamin, 1936, p. 56.
132. Benjamin, 1936, p. 56, ellipsis added.
133. Benjamin, 1936, p. 65. The relationship between the masses and the authoritarian leader was developed by Theodor Adorno in 'Freudian Theory and Pattern of Fascist Propaganda', *The Essential Frankfurt School Reader*, Eds. Andrew Arato and Eike Gebhardt, Continuum, New York 1998, pp. 118–37.
134. Ernest Renan, 'Qu'est-ce qu'une nation?', *Oeuvres complètes*, Vol. 1, Calmann-Lévy, Paris 1947, pp. 887–906, p. 904.
135. Renan, 1947, p. 892. The utility of this forgetfulness is discussed in Anderson, 1993, p. 199 ff.
136. Guéhenno, 1935, p. 603.
137. Comité national du rassemblement populaire, 1935, p. 24.
138. Comité national du rassemblement populaire, 1935, p. 24.
139. Comité national du rassemblement populaire, 1935, p. 24.
140. Gramsci, 1996, p. 173.
141. Gramsci, 1996, p. 173.
142. Cited in Berstein, 1982, p. 378, ellipsis added.
143. Comité national du rassemblement populaire, 'Programme du rassemblement populaire', Lefranc, 1965, pp. 441–5, p. 441.

3 'Free Men': The Image Contested

1. Tristan Rémy, *La Grande Lutte*, Collection 'Ciment', Editions sociales internationales, Paris 1937, p. 37, ellipsis added.
2. Léon Blum, 'Conquête, exercice et occupation du pouvoir', *Le Populaire*, 2 July 1935, p. 1.
3. Comité national du rassemblement populaire, 'Programme du rassemblement populaire', Lefranc, 1965, p. 442.
4. For the different interpretations see Gerd Rainer Horn, *European Socialists Respond to Fascism: Ideology, Activism and Contingency in the 1930s*, Oxford University Press, Oxford and New York 1996, p. 114.
5. Letter of 20 December 1934, cited in Nicole Racine, 'Marcel Martinet et la culture ouvrière', *Le Mouvement Social*, No. 91, April–June 1975, pp. 59–78, p. 70.
6. This point should not be overstated, for the right won six seats as the result of indiscipline. The Radicals, in particular, sometimes found it difficult to support Communists. For a full analysis of this situation see Berstein, *Histoire du Parti Radical: Crise du Radicalisme 1926–1939*, Presses de la Fondation nationale des sciences politiques, Paris, 1982, p. 421 ff.
7. Paul Vaillant-Couturier, 'Sarraut décide de rester pour ne rien faire', *L'Humanité*, 6 May 1936, p. 1.
8. See Danielle Tartakowsky, 'Des grèves de juin à la pause, «Le ministère des masses»au coeur des contradictions', *Cahiers d'Histoire de l'Institut de Recherches Marxistes*, Part 24, 1986, pp. 36–53, p. 36.
9. See Bernard Pudal, *Prendre parti: Pour une sociologie historique du PCF*, Presses de la Fondation nationale des sciences politiques, Paris 1989, p. 141 ff.
10. For this point see Pascal Ory, *La Belle Illusion: Culture et politique sous le signe du Front populaire, 1934–1938*, Plon, Paris 1994, p. 530. Here it should be

noted that whilst Blum was *de facto* leader of his party the general secretary was Paul Faure.

11. See Jacques Danos and Marcel Gibelin, *June '36: Class Struggle and the Popular Front in France*, Trans. Peter Fysh and Christine Bourry, Bookmarks, London and Chicago 1986, pp. 50–1. This work is the most detailed account of the strike movement.
12. For an assessment of the tactic see Danos and Gibelin, 1986, p. 130 ff. and Salomon Schwarz, *Les Occupations d'usine en France de mai et juin 1936*, E.J. Brill, Leiden 1937.
13. Marceau Pivert, 'La Parole est aux militants', *Le Populaire*, 12 May 1936, p. 6.
14. Cited in Danos and Gibelin, 1986, p. 52.
15. Julian Jackson, *The Popular Front in France: Defending Democracy, 1934–38*, Cambridge University Press, Cambridge 1988, p. 86.
16. My assessment of the coverage of the strikes is based on a detailed survey of the major daily papers as defined in David Wingeate Pike, *La Presse française à la veille de la second guerre mondiale*, Editions Richelieu, Paris 1973, p. 6. His list, in descending order of circulation for 1936, is as follows: *Le Petit Parisien, Le Journal, L'Humanité, Le Petit Journal, Le Jour, L'Oeuvre, Le Populaire, L'Excelsior, L'Echo de Paris, L'Ami du Peuple*. I have also included *Le Figaro* and *Le Peuple*, and the evening papers *Le Temps, Paris-Soir* and *L'Intransigeant*. The period of the survey is from the beginning of the strike coverage in each paper – usually 27 May – until 22 June. Regrettably it was necessary to limit the survey to the Parisian press.
17. Marceau Pivert, 'Tout est possible', *Le Populaire*, 27 May 1936, p. 6.
18. Pivert's article has received considerable attention, but its force should not be overstated. For a clear assessment of Pivert's position at this date see Pierre Broué and Nicole Dorey, 'Critiques de gauche et opposition révolutionnaire au Front populaire (1936–1938)', *Le Mouvement Social*, No. 54, January–March 1966, pp. 104–5.
19. Anon. 'Des nombreuses grèves se sont déroulées hier dans la métallurgie', *Le Populaire*, 27 May 1936, p. 1.
20. The two accounts were not necessarily in conflict. Michelle Perrot has argued that the French strikes of the late nineteenth century involved festivities as reassertions of social communication which were a precondition for struggles involving pay and conditions: see Michelle Perrot, *Les Ouvriers en grève, France, 1871–1890*, Vol. 2, Mouton, Paris 1974, p. 547 ff.
21. Léon Bailby, 'L'Occupation des usines de guerre', *Le Jour*, 28 May 1936, p. 1.
22. See for example: anon. 'Trois usines de la banlieue occupées par des communistes', *L'Ami du Peuple*, 27 May 1936, p. 1; anon. 'Les Soviets partout!', *L'Echo de Paris*, 27 May 1936, p. 1; anon. 'Tout est possible', *Le Temps*, 28 May 1936, p. 1.
23. Although the SFIO won the most seats in the elections, the PCF made the greatest gains. In the first round the vote for the PCF increased by 800,000 whilst the vote for the SFIO decreased by 30,000: see Jackson, 1988, p. 50.
24. Danos and Gibelin, 1986, p. 55. The importance of the Renault strike has led to considerable debate over its genesis. The strike began in the workshop of a Communist, Marceau Vigny: see Jean-Paul Depretto and Sylvie V. Schweitzer, *Le Communisme à l'usine: Vie ouvrière et mouvement ouvrier chez Renault, 1920–1939*, EDIRES, Roubaix 1984, pp. 182–3. Moreover, the Renault plant

had been a focus of Communist activism: see Gérard Noiriel, *Workers in French Society in the 19th and 20th Centuries*, Trans. Helen McPhail, Berg, New York, Oxford and Munich 1990, p. 156 and pp. 168–9. Yet most students of the strikes cannot muster evidence sufficient to convince themselves of a Communist plot. For the opinion of Depretto and Schweitzer see p. 196 ff. Also see Marcel Schulz, 'Les Origines de la crise ouvrière de 1936', *Le Musée Social*, No. 5, May 1937, pp. 121–39; No. 6, June 1937, pp. 153–65, especially pp. 164–5, and No 7, July 1937, pp. 185–200, especially p. 198. The greatest measure of Communist control is suggested in Bertrand Badie, 'Les Grèves de 1936 aux usines Renault', Bouvier, 1986, pp. 68–85.

25. For a series of reflections on this see Michel de Certeau, *The Practice of Everyday Life*, Trans. Steven Randall, University of California Press, Berkeley, Los Angeles and London 1984.
26. The transformation was noted in *L'Humanité*. The issue of 15 June 1936 carried a photograph of the Boulevard Marcel Cachin on p. 5.
27. Marcel Gitton, 'Tout n'est pas possible', *L'Humanité*, 29 May 1936, pp. 1–2.
28. Marcel Roy, 'Les Travailleurs de la métallurgie forts de leur unité passent à l'offensive', *Le Populaire*, 28 May 1936, p. 6, and 'Le Caractère du mouvement des ouvriers métallurgistes', *Le Peuple*, 29 May 1936, p. 1 and p. 3.
29. Roy, 28 May 1936, p. 6.
30. Roy, 28 May 1936, p. 6.
31. For one account of the conventions of documentary photography and their role in producing a passive object see Solomon-Godeau, 'Who is speaking thus?', Solomon-Godeau, 1991.
32. Steve Edwards, 'The Machine's Dialogue', *Oxford Art Journal*, Vol. 13, No. 1, 1990, pp. 63–76, p. 64.
33. On the currency and circulation of photographs see John Tagg, *The Burden of Representation: Essays on Photographies and Histories*, Macmillan Education, Basingstoke and London 1988.
34. The other four papers were: *La République*, *L'Ere Nouvelle*, *Le Quotidien* and *La Volonté*.
35. On the trajectories of the Radical press see Peter Larmour, *The French Radical Party in the 1930s*, Stanford University Press, Stanford 1964, p. 55 ff.
36. Raud was imposed on the paper by its owner, Pierre Guimier, who also happened to be owner and editor of the conservative *Le Journal*. Raud was considered by many as Guimier's instrument. On this point see Pierre Biquard, 'Rapport sur la situation actuelle de la presse', *Vigilance*, No. 61, 10 January 1938, pp. 11–13. On Raud's opportunism see Madeleine Jacob, *Quarante ans de journalisme*, Julliard, Paris 1970, p. 335.
37. Anon. 'Le Mouvement gréviste s'étend dans la métallurgie', *L'Oeuvre*, 28 May 1936, p. 1 and p. 5, p. 5.
38. One indication of *L'Oeuvre*'s delicate position during this period is given by the defensive tone of a note appended to a statement from a workers' delegation denouncing misinformation in the press: 'Is it necessary to say that this text does not concern *L'Oeuvre*, which has always tried ... to reproduce as faithfully as possible the thoughts of the delegates of the workers' organisations?' Anon, 'La Conférence paritaire s'est prononcée pour le droit syndicale et la liberté d'opinion', *L'Oeuvre*, 2 June 1936, p. 1 and p. 5, p. 5, ellipsis added.

39. See Schwarz, 1937, p. 50. There was at least one attempt to continue production but this received very little coverage in 1936. On this point see Broué and Dorey, 1966, pp. 101–2.
40. Anon, *L'Oeuvre*, 28 May 1936, p. 5.
41. Maurice Guérin, 'A propos de l'occupation des usines: ce qui est en question', *L'Aube*, 3 June 1936, p. 1.
42. Guérin, 1936, p. 1.
43. Anon. 'Les Grèves', *L'Humanité*, 4 June 1936, p. 5.
44. This designation had been introduced on 20 February 1936, when *Regards* was enlarged from 16 to 24 pages. On this transition see Claude Estier, *La Gauche Hebdomadaire, 1914–1962*, Colin, Paris 1962, p. 78.
45. Anon. 'Aux lecteurs, aux amis!', *Regards*, No. 21, 6 July 1933, n. p.
46. François Delpla has singled out the coverage of the strikes in *Regards* as a turning point in the magazine's treatment of sexuality, arguing that after the strikes traditional images of femininity were introduced. Delpla presents this as part of a retreat from an earlier militancy. François Delpla, 'Les Communistes français et la sexualité, 1932–1938', *Le Mouvement Social*, No. 91, April–June 1975, pp. 121–52.
47. Pierre Unik, 'Dans les usines avec les métallos en grève', *Regards*, No. 125, 4 June 1936, pp. 5–7.
48. Unik, 1936, p. 5.
49. Caption, *Le Peuple*, 4 June 1936, p. 4.
50. See Charles Rearick, *The French in Love and War: Popular Culture in the Era of the World Wars*, Yale University Press, New Haven and London 1997, p. 57 and p. 194.
51. For a discussion of *Voilà* and its relationship with the entertainment industry, see Adrian Rifkin, *Street Noises: Parisian Pleasures, 1900–1940*, Manchester University Press, Manchester and New York 1993, p. 62 ff.
52. Anon. 'Voilà la vie. Les grèves feminines de la région parisienne', *Voilà*, No. 273, 13 June 1936, p. 1.
53. The escape from routine through popular music was a theme frequently rehearsed during the occupations. The opportunities provided for the errand boys to reveal their talents may be contrasted with Maurice Chevalier's own account of his early life as a metalworker. Adrian Rifkin draws attention to one scene in the singer's biography: 'And once, the rhythm of the song in his head and the dully repeated rhythm of beating out the pinheads clash: the hammer comes down on his thumb, crushing it.' Rifkin, 1993, p. 36.
54. Schwarz, 1937, p. 74.
55. Schwarz, 1937, p. 78. The shifting of the strike negotiations to a national level was an aim of the employers from as early as 28 May: see Schwarz, 1937, p. 68.
56. The text of the Agreements is reprinted in Georges Lefranc, *Histoire du Front populaire, 1934–1938*, Payot, Paris 1965, pp. 454–5.
57. Adrian Rossiter, 'Popular Front economic policy and the Matignon Negotiations', *Historical Journal*, Vol. 30, No. 3, 1987, pp. 663–83, p. 663.
58. Rossiter, 1987, pp. 677–9. Of course, at this point Blum was under a great deal of pressure. A flight of capital had begun during the election campaign and was still continuing and the Matignon agreements were in part an attempt to

restore confidence. On this point see Julian Jackson, *The Politics of Depression in France: 1932–1936*, Cambridge University Press, Cambridge 1985, p. 200 ff.
59. Anon. 'Notre camarade Thorez fait acclamer notre soutien au gouvernement Léon Blum', *L'Humanité*, 8 June 1936, pp. 1–2.
60. Marcel Cachin, 'Travail et «propriété»', *L'Humanité*, 8 June 1936, p. 1, ellipsis added.
61. Karl Marx, *Capital: A Critique of Political Economy*, Vol. 1, Trans. Ben Fowkes, Penguin Books, Harmondsworth, 1990, p. 280.
62. Marx, 1990, p. 280.
63. Cachin, 1936, p. 1.
64. Simone Weil 'La Vie et grève des ouvrières métallos', *La Révolution Prolétarienne*, No. 224, 10 June 1936, pp. 5–8, here cited from Weil, *La Condition ouvrière*, Gallimard, Paris 1951, pp. 161–74. The text is considered an authoritative source not only because of its place of publication but also because it drew on Weil's experience of factory work in 1934–35. This experience was recorded in a journal, published in Weil, 1951, pp. 35–107.
65. Weil, 1951, p. 161.
66. Weil, 1951, p. 162.
67. Weil, 1951, p. 162.
68. Weil, 1951, p. 165.
69. Weil, 1951, p. 168.
70. Weil, 1951, p. 168.
71. Weil, 1951, p. 169.
72. Marx, 1990, pp. 1052–3.
73. Walter Benjamin, 'Little History of Photography', Benjamin, 1999, pp. 507–30, p. 526.
74. Weil, 1951, p. 171.
75. Caption, *L'Echo de Paris*, 10 June 1936, p. 1.
76. Maurice Thorez, 'La Lutte pour le pain. Extraits du rapport présenté par Maurice Thorez à l'assemblée d'information des communistes de la région parisienne, jeudi 11 juin', *L'Humanité*, 13 June 1936, p. 4, ellipsis added. Key extracts of the report were published in *L'Humanité* on the 12th. For examples of the reporting of this statement see anon. '«Il faut savoir terminer une grève»', *Le Petit Journal*, 13 June 1936, p. 1, and anon. 'Cafés, restaurants, hôtels, pharmacies sont rouverts en grand nombre', *Paris-Soir*, 13 June 1936, p. 1.
77. For the strike as carnival see Noëlle Gérôme, 'Images de l'occupation de l'usine à gaz de Poitiers', Bouvier, 1986, pp. 62–7.
78. Anon. 'La grève des hôtels, restaurants et cafés a bouleversé hier la vie de Paris', *L'Echo de Paris*, 12 June 1936, p. 1. This in turn was a development of arguments set out in anon. 'Chez Renault, citadelle ouvrière', *Le Figaro*, 9 June 1936, p. 4.
79. On the character of *Marianne*, see Géraldi Leroy and Anne Roche, *Les Ecrivains et le Front populaire*, Presses de la Fondation nationale des sciences politiques, Paris 1986, p. 90 ff.
80. Marcel Montarron, 'Souvenirs de «l'occupation». Chansons sur le tas', *Marianne*, No. 191, 17 June 1936, p. 3.
81. Anon. 'La Grève a gagné toute la France et a touché toutes les industries', *Les Femmes dans l'Action Mondiale*, Special issue, 1936, pp. 5–6. The issue is undated but appeared between the May and July issues. As it includes coverage of the second evacuation of the Renault factories it has to be dated after 13 June.

82. This universality is supported by the pose and lighting used in the photograph, which is in all probability the work of an advertiser rather than a reporter-photographer. The editors of *Les Femmes dans l'Action Mondiale* were certainly not above such substitutions, as is revealed by the back cover of the issue dedicated to the strikes, which carries a montage of the triumphal exit from the Renault factory. This exit is presided over by two images of smiling women. Whilst it is not impossible that these women worked at the factory and also worked as knitwear models, it is nevertheless certain that their images first appeared to advertise knitwear on page 8 of *Les Femmes dans l'Action Mondiale*, No. 8, 15 April 1935.
83. Anon. *Les Femmes dans l'Action Mondiale*, Special issue, 1936, pp. 5–6.
84. Anon. *Les Femmes dans l'Action Mondiale*, Special issue, 1936, pp. 5–6.
85. Bernardette Cattanéo, 'Notre route ... ', *Les Femmes dans l'Action Mondiale*, No. 9, 15 May-15 June 1935, pp. 8–9.
86. See André Varagnac, 'Les grévistes ont su organiser leurs loisirs', *Le Populaire*, 22 June 1936, p. 6; 'Projet de questionnaire sur le folklore des grèves', *Revue de Folklore Français et Folklore Colonial*, Vol. 7, 1936, p. 129; modified text reprinted in Arnold van Gennep, *Manuel de folklore français contemporain*, Vol. 3, Picard, Paris 1937, p. 54.
87. Jean Fréville, *Pain de brique*, Flammarion, Paris 1937. The definition of socialist realism is drawn from the first article on the technique to be published in France: P. Youdine and A. Fadeev [Pavel Yudin and Aleksandr Fadeyev], 'Le Réalisme socialiste: Méthode fondamentale de la littérature soviétique', *Commune*, No. 10, June 1934, pp. 1025–30. This text drew on the statutes of the Union of Soviet Writers of the USSR.
88. Fréville, 1937, p. 234.
89. On Fréville's ghosting see Ory, 1994, p. 204.
90. Tristan Rémy, *Porte de Clignancourt*, Rieder, Paris 1928, p. 106.
91. Louis Aragon, '*Faubourg Saint-Antoine* par Tristan Rémy', *Commune*, No. 33, May 1936, pp. 1120–2; S[imone] Claude and Henri Cartier[-Bresson], '*Faubourg Saint-Antoine* avec Tristan Rémy', *Regards*, No. 120, 30 April 1936, p. 10. On these works see Simon Dell, 'On the Metaphor and Practice of Photography: Socialist Realism, the Popular Front in France and the Dynamics of Cultural Unity', *History of Photography*, Vol. 25, No. 1, Spring 2001, pp. 52–60.
92. Rémy, 1937, p. 35.
93. Rémy, 1937, p. 103.
94. Rémy, 1937, p. 128.
95. Rémy, 1937, p. 153.
96. Rémy, 1937, p. 206.
97. Rémy, 1937, p. 235.
98. Rémy, 1937, p. 283.
99. The quotations are in fact from Marceau Pivert, 'Un mot aux sénateurs ... "républicains" ', *Le Populaire*, 10 October 1936, p. 6.

4 'The Apocalypse of Fraternity': The Image Destroyed

1. André Malraux, *Days of Hope*, Trans. Stuart Gilbert and Alastair Macdonald, Hamish Hamilton, London 1968, p. 97 and p. 100, first ellipsis added.
2. Malraux, 1968, p. 102.

3. Jacques Duclos, 'Insurrection fasciste au Maroc espagnol', *L'Humanité*, 19 July 1936, p. 1.
4. Paul Nizan, 'L'Insurrection fasciste est vaincue à Barcelone, à Séville et à Melilla', *L'Humanité*, 20 July 1936, p. 1 and p. 3, p. 3.
5. P.-L. Darnar, 'Vérité en deça comme au dela des Pyrénées', *L'Humanité*, 20 July 1936, p. 1.
6. Pierre Gérôme, *La Presse et Franco*, Comité de vigilance des intellectuals antifascistes, Paris 1937, p. 37.
7. The consequences of the Spanish Civil War for the Popular Front in France are forcefully stated in Helmut Gruber, *Léon Blum, French Socialism, and the Popular Front: A Case of Internal Contradictions*, Cornell Studies in International Affairs: Western Societies Papers, Ithaca 1986, p. 20.
8. That the first six months of the Spanish conflict were the most significant for France is the conclusion reached in David Wingeate Pike, *Conjecture, Propaganda, and Deceit and the Spanish Civil War: The International Crisis over Spain, 1936–1939, as seen in the French Press*, California Institute of International Studies, Stanford 1968, p. xvi, and see Caroline Brothers, *War and Photography: A Cultural History*, Routledge, London and New York, 1997, p. 3. My arguments in this chapter are based on a detailed survey of *Le Populaire* and *L'Humanité* during this period. For an alternative survey of the coverage of the war see François Fontaine, *La Guerre d'Espagne: Un deluge de feu et d'images*, BDIC-Berg International, Paris 2003. This work also provides a detailed account of the situation of foreign correspondents in Spain.
9. This summary is drawn from Daniel Blumé, 'Contribution à l'histoire de la politique de la non-intervention: documents inédits', *Cahiers Léon Blum*, Nos. 2–3, December 1977–March 1978, pp. 16–61. There has been considerable debate over the origins of the policy of non-intervention. Geoffrey Warner argues that the British exercised influence over Blum's decisions: see 'France, and Non-Intervention in Spain, July–August 1936', *International Affairs*, Vol. 38, No. 2, April 1962, pp. 203–20. This view is contested in David Carlton, 'Eden, Blum and the Origins of Non-Intervention', *Journal of Contemporary History*, Vol. 6, No. 3, 1971, pp. 40–55. For a balanced survey of the arguments see Julian Jackson, *The Popular Front in France: Defending Democracy, 1934–38*, Cambridge University Press, Cambridge 1988, pp. 206–9. Whilst Jackson presents the chief French diplomat Aléxis Léger as ultimately a shadowy figure, Claude Thiebaut has given him a decisive role in the formation of the non-intervention policy: see 'Léon Blum, Aléxis Léger et la décision de non-intervention en Espagne', *Les Français et la guerre d'Espagne*, Eds. Jean Sagnes and Sylvie Caucanas, Université de Perpignan, Perpignan 1990, pp. 23–43.
10. Blumé, 1977–1978, p. 23. It should be noted that Blum was intent on maintaining secret deliveries to Spain: see Blumé, 1977–1978, p. 22.
11. Paul Vaillant-Couturier, 'Les forces républicaines ont repris Almera, Almansa, Gijon, Guadalajarra, Huesca, Mahon, Tolède, Saint-Sébastien', *L'Humanité*, 23 July 1936, p. 1.
12. Vaillant-Couturier, 23 July 1936, p. 1.
13. See Robert Fuzier, 'A Barcelone parmi les héroiques défenseurs de la République', *Le Populaire*, 24 July 1936, p. 2, and Jean-Maurice Herrmann, 'En route vers le pays où les travailleurs défendent la République les armes à la main', *Le Populaire*, 24 July 1936, p. 3.

14. See Pierre Unik, 'Dans les usines avec les métallos en grève', *Regards*, No. 125, 4 June 1936, p. 5, and Emmanuel d'Astier, 'La Première Nuit des grévistes ...', *Vu*, No. 429, 3 June 1936, pp. 630–1.
15. Thorez would later draw explicit parallels between the coverage of the strikes and that of the civil war, noting how the right wing misrepresented both struggles: see Maurice Thorez, 'Au service de la liberté et de la paix! Rapport présenté par Maurice Thorez à l'assemblée des communistes parisiens, salle Huygens, le 6 août 1936', *L'Humanité*, 8 August 1936, p. 4.
16. Fuzier, 1936, p. 3.
17. Paul Vaillant-Couturier, 'L'Offensive républicaine se développe dans toute l'Espagne', *L'Humanité*, 24 July 1936, p. 1.
18. Anon. 'Les Sportifs retour de Barcelone nous disent ...', *L'Humanité*, 25 July 1936, p. 1 and p. 7.
19. The opposite of the coverage which brings the viewer and the militia eye to eye may be found in *L'Illustré du Petit Journal*. Here a studiedly neutral account of historical events is paired with wide-angled street views which place a distance between the viewer and the protagonists: see for example Jean Lecoq, 'Révolutions et guerres civiles en Espagne', *L'Illustré du Petit Journal*, No. 2381, August 1936, p. 4.
20. For Larranada see Paul Vaillant-Couturier, 'L'Offensive partout', *L'Humanité*, 31 July 1936, p. 4. For Fabra see Paul Nizan, 'Victoire à Valence', *L'Humanité*, 3 August 1936, p. 3.
21. Anon. 'Le Gouvernement français précise qu'il ne s'immisce pas dans les affaires intérieures de l'Espagne', *L'Humanité*, 26 July 1936, p. 2.
22. Paul Vaillant-Couturier, 'Salut à notre soeur l'Espagne!', *L'Humanité*, 27 July 1936, p. 1 and p. 4, p. 1.
23. Such at least was the situation in July 1936. As the civil war drew on the division between Communists and Trotskyists would become an open conflict and the legitimacy of the militia put in question.
24. Vaillant-Couturier, 27 July 1936, p. 4.
25. Vaillant-Couturier, 27 July 1936, p. 4.
26. The importance of the witness is discussed in Rose Alquezar, *L'Espagne et l'Amérique latine dans l'hebdomadaire* Vendredi, *Novembre 1935–Novembre 1938*, Doctorat de troisième cycle, Université de Bordeaux, 1985–1986, p. 61. Chamson, an editor of *Vendredi* and the exemplary witness of 14 July 1935, produced a book entitled: *Retour d'Espagne: Rien qu'un témoignage*, Bernard Grasset, Paris 1937.
27. Paul Vaillant-Couturier, 'Des armes! Pour des hommes!', *L'Humanité*, 28 July 1936, p. 1 and p. 3.
28. Parti communiste français, 'Avec l'Espagne pour la sécurité de la France', *L'Humanité*, 3 August 1936, p. 6.
29. Thorez, 8 August 1936, p. 4, ellipsis added.
30. This is not to suggest that the stance of the PCF was consistent. On the complexities of the Communist position see Silvio Pons, 'La Diplomatie soviétique, l'antifascisme et la guerre civile espagnole' and Yves Santamaria '«Noblesse oblige»: PCF, défense nationale et lutte pour la paix (1935–1936)', Wolikow and Bleton-Ruget, 1998, pp. 59–66 and pp. 75–85, respectively.
31. See anon. '400,000 Parisiens à Saint-Cloud', *L'Humanité*, 10 August 1936, p. 2.
32. Anon. 'Des centaines de milliers de manifestants ont renouvelé hier le Serment de la Paix', *Le Populaire*, 10 August 1936, pp. 1–3, p. 2.

33. On the development of the *fête de souveraineté* see Danielle Tartakowsky, *Les Manifestations de rue en France: 1918–1968*, Publications de la Sorbonne, Paris 1997, p. 398 ff.
34. Anon. *L'Humanité,* 10 August 1936, p. 2.
35. Louis de Brouckère, 'Voyage en Espagne', *Le Populaire,* 9 August 1936, p. 4.
36. Later, this renewal would be extended to 1848. The militiawomen would be seen as an incarnation of the earlier dream of women soldiers: see Roger Devigne, 'Des «Miliciennes» de 1937 aux «Vésuviennes» de 1848', *Vendredi,* No. 81, 21 May 1937, p. 4.
37. Anon. 'L'URSS adhere à la proposition française', *L'Humanité,* 11 August 1936, p. 3. In fact the Soviet Union did not formally join the non-intervention pact until 23 August.
38. André Marty, 'Il faut que cesse immédiatement le blocus de fait de l'Espagne républicaine', *L'Humanité,* 11 August 1936, p. 1.
39. Parti communiste français, 'Une Lettre du Parti communiste à la CAP du Parti socialiste', *L'Humanité,* 12 August 1936, p. 2.
40. For the details of this see Gabriel Péri, 'La Réponse italienne à la proposition française', *L'Humanité,* 23 August 1936, p. 3, and Gabriel Péri, 'Après la décision du 3e Reich, il convient d'organiser le contrôle internationale d'accord de "neutralité" ', *L'Humanité,* 25 August 1936, p. 3.
41. Letter of Maurice Thorez, reproduced anon. 'Pour l'Espagne républicaine! Pour la liberté! Pour la paix!', *L'Humanité,* 5 September 1936, p. 1.
42. On 19 September 1936, Thorez described the demonstration of the 4th as the first in which the masses adopted the line of the PCF against the position of the government. On this point see Carlos Serrano, *L'Enjeu espagnol: PCF et guerre d'Espagne,* Messidor/Editions sociales, Paris 1987, pp. 34–5.
43. Marcel Gitton, ' "Des canons! Des avions !" ', *L'Humanité,* 5 September 1936, p. 1.
44. Cited in Gitton, 5 September 1936, p. 1.
45. Gitton, 5 September 1936, p. 1.
46. Anon. 'A la République', *L'Humanité,* 5 September 1936, pp.1–2, p. 1.
47. Anon. 'A la République', *L'Humanité,* 5 September 1936, p. 1.
48. Herrmann's last report from Spain was 'Premier jour de bombardement aérien à Madrid', *Le Populaire,* 5 September 1936, p. 2. His first report on domestic affairs was published on 10 September. Herrmann's support for supplying arms is noted in Jean Prader, *Au secours de l'Espagne socialiste!,* Librairie du Travail, Paris 1936, p. 21. His work is praised in René Modiano, 'L'Evolution du 'Populaire', *La Gauche Révolutionnaire,* No. 14, 20 January 1937, p. 11.
49. Ilya Ehrenbourg, 'Visages d'Espagne', *Regards,* No. 142, 1 October 1936, pp. 4–5, p. 4.
50. The address to the familial was not unusual of course, and could be directed towards French parents in appeals for aid. Here the photographic image also played a role. For one example referring to the impact of photographs from Spain see Comité de rassemblement populaire de Billy-Montigny, *A la population billysienne,* Billy-Montigny 1938.
51. Jean-Richard Bloch, *Espagne, Espagne!,* Le Temps des cerises, Paris 1996, p. 169, ellipsis added. The passage cited was initially published in *Vendredi* on 14 October 1936.
52. For one critique of the embrace of the nation, see P. R. 'Le Communisme tricolore', *Que faire?,* No. 17, May 1936, pp. 20–1. The fate of internationalism

in this period is effectively analysed in Michel Dreyfus, 'Les Socialistes européens et les fronts populaires: Un Internationalisme declinant', Wolikow and Bleton-Ruget, 1998, pp. 21–9.

53. On the timing of Stalin's decision see Rémi Skoutelsky, *L'Espoir guidait leurs pas: Les Volontaires français dans les Brigades internationales, 1936–1939*, Bernard Grasset, Paris 1998, p. 44. For an account of intervention from the Soviet perspective see Stanley G. Payne, *The Spanish Civil War, the Soviet Union, and Communism*, Yale University Press, New Haven and London 2004, pp. 124–52. Payne stresses the incremental growth of the Soviet policy of intervention. He also stresses a distinction between the propaganda claims of the Communists and the actual position of the Comintern.
54. As with so much else concerning the Communists and the Spanish Civil War, the status of the International Brigades is largely obscure. I have relied on Skoutelsky, 1998. This is by far the most systematic and detailed account of the French case. For the formation of the Brigades see p. 50 ff. For the early presence of volunteers see the report dated 26 July 1936 which mentions French volunteers amongst those marching to Saragossa: Jean-Maurice Herrmann, 'Le gouvernement de Barcelone travaille à l'organisation d'un ordre social nouveau', *Le Populaire*, 28 July 1936, p. 2.
55. This was in fact the declaration of a position already indicated on 7 October. See Payne, 2004, p. 147.
56. Gabriel Peri, 'L'URSS dénonce la duperie de la neutralité à sens unique', *L'Humanité*, 24 October 1936, p. 1 and p. 3.
57. See Berstein, *Histoire du Parti Radical: Crise du Radicalisme 1926–1939*, Presses de la Fondation nationale des sciences politiques, Paris 1982, pp. 476–7. This is not of course to sugget that the Radicals were united over Spain.
58. See for example Jacques Duclos, 'Levez le blocus!', *L'Humanité*, 31 October 1936, pp. 1–2.
59. Paul Vaillant-Couturier, ' "Agissements" communistes', *L'Humanité*, 30 November 1936, p. 1.
60. Vaillant-Couturier, 30 November 1936, p. 1.
61. Jacques Duclos, 'La Déclaration de Jacques Duclos', *L'Humanité*, 6 December 1936, p. 4.
62. Tristan Tzara, 'Le Témoignage d'un écrivain sur Madrid en armes', *L'Humanité*, 7 December 1936, p. 7.
63. Tzara, 7 December 1936, p. 7.
64. Tzara, 7 December 1936, p. 7.
65. Tzara, 7 December 1936, p. 7.
66. Tristan Tzara, 'Aux avants-postes de la liberté', *Regards*, No. 154, 24 December 1936, pp. 10–11, p. 11, ellipsis added.
67. Malraux, 1968, p. 40.
68. André Malraux, 'Sur l'héritage culturel', *Commune*, No. 37, September 1936, pp. 1–9. According to Benjamin, Malraux had the intention of developing his reading of the essay in his next book: see the letter of 10 August 1936 to Max Horkheimer, Walter Benjamin, *Correspondence: 1910–1940*, Ed. Gershom Scholem and Theodor W. Adorno, Trans. Manfred R. Jacobsen and Evelyn M. Jacobsen, University of Chicago Press, Chicago and London 1994, p. 529.
69. Walter Benjamin, 'L'Oeuvre d'art · l'époque de sa reproduction mécanisée', Trans. Pierre Klossowki, *Zeitschrift für Sozialforschung*, Vol. 5, 1936, p. 65.

70. Malraux, 1968, p. 179.
71. And these sentiments seemed destined for Malraux's treatment. The investigation of fraternity was a feature of Malraux's writing, so much so that in August 1936, long before *L'Espoir* was published, J. E. Pouterman would describe the Spanish militiamen as heroes from one of Malraux's novels: see 'Avec les miliciens sur le front de Saragosse', *L'Oeuvre*, 10 August 1936, pp. 1–2, p. 2.
72. Malraux, 1968, p. 220.
73. Malraux, 1968, p. 220.
74. Louis Aragon, '*Espagne, Espagne!* par Jean-Richard Bloch', *Commune*, No. 41, January 1937, pp. 597–8, p. 597.
75. Anon. 'L'Espoir par André Malraux', *Ce Soir*, 3 November 1937, p. 1 and p. 6.
76. Mathieu Corman, 'Il y a un an 300 mercenaires de Franco entraient dans Madrid ...', *Ce Soir*, 7 November 1937, p. 1 and p. 3.

Epilogue: 30 November 1938

1. See, amongst others, anon. 'Physionomie de Paris', *Le Figaro*, 1 December 1938, p. 1 and p. 5; anon. 'La grève? Mais où donc étaient les grévistes?', *Le Jour-L'Echo de Paris*, 1 December 1938, p. 1 and p. 5; anon. 'Promenade dans Paris ... qui travaille', *Le Journal*, 1 December 1938, p. 3; anon. 'Dans Paris à la recherche de la grève générale', *Le Matin*, 1 December 1938, p. 2.
2. Simone Weil, 'Fragment', *Ecrits historiqes et politiques*, Gallimard, Paris 1960, p. 217.
3. André Delmas, *Mémoires d'un instituteur syndicaliste*, Editions Albatros, Paris 1979, p. 373 ff.
4. Anon. 'Contre les décrets-lois. Aujourd'hui, demonstration nationale. Mercredi, grève générale', *Le Peuple*, 26 November 1938, p. 2. The PCF made similar claims: see for example P.-L. Darnar, 'Comme au 12 février 1934 dans l'union et la discipline la grève générale se prépare pour le progrès social et la République', *L'Humanité*, 25 November 1938, p. 1.
5. This paragraph is merely a condensed version of the narrative in Lefranc, 1965, pp. 228–82. For Daladier's period of office Lefranc's narrative should be supplemented by Antoine Prost, 'Le Climat social', *Edouard Daladier: Chef de gouvernement, Avril 1938–Septembre 1939*, Eds. René Rémond and Janine Bourdin, Presses de la Fondation nationale des sciences politiques, Paris 1977, pp. 99–111.
6. See Daniel Guérin, *Front populaire: Révolution manquée*, Actes sud, Arles, 1997, offers an account of the entire period from the perspective of Pivert's Gauche révolutionnaire. For the formation of the PSOP see p. 308 ff.
7. For an account of Daladier's ascendancy see Serge Berstein, *Histoire du Parti Radical: Crise du Radicalisme 1926–1939*, Presses de la Fondation nationale des sciences politiques, Paris, 1982, pp. 535–57. The growth of Radical anticommunism is well traced in Peter Larmour, *The French Radical Party in the 1930s*, Stanford University Press, Stanford 1964, pp. 197–226. I have dealt here only with the parliamentary parties but divisions also appeared in the other organisations belonging to the Front. The CVIA was split over the nature of its pacifism; the reunited CGT experienced continual struggles between its communist and anticommunist members.

8. If one excludes 1936, the figure of 2616 strikes in 1937 is unprecedented: see Edward Shorter and Charles Tilly, *Strikes in France: 1830–1968*, Cambridge University Press, London and New York 1974, pp. 360–2.
9. The term 'trial of strength' was used repeatedly by Wladimir d'Ormesson in *Le Figaro*. Its use was deplored by Léon Blum in 'Halte!', *Le Populaire*, 27 November 1938, p. 1.
10. Daladier used decree powers to ensure the operation of the public services, thereby avoiding a repetition of the strike of December 1937, which had significantly disrupted Paris. The five-day period before the strike also provided time for the effective deployment of troops. The error in the timing of the announcement was quickly attacked by Trotsky: see 'The Decisive Hour', Trotsky, 1979, pp. 196–204, p. 202.
11. Anon. 'La République retrouvé', *Le Temps*, 2 December 1938, p. 1. The date of the 2nd is explained by the fact that *Le Temps* was an evening paper dated for the morning after its publication.
12. Anon. 'C'est le principe même de la République qui a triomphe aujourd'hui: respect des lois, respect du travail, respect de la patrie', *L'Excelsior*, 1 December 1938, p. 1.

Bibliography

Anonymous articles are listed by publication.

Unpublished sources

Alquezar, Rose *L'Espagne et l'Amérique latine dans l'hebdomadaire* Vendredi, *Novembre 1935–Novembre 1938*, Doctorat de troisième cycle, Université de Bordeaux, 1985–1986.

Boilloz, Bernard *Les Périodiques français édités à Paris de 1919–1939: Classification, description bibliographique et évolution*, Doctorat de troisième cycle, Université de Paris VIII, 1978.

Cattaruzza, Natalie *Le Rôle des patrons, rédacteurs en chef, directeurs artistiques de la presse illustrée dans le développement de certains tendances photographiques, en France des années 1920 aux années 1960 (reportage, photojournalisme, mode, publicité, illustration)*, Allocation de formation et de recherche, Mission de patrimoine photographique, Paris 1995.

Comité national d'organisation du rassemblement populaire du 14 juillet 1935, *Le Defilé du 14 juillet 1935*, Film, 15 September 1935 Paris, Vidéothèque de Paris, VDP1224.

Published sources

Abel, Richard *The Ciné Goes to Town: French Cinema, 1896–1914*, University of California Press, Berkeley, Los Angeles and London 1994.

Adorno, Theodor W. 'Freudian Theory and Pattern of Fascist Propaganda', *The Essential Frankfurt School Reader*, Eds. Andrew Arato and Eike Gebhardt, Continuum, New York 1998, pp. 118–37.

Agulhon, Maurice *Marianne into Battle: Republican Imagery and Symbolism in France, 1789–1880*, Trans. Janet Lloyd, Cambridge University Press, Cambridge and New York 1981.

Alain, Langevin, Paul and Rivet, Paul 'Aux Travailleurs', *Commune*, Nos. 7–8, March–April 1934, pp. 859–64.

Albert, Pierre and Feyel, Gilles 'Photography and the Media: Changes in the Illustrated Press', *A New History of Photography*, Ed. Michel Frizot, Könemann, Cologne 1998, pp. 359–69.

Althusser, Louis 'Ideology and Ideological State Apparatuses (Notes towards an Investigation)', *Lenin and Philosophy and Other Essays*, Trans. Ben Brewster, New Left Books, London 1971, pp. 121–73.

Amalui, Christian 'Le 14-juillet: Du Dies irae à jour de fête', Nora 1992, pp. 421–72.

L'Ami du Peuple, anon. 'Trois usines de la banlieue occupées par des communistes', 27 May 1936, p. 1.

Anderson, Benedict *Imagined Communities: On the Origins and Spread of Nationalism*, Verso, London and New York 1993.
Anderson, Perry 'The Antinomies of Antonio Gramsci', *Antonio Gramsci: Critical Assessments of Leading Political Philosophers*, Vol. 2, Ed. James Martin, Routledge, London and New York 2002, pp. 339–410.
Annuaire de la Presse, Annuaire International de la Presse, Paris 1922–1937.
Annuaire de Commerce Didot-Bottin, Didot-Bottin, Paris 1920–1938.
Aragon, Louis '*Faubourg Saint-Antoine* par Tristan Rémy', *Commune*, No. 33, May 1936, pp. 1120–2.
—— '*Espagne, Espagne!* par Jean-Richard Bloch', *Commune*, No. 41, January 1937, pp. 597–8.
Astier, Emmanuel d' 'La Première Nuit des grévistes ...', *Vu*, No. 429, 3 June 1936, pp. 630–1.
Aymé, Marcel 'Les Signes extérieurs', *Marianne*, No. 70, 21 February 1934, p. 8.
Badie, Bertrand 'Les Grèves de 1936 aux usines Renault', Bouvier, 1986, pp. 68–85.
Bailby, Léon 'L'Occupation des usines de guerre', *Le Jour*, 28 May 1936, p. 1.
Balk, Theodor *La Quatorzième*, Editions du Commissariat des Brigades internationales, Madrid 1937.
Baqué, Dominique *Les Documents de la modernité: Anthologie de textes sur la photographie de 1919 à 1939*, Jacqueline Chambon, Nîmes 1993.
Bard, Christine *Les Filles de Marianne: Histoire des féminismes, 1914–1940*, Fayard, Paris 1995.
Barral, Pierre *Les Fondateurs de la troisième République*, Colin, Paris 1968.
Barrett, Michèle 'Ideology, Politics, Hegemony: From Gramsci to Laclau and Mouffe', *Mapping Ideology*, Ed. Slavoj Žižek, Verso, London and New York 1994, pp. 235–64.
Basch, Françoise *Victor Basch ou la passion de la justice: De l'affaire Dreyfus au crime de la milice*, Plon, Paris 1994.
Basch, Victor 'Le Front populaire', *Les Cahiers des Droits de l'Homme*, New Series, No. 28, 10 November 1935, pp. 695–6.
Bellanger, Claude *et al. Histoire générale de la Presse francaise*, Vol. 3, Presses universitaires de France, Paris 1972.
Benjamin, Walter 'L'Oeuvre d'art à l'époque de sa reproduction mécanisée', Trans. Pierre Klossowski, *Zeitschrift für Sozialforschung*, Vol. 5, 1936, pp. 40–68.
—— *Correspondence: 1910–1940*, Ed. Gershom Scholem and Theodor W. Adorno, Trans. Manfred R. Jacobsen and Evelyn M. Jacobsen, University of Chicago Press, Chicago and London 1994.
—— *Selected Writings*, Vol. 2, Eds. Howard Eiland, Michael W. Jennings and Gary Smith, Trans. Rodney Livingstone and others, Belknap Press of Harvard University Press, Cambridge, Mass. and London 1999.
—— 'Little History of Photography', pp. 507–30.
—— 'The Newspaper', pp. 741–2.
—— 'The Author as Producer', pp. 768–82.
Berstein, Serge *Le 6 février 1934*, Gallimard, Paris 1975.
—— *Histoire du Parti Radical: Crise du Radicalisme 1926–1939*, Presses de la Fondation nationale des sciences politiques, Paris 1982.
Biquard, Pierre 'Rapport sur la situation actuelle de la presse', *Vigilance*, No. 61, 10 January 1938, pp. 11–13.

Birnbaum, Pierre *Le Peuple et les gros: Histoire d'un mythe*, Grasset, Paris 1979.

Bloch, Jean-Richard *Espagne, Espagne!*, Le Temps des cerises, Paris 1996.

Blum, Léon 'Conquête, exercice et occupation du pouvoir', *Le Populaire*, 2 July 1935, p. 1.

—— 'Halte!', *Le Populaire*, 27 November 1938, p. 1.

Blumé, Daniel 'Contribution à l'histoire de la politique de la non-intervention: documents inédits', *Cahiers Léon Blum*, Nos. 2 and 3, December 1977–March 1978, pp. 16–61.

Boiry, Maurice 'Nous ... les reporters photographes', *Presse Publicité*, No. 2, 21 March 1937, p. 13.

Bouqueret, Christian *Des années folles aux années noires: La nouvelle vision photographique en France, 1920–1940*, Marval, Paris 1997.

Bourdieu, Pierre *et al. Photography: A Middle-brow Art*, Trans. Shaun Whiteside, Polity Press, Cambridge 1990.

Bouvier, Jean Ed. *La France en mouvement: 1934–1938*, Champ Vallon, Seyssel 1986.

Bouvier, Jeanne *Mes mémoires, ou 59 années d'activité industrielle, sociale et intellectuelle d'une ouvrière*, L'Action intellectuelle, Poitiers 1936.

Bréval, Marcel 'Le Parti et les "classes moyennes" ', *Que faire?*, Nos. 1–2, November–December 1934, pp. 16–24.

Brothers, Caroline *War and Photography: A Cultural History*, Routledge, London and New York 1997.

Brouckère de, Louis 'Voyage en Espagne', *Le Populaire*, 9 August 1936, p. 4.

Broué, Pierre and Dorey, Nicole 'Critiques de gauche et opposition révolutionnaire au Front populaire (1936–1938)', *Le Mouvement Social*, No. 54, January–March 1966, pp. 91–133.

Cachin, Marcel 'Travail et «propriété»', *L'Humanité*, 8 June 1936, p. 1.

Carlton, David 'Eden, Blum and the Origins of Non-Intervention', *Journal of Contemporary History*, Vol. 6, No. 3, 1971, pp. 40–55.

Cattanéo, Bernadette 'Travailleuses des villes et des champs contre la misère, le fascisme, la guerre. Debout! Organisez-vous!', *Les Femmes dans l'Action Mondiale*, No. 1, undated [1934], p. 6.

—— 'Les Socialistes avec nous!', *Les Femmes dans l'Action Mondiale*, No. 2, October 1934, n.p.

—— 'Les Comités féminins se présentent aux élections avec leurs programmes', *Les Femmes dans l'Action Mondiale*, No. 8, 15 April–15 May 1935, pp. 8–9.

—— 'Notre route ...', *Les Femmes dans l'Action Mondiale*, No. 9, 15 May–15 June 1935, pp. 8–9.

Certeau de, Michel *The Practice of Everyday Life*, Trans. Steven Randall, University of California Press, Berkeley, Los Angeles and London 1984.

Ce Soir, anon. 'L'Espoir par André Malraux', 3 November 1937, p. 1 and p. 6.

Chamson, André *Retour d'Espagne: Rien qu'un témoignage*, Bernard Grasset, Paris 1937.

Chamson, André, Guéhenno, Jean, Viollis, Andrée 'Histoire de "Vendredi" ', *Vendredi*, No. 29, 22 May 1936, p. 1.

Claude S[imone] and Cartier[-Bresson], Henri '*Faubourg Saint-Antoine* avec Tristan Rémy', *Regards*, No. 120, 30 April 1936, p. 10.

Combeau, Yvan 'Les Elections municipales de 1935. Acte de naissance électoral du Front populaire', *L'Information Historique*, No. 56, 1994, pp. 195–200.

Comité de rassemblement populaire de Billy-Montigny, *A la population billysienne*, Billy-Montigny 1938.
Comité national du rassemblement populaire, *14 juillet 1935*, Comité national du rassemblement populaire, Paris 1935.
—— 'Programme du rassemblement populaire', Lefranc, 1965, p. 441–5.
Confédération générale du travail, 'Au peuple! Aux travailleurs!', *Le Peuple*, 9 February 1934, p. 1.
Constant, Etienne 'Le Droit au travail et le droit à la vie ...', *Les Femmes dans l'Action Mondiale*, No. 8, 15 April–15 May 1935, pp. 4–5.
Corman, Mathieu 'Il y a un an 300 mercenaires de Franco entraient dans Madrid ...', *Ce Soir*, 7 November 1937, p. 1 and p. 3.
Crevel, René 'Individu et société', *Commune*, No. 23, July 1935, pp. 1204–11.
Danos, Jacques and Gibelin, Marcel *June '36: Class Struggle and the Popular Front in France*, Trans. Peter Fysh and Christine Bourry, Bookmarks, London and Chicago 1986.
Darnar, P.-L., 'Vérité en deça comme au dela des Pyrénées', *L'Humanité*, 20 July 1936, p. 1.
—— 'Comme au 12 février 1934 dans l'union et la discipline la grève générale se prépare pour le progrès social et la République', *L'Humanité*, 25 November 1938, p. 1.
Decaris, Germaine 'Le Gouvernement et le cinéma', *La Lumière*, No. 482, 1 August 1936, p. 5.
Dell, Simon 'On the Metaphor and Practice of Photography: Socialist Realism, the Popular Front in France and the Dynamics of Cultural Unity', *History of Photography*, Vol. 25, No. 1, Spring 2001, pp. 52–60.
Delmas, André *Mémoires d'un instituteur syndicaliste*, Albatros, Paris 1979.
Delpla, François 'Les Communistes français et la sexualité, 1932–1938', *Le Mouvement Social*, No. 91, April–June 1975, pp. 121–52.
Denoyelle, Françoise *La Lumière de Paris: Les Usages de la photographie, 1919–1939*, L'Harmattan, Paris 1997.
Depretto, Jean-Paul and Schweitzer, Sylvie V. *Le Communisme à l'usine: Vie ouvrière et mouvement ouvrier chez Renault, 1920–1939*, EDIRES, Roubaix 1984.
Devigne, Roger 'Des «Miliciennes» de 1937 aux «Vésuviennes» de 1848', *Vendredi*, No. 81, 21 May 1937, p. 4.
Dreyfus, Michel 'Les Socialistes européens et les fronts populaires: Un Internationalisme declinant', Wolikow and Bleton-Ruget 1998, pp. 21–9.
Duchêne, Gabrielle 'Pourquoi ce mouvement', *Les Femmes dans l'Action Mondiale*, No. 1, undated [1934], pp. 1–2.
Duclos, Jacques *Le Triomphe du Front populaire. De la Conférence Communiste d'Ivry (Juin 1934) aux Assises de la Paix et de la Liberté du 14 Juillet 1935*, Les Publications révolutionnaires, Paris 1935.
—— 'Insurrection fasciste au Maroc espagnol', *L'Humanité*, 19 July 1936, p. 1.
—— 'Levez le blocus!', *L'Humanité*, 31 October 1936, pp. 1–2.
—— 'La Déclaration de Jacques Duclos', *L'Humanité*, 6 December 1936, p. 4.
Duval, René *Histoire de la radio en France*, Alain Moreau, Paris 1979.
L'Echo de Paris, anon. 'Les Soviets partout!', 27 May 1936, p. 1.
—— Anon. 'La grève des hôtels, restaurants et cafés a bouleversé hier la vie de Paris', 12 June 1936, p. 1.

Eco, Umberto 'A Photograph', *Faith in Fakes: Essays*, Trans. William Weaver, Secker and Warburg, London 1986, pp. 213–17.

Edwards, Steve 'The Machine's Dialogue', *Oxford Art Journal*, Vol. 13, No. 1, 1990, pp. 63–76.

—— 'Photography, Allegory, and Labor', *Art Journal*, Vol. 55, No. 2, Summer 1996, pp. 38–44.

Ehrenbourg, Ilya 'Visages d'Espagne', *Regards*, No. 142, 1 October 1936, pp. 4–5.

Estier, Claude *La Gauche Hebdomadaire, 1914–1962*, Colin, Paris 1962.

L'Excelsior, anon. 'C'est le principe même de la République qui a triomphe aujourd'hui: respect des lois, respect du travail, respect de la patrie', 1 December 1938, p. 1.

Les Femmes dans l'Action Mondiale, anon. 'La Grève a gagné toute la France et a touché toutes les industries', Special issue, 1936, pp. 5–6.

—— Anon. '«Tiens ... c'est moi»', Special issue, 1936, pp. 7–8.

Le Figaro, anon. 'Chez Renault, citadelle ouvrière', 9 June 1936, p. 4.

—— Anon. 'Physionomie de Paris', 1 December 1938, p. 1 and p. 5.

Fleig, Alain *Etant donné l'âge de la lumière: Naissance de la photographie comme média en France dans les années trente*, Editions Ides et Calendes, Neuchâtel 1997.

Fogle, Douglas *The Last Picture Show: Artists Using Photography, 1960–1982*, Walker Art Center, Minneapolis 2003.

Fontaine, François *La Guerre d'Espagne: Un deluge de feu et d'images*, BDIC-Berg International, Paris 2003.

Fréville, Jean *Pain de brique*, Flammarion, Paris 1937.

Furet, François *Revolutionary France: 1770–1880*, Trans. Antonia Nevill, Blackwell, Oxford 1992.

—— *The French Revolution: 1770–1814*, Trans. Antonia Nevill, Blackwell, Oxford 1996.

Fuzier, Robert 'A Barcelone parmi les héroiques défenseurs de la République', *Le Populaire*, 24 July 1936, p. 2.

Gennep van, Arnold *Manuel de folklore français contemporain*, Vol. 3, Picard, Paris 1937.

Gernsheim, Helmut with Gernsheim, Alison *The History of Photography: From the Earliest Use of the Camera Obscura in the Eleventh Century up to 1914*, Oxford University Press, London 1955.

Gérôme, Noëlle 'Images de l'occupation de l'usine à gaz de Poitiers', Bouvier 1986, pp. 62–7.

Gérôme, Pierre 'Le Front populaire', *Vigilance*, No. 25, 1 July 1935, p. 3.

—— *La Presse et Franco*, Comité de vigilance des intellectuels antifascistes, Paris 1937.

Gitton, Marcel 'Tout n'est pas possible', *L'Humanité*, 29 May 1936, pp. 1–2.

—— ' "Des canons! Des avions!" ', *L'Humanité*, 5 September 1936, p. 1.

Gramsci, Antonio *Prison Notebooks*, Vol. 1, Ed. and Trans. Joseph A. Buttigieg, Columbia University Press, New York 1992.

—— *Prison Notebooks*, Vol. 2, Ed. and Trans. Joseph A. Buttigieg, Columbia University Press, New York 1996.

Gruber, Helmut *Léon Blum, French Socialism, and the Popular Front: A Case of Internal Contradictions*, Cornell Studies in International Affairs: Western Societies Papers, Ithaca 1986.

Guéhenno, Jean 'Valeur d'une fête', *Europe,* No. 152, 15 August 1935, pp. 601–4.
Guérin, Daniel *Front populaire: Révolution manquée,* Actes sud, Arles 1997.
Guérin, Maurice 'A propos de l'occupation des usines: ce qui est en question', *L'Aube,* 3 June 1936, p. 1.
Guernut, Henri *et al.* 'Proposition de loi relative au Statut Professionnel des Journalistes', *Le Journaliste,* No. 90, April 1933, pp. 3–6.
Habermas, Jürgen *The Structural Transformation of the Public Sphere: An Inquiry into a Category of Bourgeois Society,* Trans. Thomas Burger and Frederick Lawrence, Polity Press, Cambridge 1996.
Herrmann, Jean-Maurice 'En route vers le pays où les travailleurs défendent la République les armes à la main', *Le Populaire,* 24 July 1936, p. 3.
—— 'Le gouvernement de Barcelone travaille à l'organisation d'un ordre social nouveau', *Le Populaire,* 28 July 1936, p. 2.
—— 'Premier jour de bombardement aérien à Madrid', *Le Populaire,* 5 September 1936, p. 2.
Hobsbawm, Eric 'Mass-Producing Traditions: Europe, 1870–1914', *The Invention of Tradition,* Eds. Eric Hobsbawm and Terence Ranger, Cambridge University Press, Cambridge and New York 1992, pp. 263–307.
—— *The Age of Capital: 1848–1875,* Weidenfeld and Nicolson, London 1995.
Horn, Gerd Rainer *European Socialists Respond to Fascism: Ideology, Activism and Contingency in the 1930s,* Oxford University Press, Oxford and New York 1996.
Huard, Raymond *La Naissance du parti politique en France,* Presses de la Fondation nationale des sciences politiques, Paris 1996.
L'Humanité, anon. 'Unanime, le Comité exécutif radical approuve la participation aux manifestations du Front populaire du 14 juillet', 4 July 1935, pp. 1–2.
—— Anon. 'Les Grèves', 4 June 1936, p. 5.
—— Anon. 'Notre camarade Thorez fait acclamer notre soutien au gouvernement Léon Blum', 8 June 1936, pp. 1–2.
—— Anon. 'Les Sportifs retour de Barcelone nous disent ...', 25 July 1936, p. 1 and p. 7.
—— Anon. 'Le Gouvernement français précise qu'il ne s'immisce pas dans les affaires intérieures de l'Espagne', 26 July 1936, p. 2.
—— Anon. '400,000 Parisiens à Saint-Cloud', 10 August 1936, p. 2.
—— Anon. 'L'URSS adhere à la proposition française', 11 August 1936, p. 3.
—— Anon. 'Pour l'Espagne républicaine! Pour la liberté! Pour la paix!', 5 September 1936, p. 1.
—— Anon. 'A la République', 5 September 1936, pp. 1–2.
Jackson, Julian *The Politics of Depression in France: 1932–1936,* Cambridge University Press, Cambridge 1985.
—— *The Popular Front in France: Defending Democracy, 1934–38,* Cambridge University Press, Cambridge 1988.
Jacob, Madeleine *Quarante ans de journalisme,* Julliard, Paris 1970.
Jammy-Schmidt, *Idées et images radicales,* Excelsior, Paris 1934.
Jeffrey, Ian *Photography: A Concise History,* Thames and Hudson, London 1981.
—— *Revisions: An Alternative History of Photography,* National Museum of Photography, Film and Television, Bradford 1999.
Le Jour-L'Echo de Paris, anon. 'La grève? Mais où donc étaient les grévistes?', 1 December 1938, p. 1 and p. 5.

Le Journal, anon. 'Promenade dans Paris ... qui travaille', 1 December 1938, p. 3.
Le Journaliste, anon. 'Les reporters photographes sont des reporters', No. 91, May 1933, p. 8.
Le Journaliste, anon. 'Les Journalistes de l'objectif au Syndicat National', No. 93, October–November 1933, p. 12.
—— Anon. 'Il est temps pour les journalistes photographes de travailler à leur propre contrat', No. 101, August–September 1934, p. 7.
—— Anon. 'Barême des traitments minimum des Journalistes professionnels du département de la Seine pour l'année 1936', No. 110, February 1936, p. 5.
—— Anon. 'Chez les Reporters-Photographes', No. 112, April 1936, p. 7.
Juillard, Jacques 'Le Peuple', Nora, 1992, pp. 184–229.
Kayser, Jacques 'Le Parti radical-socialiste et le rassemblement populaire 1935–1938', *Société d'Histoire de la Troisième République*, New Series, No. 14, April–July 1955, pp. 271–84.
Kergoat, Jacques *La France du Front populaire*, Editions La Découverte, Paris 1986.
Kriegel, Annie 'Langage et stratégie: L'exemple du Front populaire', *Communismes au miroir français: Temps, cultures et sociétés en France devant le communisme*, Gallimard, Paris 1974, pp. 95–114.
L., P. 'Jean Roubier', *Le Photographe*, No. 462, 20 July 1938, pp. 215–16.
Laclau, Ernesto and Mouffe, Chantal *Hegemony and Socialist Strategy: Towards a Radical Democratic Politics*, Verso, London and New York 2001.
Lanot de, F. 'La Photographie et la presse', *Bulletin de la Société Française de la Photographie et de Cinématographie*, Vol. 21, No. 2, February 1934, pp. 41–8 and No. 3, March 1934, pp. 63–8.
Larmour, Peter J. *The French Radical Party in the 1930s*, Stanford University Press, Stanford 1964.
Lecoq, Jean 'Révolutions et guerres civiles en Espagne', *L'Illustré du Petit Journal*, No. 2381, 9 August 1936, p. 4.
Lefranc, Georges *Histoire du Front populaire, 1934–1938*, Payot, Paris 1965.
Leroy, Géraldi and Roche, Anne *Les Ecrivains et le Front populaire*, Presses de la Fondation nationale des sciences politiques, Paris 1986.
Libermann, Alexandre 'La première qualité d'une photo d'actualité c'est la sincérité', *Presse Publicité*, No. 9, 9 May 1937, p. 14.
Ligue des droits de l'homme: Comité central, 'Séance du 27 juin 1935', *Les Cahiers des Droits de l'Homme*, New Series, No. 23, 10 August 1935, pp. 593–6.
—— 'La Lutte contre le fascisme et la guerre: Séances du 13 octobre 1935', *Les Cahiers des Droits de l'Homme*, New Series, No. 29, 20 November 1935, pp. 726–30.
Malraux, André 'Sur l'héritage culturel', *Commune*, No. 37, September 1936, pp. 1–9.
—— *Days of Hope*, Trans. Stuart Gilbert and Alastair Macdonald, Hamish Hamilton, London 1968.
Manevy, Raymond *La Presse de la IIIe République*. J. Foret, Paris 1955.
Marty, André 'Une grève générale sans précédent', *L'Humanité*, 13 February 1934, p. 1.
—— 'Il faut que cesse immédiatement le blocus de fait de l'Espagne républicaine' *L'Humanité*, 11 August 1936, p. 1.
Marx, Karl, *Capital: A Critique of Political Economy*, Vol. 1, Trans. Ben Fowkes, Penguin Books, Harmondsworth 1990.

Marx, Karl, *Surveys from Exile: Political Writings*, Vol. 2, Ed. David Fernbach, Trans. Paul Jackson, Penguin Books, Harmondsworth 1992(a).

—— 'The Class Struggles in France: 1848–1850', pp. 35–142.

—— 'The Eighteenth Brumaire of Louis Bonaparte', pp. 143–249.

—— 'The Civil War in France', *The First International and After: Political Writings*, Vol. 3, Ed. David Fernbach, Harmondsworth, 1992(b), pp. 186–236.

Marx, Karl and Engels, Friedrich *The Communist Manifesto*, Trans. Samuel Moore, Oxford University Press, Oxford and New York 1992.

Le Matin, anon. 'Dans Paris à la recherche de la grève générale', 1 December 1938, p. 2.

McCauley, Anne 'Writing Photography's History before Newhall', *History of Photography*, Vol. 21, No. 2, Summer 1997, pp. 87–101.

Méadel, Cécile 'Programme en masse, programme de masse? La Diffusion de la radio en France pendant les années trente', *Masses et culture de masse dans les années trente*, Régine Robin Ed. Les Editions ouvrières, Paris 1991, pp. 51–68.

Modiano, René 'L'Evolution du "Populaire" ', *La Gauche Révolutionnaire*, No. 14, 20 January 1937, p. 11.

Montarron, Marcel 'Souvenirs de «l'occupation». Chansons sur le tas', *Marianne*, No. 191, 17 June 1936, p. 3.

Nadaud, Eric 'Le Renouvellement des pratiques militantes de la SFIO au début du Front populaire (1934–1936)', *Le Mouvement Social*, No. 153, October–December 1990, pp. 9–32.

Nemeth, Thomas *Gramsci's Philosophy: A Critical Study*, The Harvester Press, Brighton 1980.

Nesbit, Molly *Atget's Seven Albums*, Yale University Press, New Haven and London 1992.

Nickel, Douglas, R. 'History of Photography: The State of Research', *Art Bulletin*, Vol. 83, No. 3, September 2001, pp. 548–58.

Nicolet, Claude *L'Idée républicaine en France (1789–1924): Essai d'histoire critique*, Gallimard, Paris 1982.

Nizan, Paul 'L'Insurrection fasciste est vaincue à Barcelone, à Séville et à Melilla', *L'Humanité*, 20 July 1936, p. 1 and p. 3.

—— 'Victoire à Valence', *L'Humanité*, 3 August 1936, p. 3.

Noiriel, Gérard *Workers in French Society in the 19th and 20th Centuries*, Trans. Helen McPhail, Berg, New York, Oxford and Munich 1990.

Nora, Pierre, Ed. *Les Lieux de mémoire*, Vol. 3, Gallimard, Paris 1992.

L'Oeuvre, anon. 'Le Congrès de Nantes, unanime, fait confiance aux ministres radicaux pour défendre les libertés démocratiques', 28 October 1934, p. 1 and p. 4.

—— Anon. 'Le Mouvement gréviste s'étend dans la métallurgie', 28 May 1936, p. 1 and p. 5.

—— Anon, 'La Conférence paritaire s'est prononcée pour le droit syndicale et la liberté d'opinion', 2 June 1936, p. 1 and p. 5.

Ormesson Wladimir d' 'Sous les yeux de l'étranger', *Le Figaro*, 27 November 1938, p. 1.

Ory, Pascal *La Belle Illusion: Culture et Politique sous le signe du Front populaire, 1934–1938*, Plon, Paris 1994.

Ozouf, Mona *Festivals and the French Revolution*, Trans. Alan Sheridan, Harvard University Press, Cambridge, Mass. and London 1988.

Paris-Soir, anon. 'Cafés, restaurants, hôtels, pharmacies sont rouverts en grand nombre', 13 June 1936, p. 1.

Parti communiste français, 'Avec l'Espagne pour la sécurité de la France', *L'Humanité*, 3 August 1936, p. 6.

—— 'Une Lettre du Parti communiste à la CAP du Parti socialiste', *L'Humanité*, 12 August 1936, p. 2.

Payne, Stanley G. *The Spanish Civil War, the Soviet Union, and Communism*, Yale University Press, New Haven and London 2004.

Peri, Gabriel 'La Réponse italienne à la proposition française', *L'Humanité*, 23 August 1936, p. 3.

—— 'Après la décision du 3e Reich, il convient d'organiser le contrôle internationale d'accord de "neutralité" ', *L'Humanité*, 25 August 1936, p. 3.

—— 'L'URSS dénonce la duperie de la neutralité à sens unique', *L'Humanité*, 24 October 1936, p. 1 and p. 3.

Perrot, Michelle *Les Ouvriers en grève, France, 1871–1890*, Vol. 2, Mouton, Paris 1974.

Peschanski, Denis *Et pourtant ils tournent: Vocabulaire et strategie du PCF, 1934–1936*, Klincksieck, Paris 1988.

Le Petit Journal, anon. '«Il faut savoir terminer une grève»', 13 June 1936, p. 1.

Le Peuple, anon. 'Contre les décrets-lois. Aujourd'hui, demonstration nationale. Mercredi, grève générale', 26 November 1938, p. 2.

Photo Annuaire, Publications photographiques et cinématographiques Paul Montel, Paris 1922–1937.

Pike, David Wingeate *Conjecture, Propaganda, and Deceit and the Spanish Civil War: The International Crisis over Spain, 1936–1939, as seen in the French Press*, California Institute of International Studies, Stanford 1968.

—— *La Presse française à la veille de la second guerre mondiale*, Editions Richelieu, Paris 1973.

Pivert, Marceau, 'La Parole est aux militants', *Le Populaire*, 12 May 1936, p. 6.

—— 'Tout est possible', *Le Populaire*, 27 May 1936, p. 6.

—— 'Un mot aux sénateurs …"républicains" ', *Le Populaire*, 10 October 1936, p. 6.

Pons, Silvio 'La Diplomatie soviétique, l'antifascisme et la guerre civile espagnole', Wolikow and Bleton-Ruget, 1998, pp. 59–66.

Le Populaire, anon. 'Ce que fut la journée', 13 February 1934, pp. 2–3.

—— Anon. 'Des nombreuses grèves se sont déroulées hier dans la métallurgie', 27 May 1936, p. 1.

—— Anon. 'Des centaines de milliers de manifestants ont renouvelé hier le Serment de la Paix', 10 August 1936, pp. 1–3.

Pouterman, J. E., 'Avec les miliciens sur le front de Saragosse', *L'Oeuvre*, 10 August 1936, pp. 1–2.

Prader, Jean *Au secours de l'Espagne socialiste!*, Librairie du Travail, Paris 1936.

Presse Publicité, anon. 'La presse de demain sera une combinaison du journalisme politique et du journalisme d'information', No. 9, 9 May 1937, p. 3.

—— Anon. 'Un journal du soir doit être un journal de loisirs, nous dit Jean-Richard Bloch', No. 10, 16 May 1937, pp. 1–2 and p. 26.

Prost, Antoine 'Le Climat social', *Edouard Daladier: Chef de gouvernement, Avril 1938–Septembre 1939*, Eds. René Rémond and Janine Bourdin, Presses de la Fondation nationale des sciences politiques, Paris 1977, pp. 99–111.

Prost, Antoine 'Les Manifestations du 12 février 1934 en province', Bouvier 1986, pp. 12–30.

Proust, Marcel 'Sentiments filiaux d'un parricide', *Contre Sainte-Beuve,* précédé de *Pastiches et mélanges* et suivi de *Essais et articles,* Bibliothèque de la Pléiade, Gallimard, Paris 1971, pp. 150–9.

Pudal, Bernard *Prendre parti: Pour une sociologie historique du PCF,* Presses de la Fondation nationale des sciences politiques, Paris 1989.

R., P. 'Le Communisme tricolore', *Que faire?,* No. 17, May 1936, pp. 20–1.

Racine, Nicole 'Marcel Martinet et la culture ouvrière', *Le Mouvement Social,* No. 91, April–June 1975, pp. 59–78.

Racine, Nicole and Bodin, Louis, Eds. *Le Parti communiste français pendant l'entre-deux-guerres,* Presses de la Fondation nationale des sciences politiques, Paris 1982.

Rambaud, A. 'Congrès National', *La Photographie Professionnelle,* No. 6, July 1936, pp. 3–31.

—— 'Parlons clair', *Le Photographe,* No. 425, 5 January 1937, pp. 10–11.

Rancière, Jacques 'The Concept of "Critique" and the "Critique of Political Economy" ', *Ideology, Method and Marx: Essay from Economy and Society,* Ed. Ali Rattansi, Routledge, London and New York 1989, pp. 74–180.

Rearick, Charles *The French in Love and War: Popular Culture in the Era of the World Wars,* Yale University Press, New Haven and London 1997.

Regards, anon. 'Aux lecteurs, aux amis!', No. 21, 6 July 1933, n.p.

Renan, 'Qu'est-ce qu'une nation?', *Oeuvres complètes,* Vol. 1, Calmann-Lévy, Paris 1947, pp. 887–906.

Rémy, Tristan *Porte de Clignancourt,* Rieder, Paris 1928.

—— 'Une grande journée populaire', *Le Peuple,* 19 July 1935, pp. 1–2.

—— *La Grande Lutte,* Collection 'Ciment', Editions sociales internationales, Paris 1937.

Rifkin, Adrian *Street Noises: Parisian Pleasures, 1900–1940,* Manchester University Press, Manchester and New York 1993.

Rim, Carlo 'Grandeur et servitude du reporter photographe', *Marianne,* No. 70, 21 February 1934, p. 8.

Rivet, Paul 'Les Intellectuels', *Vigilance,* No. 18, 10 March 1935, p. 3.

Roberts, John *The Art of Interruption: Realism, Photography and the Everyday,* Manchester University Press, Manchester and New York 1998.

Rossiter, Adrian 'Popular Front economic policy and the Matignon Negotiations', *Historical Journal,* Vol. 30, No. 3, 1987, pp. 663–83.

Roy, Marcel 'Les Travailleurs de la métallurgie forts de leur unité passent à l'offensive', *Le Populaire,* 28 May 1936, p. 6.

—— 'Le Caractère du mouvement des ouvriers métallurgistes', *Le Peuple,* 29 May 1936, pp. 1 and 3.

Sanson, Rosemonde *Les 14 juillet (1789–1975): Fête et conscience nationale,* Flammarion, Paris 1976.

Santamaria, Yves '«Noblesse oblige»: PCF, défense nationale et lutte pour la paix (1935–1936)', Wolikow and Bleton-Ruget, 1998, pp. 75–85.

Sassoon, Anne Showstack *Gramsci's Politics,* University of Minnesota Press, Minneapolis 1987.

Schulz, Marcel 'Les Origines de la crise ouvrière de 1936', *Le Musée Social,* No. 5, May 1937, pp. 121–39; No. 6, June 1937, pp. 153–65; No 7, July 1937, pp. 185–200.

Schwarz, Salomon *Les Occupations d'usine en France de mai et juin 1936*, E.J. Brill, Leiden 1937.

Serrano, Carlos *L'Enjeu espagnol: PCF et guerre d'Espagne*, Messidor/Editions sociales, Paris 1987.

Shorter, Edward and Tilly, Charles *Strikes in France: 1830–1968*, Cambridge University Press, London and New York 1974.

Skoutelsky, Rémi *L'Espoir guidait leurs pas: Les Volontaires français dans les Brigades internationales, 1936–1939*, Bernard Grasset, Paris 1998.

Solomon-Godeau, Abigail, *Photography at the Dock: Essays on Photographic History, Institutions, and Practices*, University of Minnesota Press, Minneapolis 1991.

—— 'Photography after Art Photography', pp. 103–23.

—— 'Who is speaking thus? Some questions about documentary photography', pp. 169–83.

Soucy, Robert *French Fascism: The Second Wave 1933–1939*, Yale University Press, New Haven and London 1995.

Tagg, John *The Burden of Representation: Essays on Photographies and Histories*, Macmillan Education, Basingstoke and London 1988.

Tartakowsky, Danielle 'Des grèves de juin à la pause, «Le ministère des masses» au coeur des contradictions', *Cahiers d'Histoire de l'Institut de Recherches Marxistes*, Part 24, 1986, pp. 36–53.

—— *Les Manifestations de rue en France: 1918–1968*, Publications de la Sorbonne, Paris 1997.

Le Temps, anon. 'Tout est possible', 28 May 1936, p. 1.

—— Anon. 'La République retrouvé', 2 December 1938, p. 1.

Thiebaut, Claude 'Léon Blum, Aléxis Léger et la décision de non-intervention en Espagne', *Les Français et la guerre d'Espagne*, Eds. Jean Sagnes and Sylvie Caucanas, Université de Perpignan, Perpignan 1990, pp. 23–43.

Thorez, Maurice 'A tout prix, battre le fascisme. Pour un large Front populaire antifasciste', *L'Humanité*, 12 October 1934, p. 4.

—— 'Interpellation', *Journal Officiel: Débats Parlementaires, Chambre des Députés*, Session of 13 November 1934, pp. 2294–8.

—— 'La Lutte pour le pain. Extraits du rapport présenté par Maurice Thorez à l'assemblée d'information des communistes de la région parisienne, jeudi 11 juin', *L'Humanité*, 13 June 1936, p. 4.

—— 'Au service de la liberté et de la paix! Rapport présenté par Maurice Thorez à l'assemblée des communistes parisiens, salle Huygens, le 6 août 1936', *L'Humanité*, 8 August 1936, p. 4.

Trachtenberg, Alan *Reading American Photographs: Images as History, Matthew Brady to Walker Evans*, Hill and Wang, New York 1989.

Trotsky, Léon *On France*, Ed. David Salner, Pathfinder, New York 1979.

—— 'Whither France', pp. 29–62.

—— 'Once Again, Whither France', pp. 67–128.

—— 'France at the Turning Point', pp. 135–50.

—— 'The Decisive Hour', pp. 196–204.

Tzara, Tristan 'Le Témoignage d'un écrivain sur Madrid en armes', *L'Humanité*, 7 December 1936, p. 7.

—— 'Aux avants-postes de la liberté', *Regards*, No. 154, 24 December 1936, pp. 10–11.

Unik, Pierre 'Dans les usines avec les métallos en grève', *Regards*, No. 125, 4 June 1936, pp. 5–7.

Vaillant-Couturier, Paul 'Sarraut décide de rester pour ne rien faire', *L'Humanité*, 6 May 1936, p. 1.
—— 'Les forces républicaines ont repris Almera, Almansa, Gijon, Guadalajarra, Huesca, Mahon, Tolède, Saint-Sébastien', *L'Humanité*, 23 July 1936, p. 1.
—— 'L'Offensive républicaine se développe dans toute l'Espagne', *L'Humanité*, 24 July 1936, p. 1.
—— 'Salut à notre soeur l'Espagne!', *L'Humanité*, 27 July 1936, p. 1 and p. 4.
—— 'Des armes! Pour des hommes!', *L'Humanité*, 28 July 1936, p. 1 and p. 3.
—— 'L'Offensive partout', *L'Humanité*, 31 July 1936, p. 4.
—— ' "Agissements" communistes', *L'Humanité*, 30 November 1936, p. 1.
Varagnac, André 'Les grévistes ont su organiser leurs loisirs', *Le Populaire*, 22 June 1936, p. 6.
—— 'Projet de questionnaire sur le folklore des grèves', *Revue de Folklore Français et Folklore Colonial*, Vol. 7, 1936, p. 129.
Viollis, Andrée 'Cinéma-Actualités', *Vendredi*, No. 29, 22 May 1936, p. 3.
Voilà, anon. 'Voilà la vie. Les grèves feminines de la région parisienne', No. 273, 13 June 1936, p. 1.
Warner, Geoffrey 'France, and Non-Intervention in Spain, July–August 1936', *International Affairs*, Vol. 38, No. 2, April 1962, pp. 203–20.
Weil, Simone, *La Condition ouvrière*, Gallimard, Paris 1951.
—— 'Journal d'usine', pp. 35–107.
—— 'La Vie et grève des ouvrières métallos', pp. 161–74.
—— 'Expérience de la vie d'usine', pp. 241–59.
—— 'Fragment', *Ecrits historiqes et politiques*, Gallimard, Paris 1960, p. 217.
Williams, Alan *Republic of Images: A History of French Filmmaking*, Harvard University Press, Cambridge Mass. and London 1992.
Wolikow, Serge 'Le PCF et la nation au temps du Front populaire', Wolikow and Bleton-Ruget, 1998, pp. 129–40.
Wolikow, Serge and Bleton-Ruget, Annie, Eds. *Antifascisme et nation: Les Gauches européennes au temps du Front populaire*, Editions universitaires de Dijon, Dijon 1998.
Youdine, P. and Fadeev, A. [Yudin, Pavel and Fadeyev, Aleksandr], 'Le Réalisme socialiste: Méthode fondamentale de la littérature soviétique', *Commune*, No. 10, June 1934, pp. 1025–30.

Index

Numbers in **bold** refer to illustrations